Praise for *Grateful American*

"Gary Sinise writes as he lives, and as the artist and actor he has always been: with American authenticity, purpose, and a conviction that is inseparable from his nature."

—TOM HANKS, ACTOR AND FILMMAKER

"No entertainer alive today has visited and performed more for our troops at veterans hospitals and military bases all over the world than Gary Sinise. For years his foundation has built 'smart homes' for our troops that were severely wounded in combat. The book is called *Grateful American*, and I promise that after you read it you will be grateful for what Gary has accomplished and contributed to our country. He's truly one of a kind."

—CLINT EASTWOOD, ACTOR, DIRECTOR, PRODUCER, AND MUSICIAN

"In my four years in the military, fifty years in show business, and over seventy years on this planet, I have never met a more dedicated American than Gary Sinise. Where does this kind of man come from and where did he get this boundless energy to accomplish so much and still put God, family, and our men and women in the armed forces above himself? *Grateful American* is an amazing story about a man who had a midlife 'awakening.' All who read this book will be grateful that such a man lived in our lifetime."

—TOM DREESEN, COMEDIAN, ACTOR, AND ENTERTAINER

"Gary Sinise's book is absolutely amazing and provides a clear road map of one man's journey to selfless service. He uses his personal story to highlight that journey and stirs us all to do the same. Gary is an inspiration to me and to everyone he comes in contact with—his life is the ultimate example of selfless service."

—RICK LYNCH, LIEUTENANT GENERAL, US ARMY (RETIRED), AUTHOR OF *ADAPT OR DIE: BATTLE TESTED PRINCIPLES FOR LEADERS* AND *WORK HARD, PRAY HARD: THE POWER OF FAITH IN ACTION*

"For many years, I was a huge admirer of Gary Sinise's work and the fact that when he was only eighteen he started the incredible theater company Steppenwolf. When I was a struggling actor in New York City, I saw him in terrific productions like *True West, Balm in Gilead*, and *The Grapes of Wrath*, and his incredible acting was an inspiration to me. Since then, though, Gary has become an inspiration for a completely different reason: he inspires me with who he is as a person. Gary Sinise quietly and consistently brings light and hope to people, serving his fellow man with an attitude of gratitude."

—PATRICIA HEATON, ACTOR, ADVOCATE, AND
THREE-TIME EMMY AWARD-WINNER

"*Grateful American* is an incredibly honest and revealing examination of the personal path that each one of us must take to discover our life's purpose. Millions of thankful military personnel, veterans, first responders, and their families have benefitted immeasurably from Gary's journey, and it's been my distinct honor to participate in many of his inspiring initiatives throughout the years. I'm a grateful American for knowing him!"

—GENERAL (RETIRED) ROBIN RAND, US AIR FORCE

"In singing the praises of *Grateful American*, I have the added advantage of having known the author for over forty years. This book is a reflection of someone for whom my admiration by itself would probably fill a book. In reading it you will discover why I've been blessed to have this exceptional man, husband, father, and patriot as my dear friend."

—JOE MANTEGNA, ACTOR, PRODUCER, WRITER, AND DIRECTOR

GRATEFUL AMERICAN

A JOURNEY FROM SELF TO SERVICE

GARY SINISE

with Marcus Brotherton

NELSON
BOOKS
An Imprint of Thomas Nelson

Published in Nashville, Tennessee, by Nelson Books, an imprint of Thomas Nelson. Nelson Books and Thomas Nelson are registered trademarks of HarperCollins Christian Publishing, Inc.

Thomas Nelson titles may be purchased in bulk for educational, business, fund-raising, or sales promotional use. For information, please e-mail SpecialMarkets@ThomasNelson.com.

Any Internet addresses, phone numbers, or company or product information printed in this book are offered as a resource and are not intended in any way to be or to imply an endorsement by Thomas Nelson, nor does Thomas Nelson vouch for the existence, content, or services of these sites, phone numbers, companies, or products beyond the life of this book.

ISBN 978-1-4002-0812-8 (HC)
ISBN 978-1-4002-0813-5 (eBook)
ISBN 978-1-4002-1528-7 (signed)
ISBN 978-1-4002-1474-7 (TP)

Library of Congress Cataloging-in-Publication Data

Names: Sinise, Gary, author. | Brotherton, Marcus, contributor.
Title: Grateful American : a journey from self to service / Gary Sinise with Marcus Brotherton.
Description: Nashville, Tennessee : Nelson Books, [2019]
Identifiers: LCCN 2018032657| ISBN 9781400208128 (hardcover) | ISBN 9781400208135 (eBook)
Subjects: LCSH: Sinise, Gary. | Actors--United States--Biography.
Classification: LCC PN2287.S3926 S56 2019 | DDC 791.4302/8092 [B] --dc23 LC record available at https://lccn.loc.gov/2018032657

Printed in the United States of America

21 22 23 24 25 LSC 10 9 8 7 6 5 4 3 2 1

For Moira, Sophie, Mac, and Ella,
with never-ending love and gratitude

The nation which forgets its defenders will itself be forgotten.

—PRESIDENT CALVIN COOLIDGE

CONTENTS

Stunned

I am not completely prepared for what awaits me on the other side of the doors.

On this August day in 1994, the wind is blowing hot and humid throughout Chicago. Event organizers have told me more than twenty-five hundred disabled veterans are waiting for me in the air-conditioned ballroom at the Conrad Hilton Hotel. I'm here to receive an award at the national convention of the Disabled American Veterans (DAV), an organization whose motto is "Fulfilling our promises to the men and women who served." This is my first time at the convention. I've met disabled veterans before, one or two at a time, but never so many gathered in one spot. I imagine I'll walk into a sea of wheelchairs, crutches, and prosthetics, but I don't really know what to expect.

Organizers have led me down a back way through the clatter of the hotel's kitchen. We've sidestepped waiters and food prep staff and approached the ballroom doors from the kitchen entrance. Now we wait for the cue to come in. I can hear my voice being broadcast throughout the auditorium. *Forrest Gump*, the movie where I play a character named Lieutenant Dan Taylor, has been out for about six weeks, and event organizers are showing clips in the ballroom. At this point in my career, I've been in lots of plays and on a few TV shows, including *American Playhouse* broadcasts of Sam Shepard's *True West* and John Steinbeck's *The Grapes of Wrath*. I've even had a few credited roles in movies: *Of Mice and Men*, *A Midnight Clear*, *Jack the Bear*, *The Stand*. But I've never had a role that's received as much attention as Lieutenant Dan.

It's a new experience. The movie has already exploded in popularity, and more and more I'm getting recognized in public. As a result, the DAV has kindly provided me with a suite at the hotel and kept me away from the crowds.

Lieutenant Dan is a disabled Vietnam veteran who loses his legs in combat. He carries terrible guilt after leading his platoon into an ambush where many of his men are killed or wounded, and he wishes that instead of surviving with his injury he'd been killed along with his men. His post-traumatic stress[1] buries him in alcohol abuse and dark isolation. His friend, Forrest Gump, also a Vietnam veteran, is a good-hearted and simpleminded man who receives the Medal of Honor for saving Lieutenant Dan's life, as well as the lives of other members of their platoon.

Through the ballroom doors, I hear the scene that's being shown. The characters' combat days are over, and Private Gump (played by Tom Hanks) reunites with me, his lieutenant, in New York City in 1971 during the holiday season. Christmas is in the air, and I'm confined to my wheelchair. My hair has grown to my shoulders and is unkempt. I set down my whiskey bottle long enough to probe Forrest with a sneering question:

LIEUTENANT DAN: Have you found Jesus yet, Gump?

FORREST: I didn't know I was supposed to be looking for him, sir.

LIEUTENANT DAN: [Chuckles wryly.] That's all these cripples
    down at the VA ever talk about. Jesus this and Jesus that. Have
    I found Jesus? They even had a priest come and talk to me.
    He said God is listening, but I have to help myself, and if I
    accept Jesus into my heart, then I'll get to walk beside him in
    the kingdom of heaven. [Enraged, Lieutenant Dan throws the
    bottle, glares at Forrest, and shouts:] Did you hear what I said?

---

1. Usually, this condition is referred to as post-traumatic stress *disorder*. But I refuse to call it a disorder. Take any person, put him or her in combat, and they're going to experience post-traumatic stress. The result is not a disorder. It's a natural response.

WALK beside him in the kingdom of heaven. Well, kiss my
crippled a**. God is listening? What a crock of s**t.
FORREST: [Quietly] I'm going to heaven, Lieutenant Dan.
LIEUTENANT DAN: [Bitterly] Oh? Ah, well, before you go, why
don't you get your a** down to the corner and get us another
bottle of ripple.

In the ballroom, I hear dry chuckles from the audience. A clip from
later in the film begins. Lieutenant Dan has found his way to Bayou La
Batre, Alabama, and goes to work on Forrest's shrimping boat. One dark
night, a squall comes up, a real act of God. All the other shrimping boats
sensibly return to port, but Forrest and Lieutenant Dan stay out at sea.
During the storm's fiercest moments, Lieutenant Dan climbs to the top of
the mainmast, shakes his fist at the sky, and yells out at the wind and the
waves: "You call this a storm? . . . I'm right here, come and get me! You'll
never . . . sink . . . this . . . boat!" In an utter showdown with Providence,
he vents his frustration, disappointment, grief, and rage.

In the next scene the storm is over, and the sun is out. Forrest's boat
is the only one that's survived the hurricane. Lieutenant Dan sits on the
edge of the boat. He's finally let go of the anger, fear, and resentment over
what has happened to him. He looks his former private in the eyes and says
quietly, "Forrest, I never thanked you for saving my life." After a smile to
his friend, he hops into the calm waters of the ocean and floats on his back
into the distance, finally at peace, the sun breaking through the clouds as
if lighting the way forward. In a voice-over Forrest says, "He never actually
said so, but I think he made his peace with God."

As the clips continue in the ballroom, I think about how this character
seems to have resonated with a lot of people already, especially those in
the veteran community. Shortly after the movie's release, Gary Weaver, a
Vietnam vet who worked for the DAV, invited me to the DAV convention
so that the organization could present me with an award for "an honest
portrayal of a catastrophically injured veteran who served his country."
That's why the DAV has brought me to this ballroom at the Hilton—to
honor me for my "hard work" on the film.

Hard work?! Waiting outside the ballroom doors, I stifle a snicker at the absurdity. *Compared to what the people in this ballroom have gone through, my job isn't close to hard work. All I do is find my mark, say my lines. Hard work is being far from home and up to your elbows in dust, crawling along the ground while the enemy shoots at you, wondering when the bullets will stop flying long enough so you can grab an MRE and wolf down your next meal. That's hard work.*

The scene ends. The ballroom doors grow quiet.

"Ready?" asks the organizer. His hand reaches toward the door handle.

I nod. "Ready."

He opens the doors to the ballroom and I walk inside.

The entire ballroom erupts into applause. I choke up immediately. The spotlight is focused on the podium, center-stage, where I'll give my speech. I walk up the wheelchair ramp leading to the podium and glance around. It's a massive ballroom filled with hundreds and hundreds of disabled veterans plus their family members. Some of the veterans wear their uniforms. Others wear civilian clothes with hats that show which war they fought in or the unit or branch of the military they served with. The atmosphere in the room is electric. I see a wide range of ages, wounded veterans from World War II to the present. It's a sea of men and women, many with scars, prosthetics, burn marks, crutches, and wheelchairs—and all wearing the unmistakable look of pride. They're clapping, cheering wildly, whooping, calling my name.

I am stunned. Humbled. The lump in my throat won't go down. *What have I ever done?* Here are all these wounded and disabled veterans—men and women who have sacrificed so much—honoring me for merely playing a part in a movie.

The cheering continues, and I make my way to the stage, clear my throat, and choke out a few words. "I'm not prepared for the emotion I feel right now," I say spontaneously, and I pause again. Looking out at the audience, I realize why they were applauding. Lieutenant Dan has somehow become more than just a character in a movie. To these veterans he has become a symbol of our country's collective awareness of all our injured veterans, especially the Vietnam veteran. Already this character has grown beyond anything I could ever imagine.

Somehow, I manage to finish my words, and when I'm done speaking, the DAV national commander, Richard Marbes, presents me with the award. Richard is an injured veteran, and due to his time in service he's standing on crutches with his right leg missing up to his hip. The award he presents to me is called the National Commander's Award, one of the DAV's highest honors. I make the mistake of reading the award's wording: "Your superb performance brought awareness of the lifelong sacrifice of disabled veterans back into public consciousness in a remarkably positive way." One word of that inscription stops me cold. But I don't know what to do with it at first.

Still taken aback by that word, I come down off the stage, award clutched in my hand. People make some more remarks. The event concludes. I shake hands and pose for pictures. Scribble autographs and give hugs. Smile and say to as many veterans as I can, "Thank you so much for serving our country," and I'm choked up now for a new reason. That single word has lodged itself deeply into my mind. The word has burned its collective sorrow and shame into me, and it's made me say a silent vow to do everything in my power to overturn all the wrongs it stands for. The one word is *back*.

"Your superb performance brought awareness of the lifelong sacrifice of disabled veterans *back* into public consciousness in a remarkably positive way."

That one word embodies the reality that honoring veterans hasn't always been the norm in America. When our troops came home from World War II, they were given ticker-tape parades, but when they came home from Korea, they were largely forgotten. And when they came back from Vietnam, they were greeted with anger. Spit upon. Called names. Hit with wadded-up lunch sacks filled with feces. There were no welcome home parades for our Vietnam veterans.

When our veterans returned from the first Gulf War, unlike Vietnam, they were greeted with giant parades in New York and a few other cities. Yet even though our country eventually tried to make amends with Vietnam veterans by supporting them as they created the Vietnam Memorial in DC, and with some cities hosting in the mid-1980s a few welcome home parades, now in 1994 I can still sense remnants of this rift in our country, this still-open wound for the veterans of the Vietnam War. Little do I know how significant this moment at the convention will become in my life. Seeds are being planted that will grow into a tree with many branches. For it's here that I first begin to ask myself: *How can I make a difference in restoring what's been lost? How can I help make sure our veterans are never treated that way again?*

⸙

More than two decades later, on an early Monday morning in 2018 at my foundation's office in Woodland Hills, California, I'm reviewing my schedule for the upcoming week—packed, as usual. A speech in downtown L.A. tonight. Gatherings with donors and veterans throughout the week. Meetings with foundation staff to go over the schedule for the next few months. A tribute concert to give this weekend. I take a deep breath.

It's been twenty-four years since that defining moment at the DAV national convention, the moment when I began to realize what the character of Lieutenant Dan means to many people. I gave everything I had to the role because I wanted to pay special tribute to our Vietnam veterans who never got the thank-you and the pat on the back they deserved. Over the years I've met many people whose lives have been touched by the role of Lieutenant Dan, especially people in the military and veteran community, and I'll always be grateful the role has done much good.

The years since the convention have been good to me as an actor. Today, in addition to *Forrest Gump*, I'm best known for roles in *Apollo 13*, *Ransom*, *Snake Eyes*, *Truman*, *George Wallace*, and *The Green Mile*, and for playing the lead roles of Detective Mac Taylor in the hit TV show *CSI: NY* (2004–2013) and Agent Jack Garrett in *Criminal Minds: Beyond Borders* (2016–2017). I've received an Emmy and a Golden Globe, been honored with a star on the Hollywood Walk of Fame, and been blessed to receive an Oscar nomination for Best Supporting Actor for my portrayal of Lieutenant Dan.

Yet my life's work has turned into so much more than what I've done on the stage and screen. Over the years I've grown in my relationships with our troops, veterans, and first responders. I've been blessed to visit our servicemen and -women in the distant and often dangerous places where they live and work. I've traveled to visit our troops in Iraq, Afghanistan, and around the world, and have performed with my band—the Lieutenant Dan Band—in Kuwait, Belgium, the Netherlands, Germany, Italy, the United Kingdom, Japan, Okinawa, Korea, Singapore, Diego Garcia, Afghanistan, Guantanamo Bay, Puerto Rico, Alaska, and all around the United States in an effort to help boost the morale of our troops and military families.

I've seen firsthand our service members' extraordinary skill and dedication, and my life's mission and passion today are to shine a light on those who serve and defend, the true heroes who go into harm's way, volunteering to lay down their lives so we can have the freedom to make something real and good of our own lives.

I'm still an actor—absolutely. But I realize I've become more than an actor. While this is not a term I use myself, I have heard people say I've become "today's Bob Hope"—the legendary Hollywood entertainer who began doing USO shows in 1941 and continued supporting and encouraging troops for the next fifty years. Bob Hope became the figurehead of tribute from an entire grateful nation. Other people—entertainers, reporters, citizens, and even the troops themselves—have compared me to him, I suppose because we both share an ongoing and long-term commitment to supporting and entertaining our defenders at home and abroad. But I never set my sights on "becoming" anyone, or trying to fill Bob Hope's shoes. He set the bar very high in his fifty years of entertaining and supporting our troops. I've simply tried to take action whenever and wherever I can, because I care about the men and women who are serving our country and want to do my bit to back them up.

For this work I've been privileged—astonishingly—to be named an honorary chief petty officer by the United States Navy. The Marine Corps has pinned me as an honorary marine. The New York City Fire Department named me an honorary battalion chief. The Association of the US Army presented me with the George Catlett Marshall Medal, awarded for "selfless service to the United States." I've received the Sylvanus Thayer Award at West Point, given to a civilian "whose character, service, and achievements reflect the ideals prized by the US Military Academy." And in November 2008 I received a call from the White House, inviting me to come to a ceremony to receive the Presidential Citizens Medal, the second-highest civilian honor awarded to citizens for "exemplary deeds performed in service of the nation."

The flow of praise feels exactly backward to me. As I travel to bases and military hospitals, it's humbling to see our servicemen and -women grow excited when I show up to shake their hands. I'm the one who's honored to meet them, to thank them, and I'm touched that they would want to turn their thanks back toward me. I've learned the reason they're excited to meet me or shake my hand is not just because I'm visiting or performing with my band, but mainly because wherever I go I carry a message of a nation's gratitude. I'm letting them know that the country they love hasn't forgotten about them.

The experiences of war leave an indelible impact on our servicemen and -women. As our veterans return to civilian life, the physical, emotional, and psychological challenges they face are often difficult. I've come to realize that one of our greatest shared responsibilities as American citizens is to support and honor the heroes who defend our nation. We are all beneficiaries of the freedom and security they fight to protect.

In 2011, I established the Gary Sinise Foundation to formally continue the service work I'd begun years earlier. Today, my foundation has become a rallying point for people everywhere who want to serve, support, and honor our troops, veterans, and first responders. Thousands of individuals and dozens of great companies and organizations have come together to help us. One of my foundation's main initiatives is to build smart homes for severely wounded veterans. We provide these houses and the land they're built on at no cost to the vets, completely mortgage free. Each house is individually designed and equipped with anything each severely wounded vet needs to make life more manageable. Adaptive smart technology, ADA-accessible restrooms, sometimes, if necessary, wheelchair ramps or elevators, whatever can help to restore functionality and independence to the veteran and his or her family. And the foundation does other things to help too.

The Lt. Dan Band is an important program of the foundation. We perform at bases in the United States and all over the world to support and encourage our troops. We've played hundreds of shows over the years. I don't make any money from these concerts or from my participation in any of the foundation's activities. And at my age, I certainly don't need to be out on the road performing cover tunes over and over again. But I believe I've been given a mission—a mission of service. What I love about playing music and doing live concerts is that they do some good: they bring a little joy, boost spirits, raise funds, and give me a platform to help spread a message of support and appreciation as I speak directly to the men and women who, past and present, serve our country. Seeing the smiles on the faces of the troops and their families is all I need to keep going.

There's a message I want to deliver in this book: I love my country, and I'm grateful to be an American. I know where my freedom comes from, and I do not take for granted the sacrifices of those who provide it. Because of that, I want to do all I can to ensure America's defenders and their families are never forgotten.

I want this book to help spread a spirit of joy, tribute, action, and ultimately gratefulness. In the pages to come, you'll read how a wild kid from the suburbs of Chicago stumbled into theater, how he eventually developed from an actor into an advocate, and why his passionate commitment to support our nation's defenders continually manifests into action.

As I've looked back on this life's journey and seen anew how my story unfolded over the years, what I've seen has surprised even me. There have been any number of ups and downs in my life, and there was a time when I wasn't concerned about too much more than my own career. But slowly things changed. It's my hope that as I share these stories from my life, you will be entertained and maybe even inspired too—empowered to overcome obstacles, embrace gratitude, and engage in service above self.

So let's go. First up: the vineyards of Ripacandida, a trip through Ellis Island, and a man who would have three wives.

Wait a minute.

What did he say?

CHAPTER 1

Yearning to Breathe Free

Let me take you back to old Italy, to the little village of Ripacandida in the province of Potenza. I want to look at how certain decisions, moments, and events in the past can shape and mold the present—and even the future—in uncanny ways.

While I've yet to travel there myself, I'm told that in Ripacandida you can see lush valleys and large cliffs, bright sunlight on the whitewashed houses. You smell fresh-baked bread and catch in the air the fruity tang of grapes. In the late 1880s, my great-grandfather Vito Sinisi (spelled with an *i* at the end) lived in Ripacandida with his family. My last name was pronounced *Sin-NEEZ-zay*. Say it out loud like a good Italian would.

The land was beautiful, the people vibrant and industrious, yet times were tough for Vito in the old country. So he traveled to Brazil and settled there for a while to try and make a buck working in the coffee fields. He then headed back to Italy, and when he was twenty-three, on January 22, 1887, he married a sixteen-year-old from the village named Anna Maria Fusco. They were happy, but times were still tough. He needed a land of opportunity. He needed a land that welcomed the tired, the poor, the huddled masses. Four years and two children later, in 1891, Vito and his young family came to America. They sailed past Lady Liberty, headed through Ellis Island, and when the American clerk who stamped forms saw the last name, he mispronounced it, saying it softer, like a whisper—*Sineece.*

Rhymes with *niece*. Vito figured that's how good Americans say his last name, and Vito wanted to be a good American, so the *i* was changed to an *e*, and ever after the Sinise family has said its last name the way that nameless clerk did.

Vito and his family wound up on the south side of Chicago, where he was soon able to buy a little house with a bakery and store out front. He created his own job, running his little grocery store and baking Italian bread twice a day. He sold his bread for ten cents a loaf as fast as he could bake it. Vito had nine children—the first two born in Ripacandida, and seven born in America. My great-grandmother Anna passed away in 1918, and after a period of mourning, Vito met and married Adiela Labriola, who had immigrated to Chicago from Italy in 1910. Adiela went by the more American name of Ethel. Sadly, a little over eighteen months after their marriage, she also died, so Vito returned to Italy in hopes of finding a new wife, this time meeting Maria Lucia Giambersio. They married in Ripacandida on December 30, 1920, and returned to America. Neither Adiela nor Maria Lucia had any other children with Vito. In later years, Vito worked in Rock Island, Illinois, as a crossing watchman, the person who flags automobile traffic when trains run through crossings, then for the city of Blue Island on a horse-drawn garbage wagon before he retired in 1940. He died in 1946, old and full of years in this new country, his family welcomed by the mighty woman with a torch.

My grandfather Donato Louis Sinise was called Daniel by everyone. He was one of Vito's kids born in Chicago. Grandpa Dan arrived in 1900 and quickly grew into a hardworking kid who sold newspapers and peddled bread. He left home at fifteen to work in a glass factory. In 1917, Grandpa Dan joined the US Army to fight in World War I, and at eighteen found himself on the front lines in France in the Battle of the Argonne Forest. This huge, bloody battle saw some 26,277 American troops killed, more Americans than were killed in the entire Revolutionary War (25,324), or about six times the number of American troops killed on D-Day (4,414 killed on June 6, 1944).

After the war, Grandpa spoke little about his battle experiences except to tell one story. He served for a time as an ambulance driver, shuttling wounded from the front lines to the hospitals. You'd think that would be a safer job in a war, but the enemy targeted the big red crosses on the ambulances while Grandpa drove in convoy, and the shells began to whistle in. *Kaboom!* The ambulance in front of Grandpa blew up. More shells whistled in. *Kaboom!* The ambulance behind Grandpa blew up. More shells whistled in. Grandpa braced for the inevitable. But somehow—miraculously—Grandpa Dan's ambulance wasn't touched.

In 1920, during a second epidemic of flu at US Army Facility Camp Grant in Rockford, Illinois, a young registered nurse named Vesta Lambertson worked at night in the pneumonia ward. Grandpa Dan became night supervisor and met her. Bells went off and they married three months later on April 23, 1920. Whenever Grandpa told this story, he said jokingly, "It was either marry me or else," but he never explained what the "or else" meant. It cost two bucks to get married. He remembered that. A buck fifty for the license and fifty cents to the judge.

In August 1920, Grandpa Dan became a switchman on the Indiana Harbor Belt railway line and a year later was promoted to conductor. He was a hardworking heartland railroad man until he retired, when he gave me, his firstborn grandchild, his pocket watch. On the back he had engraved a simple inscription: "To Gary from Grandpa, June 1969." I treasure that watch to this day.

By the time I knew my grandparents, everybody called Vesta "Grandma Betty." Grandpa Dan and Grandma Betty had three children: my uncles Jack and Jerry, and my dad, Robert. During World War II, Uncle Jack flew thirty missions as a navigator on a B-17 bomber over Europe, while Uncle Jerry, at just eighteen years old, served on a US Navy ship—a landing ship tank (USS *LST-811*)—in the Pacific, arriving just after the battle for Okinawa ended in mid-June 1945. After Imperial Japan surrendered, Uncle Jerry traveled to the Palau Islands to pick up Okinawan families to return them to their homes. Mostly women and children, they'd been used by the Japanese as slave labor. He fed Hershey bars to the kids and on the ship bought them everything he could think of. The children sang for him in return, and years later he still said they were the most beautiful voices he'd ever heard. He spent that summer and fall traveling between the islands of Okinawa, Iwo Jima, Guam, Saipan, Leyte, and Tinian, and took part as a member of the occupation force of mainland Japan.

Uncle Jerry was remarkable. He signed up for the military right after high school graduation in 1944 but was told he was 4F because his ears were badly scarred from the scarlet fever and chicken pox he had simultaneously as a child. But Uncle Jerry convinced the recruiters he was fit for service. When he reached boot camp in Coeur d'Alene, Idaho, doctors examined him once again and told him to get back on the train and go home. Uncle Jerry refused. He insisted on doing his duty. They let him stay. After the war, he would be discharged in June 1946, only to be drafted back into the navy again during the Korean War. In January of 1951, he began serving aboard the USS *McCoy Reynolds* until being discharged on February 14, 1952.

By the time I was old enough to understand and appreciate what my grandfather and Uncle Jerry had experienced during their war years, their service was long behind them. They also never spoke much about their military days. I did talk to my uncle Jack about his service during WWII before his passing in 2014, but this only came after I was an adult. I regret that I was never able to ask my uncle Jerry and my grandfather more about their service days before they passed away.

Dad was still a young teenager when World War II ended. After he graduated from high school, he tried college for about three months before deciding it wasn't for him. He joined the navy and in 1951 went through boot camp at Naval Station Great Lakes near North Chicago. He then trained at Naval Air Station Jacksonville in Florida where they asked him if he wanted to go on a ship or if he'd like to take pictures for the navy. Dad chose the camera, so he was sent to Pensacola for more training, and then to Naval Support Facility Anacostia near Washington, DC, during the Korean War. Dad's job was to develop the film and photographs that came back in cans from the war zone. The film and photos were sent to all the high-ranking generals at the Pentagon for analysis, so Dad had top-secret clearance. This was where he learned the film business.

Dad had met Mom back at Dwight D. Eisenhower High School in Blue Island, Illinois. Mom's name was Mylles Alsip. Her parents had come up with the name Mylles when they combined her mother's name, Mildred, with her father's name, Leslie, throwing out the *i* and spelling it with an artsy *y* instead. We never knew much about my grandpa Les's side of the family, as he and my grandmother divorced when I was young, and we didn't see him much after that. I do know he didn't serve in the military because of medical reasons, but his father, Walter Alsip, served in WWI, as did my grandmother's father, Elmer Percival Blomberg.

After Mom and Dad tied the knot, I was conceived on the naval base Anacostia. A few months before I was born, Mom, pregnant with me, went home to stay with her mother and father on the south side of Chicago because she didn't want to give birth on base. I was born at Saint Francis Hospital in Blue Island on March 17, 1955, eight days before my dad was honorably discharged from the navy. Does that mean I'm a navy brat? Well, just barely, I guess. Mom and Dad soon moved into a rental on the south side and eventually had two more kids. Three years after me came my sister, Lori Allyn, and a year later came my brother, Craig Randall. We called him Randy growing up, though today he goes by Craig.

Having served his four years in the military, Dad wanted to do something different, so right after I was born he went into the film business. Filmmaking was then a burgeoning industry in Chicago, with an entrepreneurial and forward-thinking workforce. The great Bob Newhart started in Chicago. So did Bill Friedkin, who won an Oscar for directing *The French Connection*. And today, the Chicago International Film Festival is the longest-running international film festival in North America.

Dad worked for other people as a film editor before launching his own company, Cam-Edit, when he was about thirty years old. He was the first person in Chicago to have his own editing business, and years later he was inducted into the Chicago Editors Hall of Fame. But in those early days, he edited documentaries, commercials, and industrial films—whatever came to him—and found himself immersed in the real-time *Mad Men* culture of the era: the 1960s, hard-driving, wisecracking, three-martini lunch crowd. Dad left home at seven most mornings and returned late, sometimes at midnight. And he worked many weekends. I knew Dad loved me, but in my growing-up years he simply was not around much.

My mom's sister, Aunt Nori, married Bill Smith, an army guy. Bill was stationed in Japan, and when I was about five years old, Bill brought back a little army uniform for me to wear. My eyes widened when I saw it, and I put it on immediately. I loved it. I wore that uniform as much as Mom allowed. To the store. To kindergarten. On Halloween. I even slept in it. Whenever, wherever—I wore that army uniform.

When I was just a little kid, I visited Dad in his office where he cut films on the old Moviola editing machines. Dad was working on the World War II documentary series *Victory at Sea* for NBC, and had also been hired by a director named Herschell Gordon Lewis, who shot very low-budget horror films, "splatter films" my dad called them. I couldn't read yet, so Dad told me the titles: *Color Me Blood Red, Two Thousand Maniacs!, Blood Feast.* Dad showed me a clip of a Lewis movie where a monster came out of a swamp and chased two hunters down the road, and he later pointed out his name on some movie posters. Dad told me once that the film was so low budget they would just run down to the local meat market for some cheap special effects to use for the blood and guts. So I imagined a director yelling at the people around him, ordering them what to do: "We need some more gory stuff—go down to the store and get some hamburger and lots of ketchup! Get tons of ketchup! This movie is called *Blood Feast* for cripes' sake." I looked on as Dad ran the inky film through a machine about the size of a breadbox and pressed a button, and I watched the film on the machine's little screen. He would stop the film often, tamp down on either side of the film, cut it with a blade, and put a piece of tape over it.

"There," Dad said. "That's how you edit film, Gary." I took note and grinned.

Years later, Mom and Dad moved out to California where Dad opened a West Coast office of his new editing firm, then called The Reel Thing. Mom came up with the name. Among the many TV series he worked on were *Miami Vice, Hart to Hart, Dawson's Creek, Baywatch,* and Michael Mann's *Crime Story,* which happened to be the first time I directed episodic television. In 1992, my dad edited *Of Mice and Men* for me.

I think it's very cool that he was so deeply involved in an industry so new in Chicago. When Dad started out, television had only been around for about twenty years—and already the industry was exploding. What's more astounding to me, though, is when I think how Dad got his start in the business by developing film for the navy, which means in some ways *my* roots in film go all the way back to the United States *military*.

———⚬⚬⚬———

When I grew up in Chicago, the North Side / South Side rivalry was as old as the city itself. Depending on who you talked to, the rivalry might be serious or only a chance for some good-natured ribbing. Even then, few people agreed completely on what the rivalry was about. The White Sox came from the South Side, Comiskey Park. The Cubs played on the North Side, Wrigley Field. The South Side of Chicago, where I was born, made its mark in industry. Railroading. The blue-collar working stiffs. The North Side, or northern suburbs, had more money. More white-collar business types. This part of Chicago was right on the lake, so folks from the North Side liked to go to the beach in the summer. The South Side suburb of Harvey, where I first lived, was actually so far south it was south of the South Side. But it was still gritty as could be. The address of the two-bedroom, one-bath, one-thousand-square-foot house my parents owned in Harvey was 14419 Sangamon Street, and my folks beat that address into my brain so I didn't forget. As a kid I was free to roam the neighborhood, and they didn't want me lost.

My grandpa Dan was a South Side man—a big-framed, tough Italian guy who'd been through the war and worked for the railroad. Not a cuddly grandpa at all. He was never mean. He was just tough. And a little scary. As a kid, I was a little afraid of Grandpa Dan whenever my parents took us for a visit. But years later, when I started acting in high school plays, Grandpa Dan and Grandma Betty came to see me in the restoration comedy *Tartuffe* by Moliére. I was playing the title character and had all kinds of makeup on, a funny nose, and a crazy wig, and from the stage I could clearly hear one voice in the audience. Grandpa Dan wasn't the kind of guy who laughed a lot. But I heard this bold belly laugh from the crowd, and I knew it was Grandpa Dan—strong, rich, and vibrant. Hearing his laugh was so affirming. I thought, *Well, if I can get Grandpa Dan laughing like this, then maybe I'm not half bad as an actor. Maybe I'll keep going.*

For first through third grades I walked to school by myself. Every morning, I passed a big mound of sticks, dirt, weeds, and thorns that beckoned to me. I liked to climb that mound and stand on top like a king. One morning I was messing around on top of the mountain and tumbled off. A thorny bush broke my fall, driving a huge thorn into my leg. Bloody, I got to school where they patched me up. My leg healed, and I forgot about it. Two years later, I looked down at my leg one day and saw something sticking out. The tip of a sliver of wood. I reached down and yanked it out. My eyebrows arched in disbelief. I had pulled out a two-inch-long piece of thorn that had lived in my leg unseen for two years. The scar is still there, a little indentation in my left calf muscle, to remind me. Perhaps it was some sort of life metaphor. Something dirty and thorny can live unnoticed in a person for a long time. Little by little, you hope, it works its way out, never to return.

This was the height of the Cold War. The nightly news didn't mean much to me as a kid, but I frequently heard about the tensions between Russia and the United States. In elementary school we had atomic bomb drills where we were all ordered to "duck and cover" underneath our desks. On the news, I heard about the Cuban Missile Crisis, a serious standoff between Khrushchev and Kennedy, and everybody prepared for nuclear weapons to land. I didn't understand all of this, and I wasn't fearful—but all the adults around me sure looked concerned. Even paranoid. *What's the big deal?* I thought. *If an atomic bomb explodes over your city, you just duck and cover under your desk.*

On November 22, 1963, I was walking to school near that same mound with the thorny bush, and another kid was climbing on the mound. He had a strange look on his face, and he chanted something over and over.

"*Kennedy's dead. He got shot in the head.*
Kennedy's dead. He got shot in the head.
Kennedy's dead. He got shot in the head."

The little kid was chanting naively. I thought he was just sing-songing nonsense. When I reached school, the teachers sent us all straight home again. Now I knew something big was up. We watched the news on our little black-and-white TV on Sangamon Street. Lee Harvey Oswald had shot and killed President Kennedy, and everybody in my family was sad. I walked outside; everybody was sad. We went to the store; everybody was sad. The whole country was grieving. I didn't know anything about politics, but I knew that my president had just been shot. I was sad too.

Not long afterward, Jack Ruby killed Oswald on live TV, and I watched the violence unfold in front of my eyes. As an eight-year-old, I didn't know what to think about what I'd just seen. About all the turmoil in my country.

About all the changes happening to America.

———⟨∞⟩———

Life wasn't all sad. At the end of third grade, we moved from the South Side to a big old historic house in Highland Park, the north suburbs of Chicago, and in the fall of 1964, I started fourth grade at a new school called Indian Trail Elementary School. For Christmas I received my first guitar. Acoustic. I had no idea how to play, but I loved it. The Beach Boys had become my favorite band. My first record was *Beach Boys Concert*, a live record, and as the songs spun on my record player, I loved to hear the crowd cheering in the background.

We lived four blocks from Lake Michigan, with a park at the end of our street. A lot of neighborhood kids went to the same school, so some of the guys and I grabbed our guitars and formed a band. We called ourselves the Beach Dwellers, an homage to my favorite band. We tacked up cardboard signs around the neighborhood and invited all the little kids to our first concert in my living room. None of us Beach Dwellers knew how to play, but a grand total of six kids came to the show (standing room only for a living room), and we put my *Beach Boys Concert* album on the turntable, wailed away with our guitars in our hands, and lip-synced along with the tunes. By the time we reached "Little Deuce Coupe," everybody was dancing like crazy.

Mom and Dad eventually invested in guitar lessons for me in fourth and fifth grade. My teacher played an electric and always dangled a lit cigarette from his mouth, and I emerged from each lesson with a headache and reeking of smoke. But he taught me scales and chords, and in sixth grade I formed another band, a real band this time. With a drummer. We played for some kid's birthday party in my backyard, and we weren't lip-syncing anymore. Performing felt fun and cool, and we sounded terrible, but at least we were actually playing. In seventh grade, I realized everybody and his dog plays the guitar, so I picked up the bass instead. As a bassist, you're always in demand. We played the Kinks and the Yardbirds. I took to the bass naturally.

I've always had curly hair, but all the cool kids in school—not to mention my musical idols, the Beach Boys—had straight hair. *Cool* straight hair. I began to hate my curly hair and felt like a dork, so I tried plastering it down with gel. That didn't work. My hair looked frozen like plastic, but it still curled up on the ends. I noticed that after I wore a baseball cap during a ball game and took it off, the hat hair was there, but the curl was minimized. One morning Mom woke me for school and there I was, sleeping with a stocking cap on. I jumped up, took it off, and looked at myself in the mirror. Ha! The curl was gone! I felt just a little cooler at school that day.

In sixth grade I went to another new school, Elm Place, across the street from Indian Trail, and right away earned a name as a terrible student. Every report card I brought home stunk. This had been going on since the first grade. Reading and writing didn't come easily to me, and my handwriting was a mess. In fact, my handwriting remained a mess all the way through my teen years and into my twenties. Today, they'd probably diagnose some sort of learning disability. But maybe I just never learned the fundamentals. Mom was always kind, fun, and loving, but she carried a load at home, not only raising three kids, but also taking care of her mother and her sister, who lived in a couple rooms in our basement. Mom was very pretty, and at one time—while we were living in Harvey and I was still really young—she even worked as a part-time model. I remember seeing her on our little black-and-white television set on a show called *Queen for a Day*, walking out wearing a cute little outfit and displaying one of the prizes, a toaster or a blender or something similar. Dad, meanwhile, was always at work downtown in the city. Our house in Highland Park was a larger house, and I think Dad probably overextended himself financially, and that's why he worked all the time. He loved us as a family. He just always needed to work to pay the bills since moving up to the northern suburbs was more expensive. So with Mom and Dad having their hands full, it was a rare moment that anybody was ever able to sit and do homework with me. At school I had trouble paying attention. I was always daydreaming, looking out the window, but somehow, I kept passing each grade with something like a straight D average.

A big Jewish community lived in Highland Park, and lots of my friends went to synagogue on Saturday and had bar mitzvahs and things I didn't quite understand as a kid. Summers, the older kids traveled to Israel to work on a kibbutz. Israel was less than twenty years old as a state then, and all the Jewish families I knew wanted to be connected to the Holy Land. But I wasn't raised with any sort of strong religious faith. We went to Sunday school until I was about six, but that was it. My great-grandfather Vito Sinise was Catholic and had raised his family Catholic, but when Grandpa Dan married Grandma Betty, she was Presbyterian, which caused a bit of a stir. I don't remember having any big thoughts of God at a young age. God, faith, service—the things that became so important to me later in life—weren't on my radar as a kid.

Halfway through my seventh-grade year, my parents moved us to Glen Ellyn, a western suburb of Chicago. Dad's business partner, Frank Romolo, and his family lived in Glen Ellyn, and Dad and Mom had fallen in love with the area. Dad's business kept growing, and I was surprised to learn the big house we moved into was once owned by the Morton family, of Morton Salt fame. But the move felt rough to me. I was a lousy student in a new school where I didn't know anyone, and I felt very out of place. I found some kids who played guitar, and we formed a band where I played bass, and music helped me make the adjustment. Music always helped me cope, and I played in a string of different bands: the Olde Molde, spelled in the Old English way; Uproot Confusion; and the Dirty Brain, named for a piece of brain coral I found while snorkeling on vacation with my family in the Virgin Islands. I brought it back home as a memento of the trip, and during our concerts we placed the spherically shaped coral on top of our rock organ and shined a spotlight on it. With its grooved surfaces, it looked just like a human's brain, and after thousands of years in the ocean, it stunk like a dead fish.

My future lay in either music or sports. I could have tossed a coin. I loved sports. In Highland Park I played baseball each spring. Winters, they'd freeze over the parking lot at my school, and we all played hockey. I was a huge Blackhawks fan, and Bobby Hull was my favorite player. I also loved football and rooted for the Bears. We organized a local football league for kids and played each other on weekends. I was a fast runner, always the quarterback or one of the halfbacks, and I was usually the kick-off return guy, running for a touchdown every chance I got.

I played football through eighth grade in Glen Ellyn, but I was an undisciplined kid and never showed up for practice, so I never knew any of the plays. The coaches would just put me in to return the kickoff because of my speed—and nine times out of ten, I'd get a touchdown. When I reached high school at Glenbard West in 1969, I tried out for the team but realized every kid was twice as motivated as me—and twice as big, so that ended my football career.

I played baseball in school through eighth grade too. Ron Santo, the third baseman for the Cubs, was my favorite, and the Cubs were in the playoffs in 1969. Even though I was born on the South Side, I've been a Cub fan since I was five years old watching them on WGN on the little black-and-white television in our living room. I dreamed of being a Major League Baseball player someday and wanted to play second or third base. But all that changed during the summer of '69 after my eighth-grade year when I blasted a double into the outfield and rounded first, heading for second. Sprinting hard, I slid headfirst, my arm stretched long. The second baseman saw me coming, and right when I dived into second, he caught the ball and came down hard on my back with his knee. *Thud!* When the dust cleared, I couldn't get up. They carried me off the field, and my dad took me to the ER. I was bruised, not broken, but for weeks it was hard to walk, and I didn't play baseball anymore after that.

That left music and my dreams of being a rock star. And I figured musicians all needed to be hard partiers—right? *Woodstock! Rock and Roll!* My parents liked to entertain and kept a bar stocked with various bottles of liquor. At the end of eighth grade, I decided to experiment. I had a metal box with a latch on it, so I gathered empty peanut butter jars with lids, cleaned them out, and stashed them in my box. When no one was looking, I sneaked small amounts of liquor out of my parents' bar. Whiskey into one jar. Vodka into another. Vermouth into another. Wine into another. Always just a bit, so Mom and Dad didn't notice.

One Saturday night I decided it was time. Randy and I shared a bedroom, but there was a small attic room connected to our room that was private where I kept some of my music gear. When Randy was asleep, I went into the attic room with my metal box full of jars, shut the door behind me, and tasted the vodka. The whiskey. The vermouth. The gin. The wine. Next thing I knew, I was plastered, sick as a dog, puking into my metal case everything I'd eaten for the past month. My head spun, and I wanted to lie down somewhere, but thought I'd better clean out the box so no one would find out what I'd been up to. I bobbed and weaved down the front stairs, heard the TV on in the other room, and figured the coast was clear. I crept into the kitchen and started dumping the vomit into the kitchen sink. I was dizzy and nauseous, and as I looked up, suddenly my mother was standing next to me, her arms folded. She looked puzzled and concerned and angry at the same time.

"Oh, hello, Mother," I said, my voice sugary. "I'm just cleaning out my box. It was a little messy. How are you this fine evening?"

The room started to go dark, and I realized I was passing out. Next thing I knew, Mom and Dad were wiping off my mouth, putting me to bed. I was grounded for a week. And no more box.

You'd think I would have learned my lesson. But that was only the start for me. The times were changing, and the drug culture had begun its rise. America was exploding in a million different directions just as I entered my teen years, and it felt like the entire country couldn't contain itself. We were at the peak of the Vietnam War, and it was going badly. We found ourselves in the age of revolution, the rise of the hippies. Everybody was anti-authority. Antiestablishment. I heard about Woodstock. The sexual revolution. Pot was everywhere, and by the end of eighth grade, although still on the football team, I felt caught between the athletes and the pot smokers.

At thirteen, fourteen, I went to parties where the drug scene was "happening." Kids sprayed oven cleaner into plastic bags and sniffed it, so of course I figured I needed to try. It's a wonder anyone survived. Kids dumped spot remover onto rags and walked around sniffing wet rags, so I tried that too. Snorting spot remover gave me a crazy buzz. And since older kids were at these parties too, beer flowed everywhere, and the air was thick with pot smoke. But at that time, I stuck to taking a few sniffs on my wet rag and that was it.

For a couple of years, I went crazy. When we lived in Glen Ellyn, this buddy of mine told me how his dad drove his car to the train station, parked, and rode the train to work. My buddy knew his dad kept a spare key inside the engine compartment. So I hiked over to the train station, lifted the hood, found the key, and took the car. I didn't have any particular place to go. Like an idiot, I made a left turn next to a sign that said, "No Left Turn," with a cop right behind me. Red lights flashed in the rearview mirror and I pulled over. The cop came to my window and said in a low voice: "Driver's license."

"Oh, yes sir," I said, my voice as proper as a lieutenant's, and I handed him my license. A fake. The name on the license was Carlos Huizinga. Age twenty. I was fourteen, looking twelve.

"Well, Carlos," the cop said. "This driver's license has expired."

"What? That can't be right." My heart pounded.

"Let's leave the car right here." He opened my door. "We'll go down to the police station and figure out what's wrong."

He took me down to the station, put me in a room, and stared straight through me. Clearly he knew I was full of crap.

"Carlos. Is your name really Carlos?"

"Oh yes, Officer. I had no idea my license was expired."

"Carlos. Can we call your mom and dad?"

"Um. I don't think they're home."

"Carlos. What's their number?"

I broke, and my words tumbled out in a rush—"Officer, I'm so sorry, I'm sorry, I'm sorry. That's not my name. It's Gary. Gary Sinise. And that's not my license. It's not even my car. It's my friend's dad's." I was wailing now, my voice cracked and pleading. "I'm sorry! I'm sorry! I'm sorry . . ."

They called my dad. Dad came to the police station. Dad drove me home. Dad wasn't happy. I was grounded for a long, long time.

I mean, c'mon. What was I thinking? Did I look like a twenty-year-old *Carlos*?

⁂

Not all my shenanigans contained even an element of humor. Dad had a big Buick Electra, and when I was fourteen I regularly lifted the keys, crawled out my window at night, and drove the Electra around town. One time a buddy said, "Hey, my dad owns a music store. We could use some speakers for our band." So one night I sneaked out and picked up my buddy in the Electra. We drove over to his dad's store. My buddy opened it with a key. We stole some big column speakers and put them in the Electra. I dropped him off and took the equipment back to my house. It was five in the morning when I unloaded the speakers into our garage. I'd just closed the trunk of the Electra and was walking into the garage for the last time when my dad came out.

"Gary. What are you doing?" His voice boomed.

"Uh. Oh, good morning, Dad. Um, my buddy was moving. We needed to get the equipment out of his house." I talked fast, caught in a web of deceit.

Dad took one long look around his garage. He didn't ask how I got the speakers from my buddy's house over to our house. He just shook his head and walked back inside.

Eventually I carried the speakers up to my room, hooked them up to my record player, and blasted music through the house. I'd become a thief and a liar and a near-failing student—and as a fourteen-year-old I couldn't care less about any of it.

Today, I know I was heading down a dark path. My mom had her hands full, and my dad was often gone, so I usually had to figure things out on my own. Sometimes my conclusions weren't so great.

At my best, I developed initiative as a kid. I don't mean by stealing stuff. I mean by forming my own bands, by drawing people together. I was often the neighborhood organizer, and if I wanted to play baseball, football, or hockey, I simply gathered some kids together and we'd play. I developed a mind-set that if something needed to get done, then I needed to do it; otherwise, it might not happen. It's a mind-set that's carried me a long way. If you can think it up, if you can dream it up, then get off your butt and make it happen. Good things come from focus and effort.

At my worst, I learned lessons the hard way. When I look back, I see how I did stupid and even dangerous things like sniffing oven spray and stealing cars (well, *borrowing* cars, just without asking to use them), and I wonder how that stupid kid doing stupid kid stuff ever survived. It's no excuse, but the country itself was going crazy in those years. In the late 1960's climate, if all the tie-dyed rock stars I knew were blowing weed and doing drugs, then it felt easy as a kid to conclude that I'd better do drugs too. That's what was going on in America in those days, and even though for a time I went back and forth trying to avoid it, like a lot of teenagers, I got caught up in all that craziness.

Later in life, I would grow to realize that I'd been born into a land of opportunity, just like Vito Sinise envisioned when he came through Ellis Island and arrived at America's sea-washed, sunset gates. The true freedom I eventually discovered in my later youth wasn't a license to do whatever I wanted, whenever I wanted. The true freedom acted as a force beckoning me to do something meaningful with my life. All I needed to start on that path was a push in the right direction.

But all that would come later. Midway through high school I was still caught. Thankfully, I would begin to channel my energies differently during my junior and senior years. I'd find a new road thanks to an incredible teacher named Barbara Greener Patterson—and thanks to a moment I'll never forget with Bernardo, leader of the Sharks.

CHAPTER 2

Baptism

It was February 1971, Mom and Dad had moved our family back to Highland Park, and I'd changed schools yet again. All the hippies at Highland Park High School hung out in the "Glass Hall," so named because it had lots of windows and a door that opened to the school's parking lot. Kids used to sneak out that door, go into the parking lot, jump into their cars, and smoke doobies between classes. This winter day the door was closed against the Illinois wind, blowing hard and unsympathetic from across Lake Michigan. I was a sophomore and played lead guitar in a new band, and me, the bass player, and the drummer all slouched against the wall in the Glass Hall. We called ourselves Half Day Road after a stretch of highway that divided our two northern Chicago suburbs, Highland Park and Highwood. We thought we were the real stuff. More than anything I just wanted to fit in at this new school and jam with my new band. But the life I hoped for was all about to change.

She walked straight toward us, a teacher named Mrs. Barbara Patterson. She was a powerhouse of a gal, a tornado of a woman. Blonde hair. Set jaw. The power of poetry running through her veins. She slowed when she neared us, stopped, and gave a diminutive sniff. Our clothes were cool and raggy, and my bandmates and I all wore scruffy jackets. I'd let my hair grow crazy and curly; it sprung out horizontally in a wild mass of thicket.

Mrs. Patterson was the theater teacher. She looked at us and said, "I'm directing *West Side Story* for the spring play. You guys all look like you could play gang members. Come and audition for the play." It sounded more like a dare than a request. Then she was off and walking fast on her way down the hall, and we shrugged it off and laughed, and one of us scoffed, "Who cares about plays?"

We *needed* to display bravado among ourselves, we three boys. Rebellion was the unwritten rule of 1971. None of us had ever been in a play before. But on that cold winter day, a warmer thought began to blow in the back of my mind. The previous year, when I was a freshman over at Glenbard West in Glen Ellyn, the school had put on *West Side Story*. All the kids went, so I did too. And you know what? That play wasn't half bad. All those Jets and Sharks running around, fighting with knives, rumbling in the streets. *Pretty cool,* I'd thought. Me and my ragtag buddies at Glenbard went out and bought jean jackets afterward so we could dress like the Jets in the play.

The bell rang and I didn't move. As a rule, I skipped most classes, but that day I thought twice, sighed, and ambled into history class and slid into a seat near the back. The teacher was saying something about a book I hadn't read. My eyes glazed and I stared out the window, working hard to become invisible. Years later, I came to love history, but that day in the classroom, I was still a horrible student. Yet for some reason teachers kept passing me year after year. I was sixteen years old, and I still didn't read or write well. My sister and brother were both better students than I was, and they were into sports: Randy played football and Lori was a cheerleader. Nothing much made sense to me except the Who; Jimi Hendrix; Crosby, Stills & Nash; *and the fringe jacket I always wore.*

The hour passed. Class ended and school was over for the day. One of my bandmates found me, and I said, "Hey, let's see what's going on at this audition." He said sure, so we ambled over to the cafeteria where the audition was taking place. We didn't know what to do or even what an audition was, but we spotted a line of girls heading into the cafeteria. Every girl's hair was flowing and parted in the middle, and they all wore beads with their bell-bottoms cut low at the waist. The groovy sight was all the prompt we needed to head in there with them. We scribbled our names on the sign-up sheet and found seats.

Kids packed themselves tight inside the makeshift audition hall. Someone shouted a handful of names, and a bunch of kids went up to the stage and were handed scripts. The first kids read their parts and sat down and another handful of names were called. *Hey, that's me.* I jumped onstage, grabbed a script, and found out which character I was supposed to read. One of the kids in my lineup started reading his character's dialogue. Pages rustled and turned. Another kid started reading his lines. Another kid. Another. *Man, they're really blowing through their lines fast,* I thought, when suddenly dead air blasted against me and silence filled the room. A lone cough echoed off the back wall.

"Hmm-hum, hey there," I said, glancing about me. I was at least four lines behind. "Hang on, *Jason.* I gotta find my place. You guys are going too fast."

The kid who'd just read wasn't named Jason. I didn't know his name, but I'd delivered my retort in such a good-natured nasal twang that my faux confidence cracked everybody up. The kid was smiling. The audience was chuckling. Even Mrs. Patterson grinned. So I ran my finger down the page, found my spot, and read my line. Everything cranked up again as the others continued reading their dialogue. In a flash it was finished. *So that's an audition,* I thought. *Well, that wasn't half bad.*

Next morning in the hallway near the drama department, a list was posted. Everybody crowded around to look. Me too. I scanned down the list—way, way down. I kept scanning but didn't recognize any of the names. *Well, who cares?!* I thought, but kept reading. My eyes kept scanning down, scanning down. Toward the very end, when I saw this, a soft light came on inside my soul:

PEPÉ---GARY SINISE

Pepé was a Shark. A gang member. He was in the chorus and had to dance a little and even had a couple of lines. The role required an actor's touch. I tried to take in all it might mean, seeing my name on the hallway list. I didn't know anything about acting, and I knew I fumbled my lines in the audition because I couldn't keep up with the other readers. But maybe, just maybe, my ability to entertain the crowd had caused Mrs. Patterson to see I'd taken her up on her dare. Maybe she saw some sort of potential I didn't see in myself yet. Because the words on the hallway list didn't lie.

I was in.

———⊗⊗⊗———

Let's backtrack in time, back before the audition. Maybe a couple months earlier.

I'd come to this new high school and fallen into a pattern of smoking dope and skipping class and smoking more dope, all the while trying to find friends. Just another kid caught up in this American craziness. At Highland Park I tried acid once when my parents weren't home, and I was high for about ten hours. Paranoia stalked me the whole time. I told my sister, and she sat with me for a while. Her face turned into a skull, then into a witch's face. I grew scared, threatened to throw myself into the pool, and never dropped acid again. But I still scored pot anytime I wanted.

There wasn't much to hold any of us together. Culture? That was changing. Morals? What were they? This was 1971. Religion? My family stopped going to church when I was a little kid, and we weren't raised with any sort of faith, nothing to provide an anchor. As a family—as a *nation*—these were tough times. Most days, I was floating on the open sea. Every evening, images of the Vietnam War splashed across our TV screens. It was the first war shown on television, and every night that screen showed only bad news. Since the Gulf of Tonkin incident in 1964, America had been involved in the war in a serious way, and it continued to kill plenty of Americans each day of each week of each month of each year. My folks were scared the war was never going to end. They figured due to the constant bevy of Ds and Fs on my report cards, I'd be drafted within three years and sent to Khe Sanh.

I'd lived in Highland Park years earlier, before all the moves across the city, back and forth to here and there and God knows where else. The last time I'd lived near Highland Park I'd had a couple of friends, but they didn't want anything to do with me anymore, and I didn't know why. Kids don't talk about these things. So I needed to find new friends. As a sophomore, then, I was a bit of a loner in a new high school, lost and wandering and having trouble connecting with new friends. The only thing that ever remotely worked for me was rock and roll. Music at Highland Park High School ushered me into the Zeppelin crowd. We formed our own band, and then I had two pretty good friends in high school. Two guys who shared the love of music.

Every so often during afternoons at Highland Park, I actually shuffled off to a few anti-war "moratoriums," as they were called. Students wore black armbands and noodled away on guitars and crooned Peter, Paul and Mary songs. All over our country at universities and high school campuses these protests were happening. I didn't go to these moratoriums because I actually protested anything. I went because if you told your teachers you were at one of these protests, then it was okay to cut classes. Plus, there were girls there.

High school proved a struggle for me every day. Ravines bordered Highland Park High School. One Thursday I ditched my second-to-last class and climbed down into one of the ravines, hid under the bridge that spanned it, and sparked up a joint. Inhaled it down. Sparked up another. When I came back for my last class, my eyes were bloodshot and my heart rate racing. I felt a strong urge to eat a bag of potato chips.

The next day after school, I went back to the ravine with my two bandmates in tow. Somehow the three of us had laid hold of three bottles of Boone's Farm apple wine, and we drank a bottle of wine each while simultaneously puffing away on joints. We had a gig scheduled in half an hour, and this was what rock and rollers did, man. The mighty Half Day Road was performing at the high school dance, and we had to get loaded before we rocked.

My bandmates and I finished our wine, smoked the last of our pot. We wobbled up to the school and headed up onstage. Grabbed our instruments. I yelled, *"Hello Highland Park!"* and our drummer started banging away on his kit. The bass player jumped in with me and my guitar, and we blasted away on our instruments for a while with the room still good and blurry. The tube top girls in the front row danced with their arms toward the stage. But something wasn't right. I glanced at my bass player, and he glanced at me, and we both started cracking up. We were halfway through our first tune, and it hit us that we weren't playing the same song. We had no idea what our drummer was playing. It might have been a third, completely different song altogether. He never told us.

We laughed about that one for days. A couple of weeks later Mrs. Barbara Patterson met us in the hallway, and I started inhabiting Pepé the Shark. Something genuinely began to change in me.

Play practice was after school every day for five weeks, and you couldn't go to play practice unless you'd been at school during the day. So for the first time in a long while, I started going to classes regularly. I found myself meeting a whole new crowd of folks, theater kids. I discovered they were smart. Cooler than I'd first thought. Funny. Passionate. Driven toward acting with the same drive I'd always poured into music. I noticed that since starting play practice, I was smoking far fewer doobies.

But my old life still pulled at me. Two weeks into rehearsals, somebody threw a huge party. Not a theater kid. Just a kid whose parents were out of town. By the time I rolled in, fifty or sixty teens were already drinking, smoking, dancing, making out in the stairwell. I had a dime bag and pulled a couple of other kids into the laundry room with me because it's good to share. We all lit up my joints, and I recognized four of the kids but not the fifth. He was a strong-looking dude, maybe nineteen. *Must be somebody's older brother,* I thought, but the fact that I didn't know him didn't concern me, because, *Hey, he's at the party—somebody must know him. Right?* He said he was a dogcatcher for the city, and he smoked pot right along with us, or at least it looked like he was smoking. We puffed away, and all told stupid jokes and laughed, and I didn't watch him too closely as the high set in. He brought the joint up to his face again. Puffed. I guessed. Everything was cool, particularly when the dude glanced around the circle and said, "Hey, where can I buy some pot for myself?"

I said in a cool, gravelly voice, "Well, I have some. I'll sell it to you."

He nodded and I nodded, and when all the joints were smoked, I sold him a nickel bag, and he followed me outside the laundry room, outside the house to my car. Followed me all the way. He said, "Man, that was really good pot. Thanks for selling it to me."

Why's he following me? "Sure, sure. Okay," I said. And I brushed him off and went home.

Man, the things you don't realize when you're stoned.

An hour later I got a phone call from a buddy who'd been at the party. He sounded worried and he talked all jumbled, breathless, like he'd been running. "Dude. The police raided the party. Came in with a real show of force. Rounded everybody up."

"What are you talking about?!" I said. Then it clicked. The dogcatcher wasn't lying about what he did for a living. It was just slang. He worked for the city all right—the police department! And I'd gone and sold pot to the dogcatcher. I was the source of the weed!

"Yeah." My friend's voice dropped on the phone. "And they're looking for *you*."

I hung up, totally freaked out. As the night wore on, I paced around my bedroom, trying to think up a plan. I didn't sleep. Early the next morning I went over to my new girlfriend's house. We lurked around in her basement together, then a knock sounded on the front door. She climbed the stairs, and I heard the front door creak open. Words. I strained to hear. Two policemen. They were there to get her, to take her down to the police station so they could question her . . . about *me*. My heart thumped.

She came downstairs to get her coat, her face white as a ghost. Looked me straight in the eyes, didn't say a word. Left. I hid out downstairs for ten minutes, made sure the coast was clear. My car sat around the corner out of sight, and I ran to the car, jumped in and drove to the train station, bought a ticket on the Northwestern, and headed into the city. I caught another train and headed out to Glen Ellyn, where I used to live. I knocked on the door of an old friend's house and asked if I could lay low for a few days until the heat blew over. Saturday passed. Sunday. I kept calling classmates who'd been at the party to ask what was happening back home. Word was the police were questioning everybody. They knew who I was. It was the height of the drug culture, and police were busting people left and right. I was a fugitive hiding out in Glen Ellyn, and the police were hunting for me. *Holy crap! I'm actually on the lam.*

By Monday I realized I couldn't hide forever, so I took the train home and admitted to my folks what had happened. They looked relieved when I told them. Even glad. I began to suspect they were aware I partook of cannabis from time to time. We talked for a long time and concluded that the best course of action for me was to turn myself in. Mom and Dad drove me to the police station, to the juvenile department. To Officer Rash. Yep—his real name. Officer Rash wore a black trench coat and had dark hair and glasses. A known commodity among teenage pot smokers, he was the guy keeping an eye on all us youngsters who struggled walking the line.

Officer Rash sat me down under the hot fluorescent lights, and I told him a bit of my story. I was honest. I told him about the moves to new schools, about my struggles to find new friends. He knew marijuana was everywhere, and I told him how a year earlier, before I'd ever taken my first puff, a friend and I had actually walked into a police station and asked for help in avoiding marijuana. We'd sincerely wanted to know what to do. Well, that really worked. A year later I was a full-on pothead selling dope to a narc. But I wasn't a delinquent—at least, I didn't think so—and the play was the clincher. I told Officer Rash all about *West Side Story*. We still had a couple of weeks to go before performances, but already I felt like things were turning around for me. I was trying harder. Feeling better about school. Staying out of the ravine.

"The play's really important to me," I said. "Really, really important. Please don't bust me. Please."

Yes, I was begging, but it wasn't a line. The play was truly important to me. I didn't want to be busted, because I genuinely wanted to appear in the play. *West Side Story* seemed to be all that was saving me back then. It was the only thing showing me a clearer path forward.

Officer Rash gave me a stern talking-to. I would have a mark on my record, he said, and I'd better not do it again. I nodded profusely. Then, by some unexplained near-miracle, I was free to go.

I never sold pot again. I smoked it once or twice—well, maybe more than once or twice—but I never sold it again. And the show was still on.

Teachers noticed this genuine change in me. In English, Mr. Allison knew I sucked at taking exams, but one afternoon he gave me a protracted side-long glance and asked me to tell the class what had been happening in play rehearsal. I didn't normally speak up in class. Ever. But on the spot I opened up and told everybody about the play. My words were enthusiastic, my voice clear, and I was surprised later when Mr. Allison handed me a solid grade for "giving an oral report," as he called it. That grade helped me pass his class that year.

Lots of kids in *West Side Story* had appeared in plays before. Many were seniors, two years older than me. But Jeff Perry, also a sophomore, had landed a lead role in the play—Tony, the former Jet who falls in love with Maria. I quickly pegged him as a leader: supersmart, a hilarious goofball, obsessed with theater, and an incredible singer. When we weren't rehearsing, I noticed that although I walked down the hallways with my hands stuffed in my pockets, his arms were loaded with books. And not just textbooks he needed for class, either. He read Shakespeare for fun, Chekhov—a Russian writer I knew nothing about—for kicks. I'd never met anyone like him, and he fascinated me.

A senior named Jeff Melvoin played Bernardo, leader of the Sharks. Jeff Melvoin came from a superacademic family. Later, he graduated magna cum laude from Harvard, and much later he became a Hollywood producer and writer for the hit TV shows *Remington Steele*, *Northern Exposure*, *Alias*, and *Army Wives*. Even in those high school play rehearsals, Jeff Melvoin was solid. He became someone to look up to, to emulate. This was important because with no experience or training, I needed to throw myself into *West Side Story* by instinct only, acting on intuition. I was totally raw, with nowhere to go but up.

After five weeks of rehearsals, it was showtime. The house lights came down, the curtains parted. Two star-crossed lovers from opposite sides of the street, Tony and Maria, fell hard for each other, and just like Romeo and Juliet, they were meeting in secret, avoiding their familiar friends. The play is shot through with hate and passion and rage. Chino shoots Tony, and Maria holds Tony in her arms as he takes his last few dying breaths. We presented four shows only—and we hit every line on Thursday and Friday nights, nailed it completely on Saturday, and on Sunday night blew the house wide open. And then it was all over. The show. My new community. Me.

The lights came down. The audience burst into applause. As one of the Sharks, I was part of the gang that carried Tony's dead body offstage. We Sharks set down the body behind the curtain, and Tony came to life again as just good old Jeff Perry, a high school kid who was quickly becoming one of my best friends. Jeff gave me a huge hug, and I burst into tears, and in glorious pandemonium offstage everybody was hugging and slapping each other on the back, with no chance to blow away the snot because it was time for the curtain call.

Out in the auditorium, the audience continued their applause, cheering, shouting, whistling their congratulations, and all the supporting players and chorus members came out onstage in a pack. Including me. As a member of the chorus, I stood far in the back of all the people on stage, and we all took our bows while the audience continued to pound their applause. And then the leads each came out one by one and bowed. They stood at the front of the pack. Tony. Maria. Bernardo. Riff. Chino. Anita. The decibel level in the auditorium notched higher with each lead. Everybody stood to their feet. A standing ovation. The leads all took their bows together. I still hung far in the back. Sobbing harder than ever. My eyes scrunched tight against the tears. Then, in the midst of all the commotion, I felt a hand on my shoulder.

Opened my eyes.

The hand was Jeff Melvoin's. Jeff the senior. Bernardo the Shark. He reached back, grabbed me. Pulled me up toward the front of the pack where the six leads stood. He shouted in my ear to take a bow with all the leads. So I did. Me, this sophomore screwup. Still bawling my eyes out. I stood at the front of the pack, and the audience was still standing, still applauding. Cheering for all of us. I took one long, glorious look around, trying to wipe my nose with my sleeve, and we all bowed again, all together, and I suddenly realized I'd fallen in love with this new community of students. With this new life of theater. It was almost too much to take in.

Later that night, back in the quiet of my room, I flopped on my bed and wondered if maybe Jeff Melvoin had seen far off into the future, to the person I had the potential to become. Because he'd grabbed me on impulse, I was pretty sure, and I doubted if the audience ever knew the fuller story of why he'd pulled this crying sophomore up to the front of the pack. In the last couple of schools where I'd been enrolled—including this one—if I was known by anyone, I was known as a kid who smoked a lot of pot and struggled to find his way in school. But in the past five weeks this play had morphed into a tent revival of sorts. Theater had pointed me toward redemption. The performers in the play had drawn me toward the river, plunged me under, pulled me up, and pushed me forward. Dripping and new. I'd been handed a fresh start, and I felt hopeful.

Grateful.

I realized theater had become my second chance at life, and this second chance caused me to understand I had a lot to be thankful for. A wide-open future. Boundless opportunity. My newfound buoyancy made me want to do something far more with my life than I'd been doing.

Ah. But here I was on my bed, exhausted. Poured out. The morning after I couldn't move. I felt like I was in the valley now, after standing on the mountaintop, and I was a wreck. I'd told my mom I didn't feel good and asked her if I could stay home. She said okay, so for the rest of the day I moped alone in my pajamas on the sofa in front of the TV. Occasionally I would get up, go to the record player, and put on the record from *West Side Story*—and it just made me sad. So I'd take it off and go back to the couch. I was brokenhearted that the play was over. This life-changing moment in time. I felt completely emotionally spent.

Later that afternoon, Barbara Patterson came over to my house, along with some of the kids in the show. They cheered me up, nudged me in the ribs, told me to knock it off and get to school tomorrow. There were more plays ahead, they reminded me. I couldn't help but buck up and grin. Their love felt so wide. Their support so broad. My first play and the lead guy had grabbed me, one of the chorus guys, to take a bow with the stars of the show. That entire cast had seen who I was before the play and what had happened to me during those five weeks. Now I had so many new friends. It was powerful. Something had really changed for me. I was going forward again. I had been baptized.

My life of purpose had begun.

CHAPTER 3

The Start of Steppenwolf

The summer of 1973, I was eighteen, and Dad was inching a big ole rented RV up the side of some mountain in Colorado. Holed up in the RV's bathroom, I buried my nose in the pages of *Cyrano de Bergerac*, a play I was supposed to be learning because Barbara Patterson wanted us to perform it in the fall. I wasn't happy about reading the play. I wasn't happy about this trip. And I definitely wasn't happy about returning to high school. After the incredible experience with *West Side Story* at the end of my sophomore year, during my junior and senior years, theater had become my primary purpose for showing up at school. While I continued to play music in an expanded version of Half Day Road, now with me as lead singer and six rock and roll buddies from Glen Ellyn, my central focus at Highland Park High School was acting. I'd been involved in every play I auditioned for, playing leading roles in plays such as *Tartuffe*, *Guys and Dolls*, *Look Back in Anger*, and *A Thousand Clowns*. Acting had lifted me up, and I couldn't get enough of it.

But there I was, the class of '73, the end of my senior year, and all my friends had graduated except me. I didn't have enough credits. I'd aced all my theater classes but bombed everything else. So I needed to return in September for one additional semester. I felt like a failure.

This RV trip turned out to be the vacation from hell. Everything went wrong. The air conditioner broke down. The plumbing got backed up. We ran out of gas. For most of the trip I tried to escape by hiding in the RV's bathroom reading my script. The last thing I wanted was to be on this family vacation. One afternoon, when things were particularly hot and tense, the RV chugged along, and everybody was cranky. From inside the bathroom, the family heard me say, "Whose idea was this anyway?" I'd voiced what everybody was thinking. Dad snickered. Mom chuckled. The crankiness vanished. My brother and sister doubled over laughing. Even I couldn't hold it back. Soon we were all howling.

When I started back to school in September, I'd forgotten about laughing. All my friends had gone to university, but *I'm the dummy,* I told myself. Depressed, I auditioned for *Cyrano* while still feeling ashamed for having failed my senior year, and I fumbled through my lines. I tried to get back on track, but my heart wasn't in it and I fumbled again. *Loser!* Halfway through my audition I fumbled a third time, stopped, and muttered, "I can't do this." I shuffled my feet in frustration. Barbara Patterson looked uncharacteristically confused. I shook my head, walked out of the room, and headed home.

I simply couldn't stand the thought of being back at high school again.

That evening Barbara Patterson phoned and said, "Well, Gary, you didn't do very well today, did you? But you can play this part, so I'm going to give you a callback. You don't deserve another audition, but we are going to do this play, and you need to finish this semester whether you're in the play or not. So you'd better get in gear and give it your best shot."

I didn't say a word. She hung up, and I slept on her words. Barbara Patterson had helped me make many changes in my life since I first stumbled into *West Side Story.* Under her guidance, I'd seen how acting wasn't about sitting in class and taking tests. It was about relying on instincts, going with your gut, and giving it everything you've got—all things I actually excelled at, I thought. Even though I was still a lousy reader, I'd found I could memorize lines easily. Onstage, I acted intuitively. Onstage, I felt free. Confident. At home.

During the previous two years, I had taken every theater class I could take—not only the performance classes, but the technical classes as well. I'd learned about lighting and set building. I'd painted sets and pounded nails.

Theater had become my life. Each of the past two summers, Barbara Patterson had gone to Beloit College in Wisconsin to perform in a professional summer stock theater company, doing eight plays in eight weeks—and she'd asked me to intern there twice. They gave me a dorm room, some food, and thirty bucks a week. I'd worked around the clock, hanging lights, running sound, painting sets, whatever needed to be done. I'd even played small parts in a couple of their plays when they needed a kid.

One of the plays they did was *Philadelphia, Here I Come!*, about a son in Ireland ready to move to New York to live with his aunt. On the last night before the son leaves, he tries to break through to his father. The two have never connected. The part of the young man is played by one actor while his thoughts are played by a different actor. The play was so beautiful, so moving, that I'd called my friend Jeff Perry and urged him to come to Wisconsin and see the play with me. Jeff had driven up and been blown away by the play too.

The previous year, when I'd been a senior for the first time, Barbara Patterson began teaching a directing class, which had never been done before at Highland Park. Each student's final project consisted of directing a play. It didn't matter what play or where it was performed; she just wanted us to direct. Jeff and I were still so moved by *Philadelphia, Here I Come!* that we asked if we could codirect it. She gave us the green light, so we went to our principal and asked if we could use the cafeteria's stage. Teachers used the stage for announcements, never for theater, but he said yes.

So we turned the announcement stage into our backstage area and built a theater-in-the-round in the middle of the cafeteria. We went to one of the technical guys in the school, a real electronics whiz, and asked him to build us a lighting board complete with dimmer switches. We built a lighting system by inserting floodlights into coffee cans. Somebody's father owned a cable business, so we asked him to donate wire, and somebody else's dad had a business that sold conduit piping. We secured the conduit to the ceiling, hung our lights from the piping, and ran the cable wiring from our coffee-can lights down to our makeshift dimmer board. We cast the play and rehearsed it, and that spring we performed the play in the cafeteria, four shows, and brought down the house. Jeff and I both received top grades, and the following year Barbara ended up turning the cafeteria space into a permanent theater. For once, I'd felt at the top of my class.

Jeff had graduated in the spring and gone to Illinois State University where he quickly became a rising star in their drama department. At one point, I contemplated going to college, maybe even to Juilliard, to study theater. I never told anyone about my dream, because report cards came out and I needed to go back to high school again. *Who was I kidding?* I whispered to myself. *Juilliard?!*

Fast-forward to the fall and the audition I'd bombed. The day after Mrs. Patterson's call, the callbacks were held at school. I went in and read with two friends, Bob Lovitz and Barbara Brandt, both great actors. We read the famous scene where Cyrano is under the balcony. Cyrano is an older man, big-nosed and not handsome, but a poet inside—and he loves the beautiful Roxane, who's being courted by the young, handsome Christian, a muscle-bound bumpkin. Christian is under the balcony looking up at Roxane, trying to woo her, and Cyrano skulks in the shadows feeding Christian lines that eventually win Roxane's heart. I was playing Cyrano, Bob was Christian, and Barbara Brandt was Roxane—and the three of us crushed it. We finished the scene, and I looked out at the seats. Barbara Patterson was sitting there, eyes closed, a bemused smile on her face, and she didn't say anything for a moment. I knew she'd been deeply moved.

Once again, theater had snapped me out of my darkness. Barbara Patterson had shaken all the self-pity out of me. She'd gotten me back on track.

Barbara Brandt was cast as Roxane. Bob had auditioned so well that Mrs. Patterson did something she'd never done before. She cast both Bob and me as Cyrano and also cast both of us as Christian. We learned both parts, and each night we swapped roles.

We performed the play in the cafeteria. School officials had built a real theater there by then, with a stage, proper risers, and real lights, not coffee cans. It was a tremendous experience, being an eighteen-year-old playing Cyrano de Bergerac. I couldn't help but feel part of something larger than myself. The confidence I gained by having the chance to play this great part in this wonderful play made all that angst over having to return to high school fade away. I thought, *This acting thing is something I want to do for a long, long time.*

∞∞

In January 1974, I finally graduated from high school. Today, if people ask, I just laugh and tell them I was part of the class of "1973 and a half."

College wasn't on my radar anymore. I just wanted to keep doing plays with these pals of mine. So with two friends who were still in high school, Rick Argosh and Leslie Wilson, we gathered some other kids we knew and we got ready to do a show. My parents knew the architects of a Unitarian church in Deerfield with a big open space. I asked them to ask the church folks if they would let us do a play there, and they said yes. We started rehearsing a play called *And Miss Reardon Drinks a Little*, a complex comedy about three middle-aged sisters who face their problems after the death of their mother. Since everyone was still in school except me, we rehearsed after school hours and into the night. It felt great to be working on a play again, in our own little space, an idea that was all our own doing.

During rehearsals, we got ready to print the programs and I said, "Okay, we need to call this outfit something." We threw out all kinds of names. Rick was reading a Hermann Hesse novel called *Steppenwolf*, and while everyone was making suggestions he didn't say anything. He just held up his novel, and pointed to it, and I said, "Great, Rick! Let's put that on the program." I hadn't read it, but it sounded good. *Steppenwolf Theatre Company*. We needed to print the programs quickly, so Steppenwolf it was. I felt so hopeful about what we were doing, excited to think we were creating a company. We pooled a few bucks together to buy a rubber stamp with "Steppenwolf" inscribed on it and stamped our name everywhere we could.

Stamp. Steppenwolf.

Stamp. Steppenwolf.

Stamp. Steppenwolf.

What none of us grasped yet was the magnitude of the moment when Steppenwolf was named. What we couldn't see was a future bigger than any of us could imagine, something that would last for decades and is still going strong today—the Steppenwolf Theatre Company of Chicago.

Our first play opened in March 1974. We were simply an impassioned group of teenage actors doing plays under our own steam. How could we possibly see that our actions would eventually result in the creation of one of the most prominent theater companies not just in America, but in the world? Over the years Steppenwolf would open shows in London, Australia, Ireland, and on Broadway, would win Tony Awards, and eventually would build its own multimillion-dollar state-of-the-art theater on the North Side of Chicago. Steppenwolf would help launch the careers of many prominent actors, including John Malkovich, Joan Allen, John Mahoney, Laurie Metcalf, Tom Irwin, Gary Cole, Glenne Headly, and many more. The company would be a place where we would work hard to entertain, inform, and inspire—and it eventually would become an internationally recognized Chicago institution. But we didn't know any of that then.

At first, Steppenwolf was completely grassroots. After our very first play was over, Rick, Leslie, and I sort of collectively shrugged and said, "Okay, let's do another." *Grease* became our second play because we'd all seen it before, and it was so much fun—and I thought I could direct it. We used the gym at one of my old elementary schools, Indian Trail, and did five performances of *Grease* over a weekend. We were on our way.

On opening night of *Grease*, we were packed. A line of people even stood out the door. In fact, we were so packed the fire marshal showed up. He walked around the edge of the crowd during the show shaking his head, muttering to himself. Fortunately, he didn't stop our play, but afterward he gave me a stern lecture about seating capacities.

In the beginning we didn't charge for tickets. We just wanted to do plays. Still, it costs money to put on any play, so we needed to figure out something. During the day I worked for my dad downtown at his film-editing business, putting cassettes together, so I took $1,000 of my own money and used it toward building sets and lights and putting a band together so we had music. I wanted to get some of my money back, so I had the grand idea of putting a shoebox in the lobby with "Donations" scribbled on the side, hoping folks would toss in some bucks. Very little money landed in the shoebox the first night. So the second night of *Grease* I came up with a better idea.

At the start of intermission, I came out onstage and made a shameless plug. I said, "Hey, everybody, we had to spend our own money so the show could go on—please consider making a donation. If you do, we'll even give you the second act tonight." Everybody laughed and started pulling money out of their wallets. In the show, we used hubcaps as pretend steering wheels, so our ushers—girls dressed in poodle skirts with their hair in ponytails—passed around the hubcaps like we were at church. People threw in lots of money, and we ended up with $1,500. Not only did I get my money back, but now we had an additional $500 to produce our next play. *Grease* ran in April and went so well that we recast certain parts and put it on again in May.

Before the show closed, I called up Jeff Perry, my good buddy at Illinois State, and told him to come see it on the weekend. He brought his new pal, Terry Kinney. I liked Terry right away and soon discovered that he was smart and an incredible actor. I asked them both to be in our next show, the existentialist tragicomedy *Rosencrantz and Guildenstern Are Dead*. So, in June of 1974, when Jeff and Terry were done with the school year, they returned, and we headed back to the Unitarian church to put on the play. Our third Steppenwolf production proved another hit in the community.

We had done really well with our first three plays, but as the summer was coming to a close, it was clear that most of the kids in the company were going off to college and things were going to break up. One night after *Rosencrantz*, Jeff and Terry and I sat on a bench outside the church, talking about the future. None of us knew exactly where we were headed or how to get there. But we all knew we wanted to do something more with theater and that it would be great to keep Steppenwolf going. That night, we made a pact that when Jeff and Terry graduated from college in 1976, we would pump our energy into this theater company and make a bigger go of it. In the meantime, I had the rubber stamp, and I would use it.

Jeff and Terry returned to college. In the fall of 1974, a few of us tried one more play. In the Highland Park cafeteria, we put on Tennessee Williams's *The Glass Menagerie*, with Barbara Patterson playing the lead role of Amanda, me playing her son, Tom, and Rick Argosh directing. I still have the little paper program from the production. This was the fourth Steppenwolf show. In 1975, we figured out how to incorporate as an official nonprofit, and that summer we put on the final production with this original group, the Pulitzer-winning drama *The Effect of Gamma Rays on Man-in-the-Moon Marigolds*. Barbara Patterson directed, and I wrote the music for it, although I didn't act in the play.

All the while I worked for my dad, as well as played in a band for the Free Street Theater, a group of actors who performed basically anywhere— stages, street corners, parking lots. They had a mobile trailer they towed around that would fold out into a stage, where they'd perform. Meanwhile, I moved into a beat-up old house with four buddies. The rent was $275 per month, and one of the guys, Ira, was an artist who blew glass and sculpted. Ira lived in our basement and had a day job working for the city in the sewers. He once found two baby raccoons in the sewers and brought them home to live with us. My band rehearsed in the basement where Ira and the raccoons lived. As the raccoons grew bigger, they started chewing on cords, guitar straps, whatever, so we gave Ira an ultimatum: either the raccoons or you, buddy. The raccoons went.

In 1975, Jeff quit college and moved up to Minneapolis to do theater there, but before long he reenrolled at ISU. Then, shortly after, his father was diagnosed with cancer, so Jeff quit school again to move back home to Highland Park to be with him in his final days. Later that same year, Jeff, Terry, and I decided it was time to make good on that pact, and we started discussing what we wanted to do. First item on the agenda: assembling a larger company. We needed more actors. The three of us loved the films of Martin Scorsese, John Cassavetes, and Elia Kazan, and we wanted to create theater like the work of those directors. So we needed brilliant actors. Hard-driving actors. Actors who would give it all on the stage. And perhaps most important, actors who would work for free.

In January 1976, Jeff, Terry, and I began meeting with other students in the theater department at Illinois State to start forming our new ensemble. Jeff and I traveled down to ISU from Highland Park in my 1969 Camaro convertible. Once, on the way home, I forgot to put oil in the car, the engine blew up, and smoke billowed everywhere. Dead. My dad had to come get us on the South Side, not a great neighborhood for two young kids to fry the engine and get stranded in. But we got the car repaired, and before long we were headed back to ISU. The meetings went on for weeks, from January through April. This new project was so important to us. All our sessions were free-form, with lots of talking and debating and passion and arguing and hanging out—all in our quest to determine who would join us. Eventually, we ended up with a total of nine people for our new Steppenwolf, and today these nine are sometimes referred to as the original members, even though the name Steppenwolf had already been in use since 1974. The nine original members were John Malkovich, Moira Harris, Nancy Evans, H. E. Baccus, Laurie Metcalf, Al Wilder, and the three founders—Terry Kinney, Jeff Perry, and me.

My pals were all highly educated about theater and playwrights and acting techniques, and I didn't know much about any of that stuff. Some days, I felt intimidated by my friends, but I made up for it by taking action and working hard.

Right away, we made plans for a full summer season. I went to the Highland Park Chamber of Commerce, informed them we'd started a theater company, and asked for their ideas about a space in town we could use. They were excited about the idea of young people doing something positive in the community, and the head of the Chamber's youth commission mentioned a basement over at the Immaculate Conception Catholic School. The school had recently closed, and a big open space in the basement, once a teen center, now stood vacant. I talked to the priest, explained what we were doing, and he agreed to rent us the basement for the exorbitant price of $1 per year as a tax write-off for the parish. Thankfully, the priest never saw any of our plays, because we ended up doing some pretty wild stuff. He might have kicked us out if he knew what was really happening in the basement.

In June of 1976, everyone from ISU moved up to Highland Park, and we began building our theater. We had a small stage on the cement floor of the basement and built risers with seating on three sides. Someone's dad knew about a downtown building that had caught fire. The theater-style seating inside had survived, so we got eighty-eight seats for free and put them into our space. On half a shoestring budget, we brought in some real theater lights, began building a few small sets—mostly just a few pieces of furniture bought on the cheap from thrift stores or borrowed from Jeff or my parents' hand-me-downs—and started rehearsing four one-act plays: *The Indian Wants the Bronx*, *The Lesson*, *The Lover*, and *Birdbath*. We put up posters all over town using the Steppenwolf stamp; we stood on street corners and handed out flyers; we tried to get free publicity in the newspaper—we did everything we could think of to inform the public there was a new theater opening in town.

We put together a governing board of grown-ups who wanted to support local kids. One board member had an old fire truck. We painted a big sign advertising Steppenwolf and put it on the side of the fire truck. A bunch of us rode on the truck—waving, shouting, screaming, howling like sirens—in Highland Park's Fourth of July parade. We even wore whiteface, like a bunch of mimes. Anything to get some attention for what we were doing. Our opening was set for July 21, 1976.

During this time, we were all working summer day jobs to support ourselves. Jeff made egg rolls in a fast-food restaurant. Terry sold men's suits. Malkovich drove a bus for a children's summer camp, and I often wondered how those children turned out. I had a few different jobs in those early days. One was unloading boxes from trucks on the loading dock at the newly opened Nieman Marcus in Northbrook, Illinois. Another was as a groundskeeper and a maintenance man at the Ravinia Festival in Highland Park, where outdoor concerts rang out all summer long. Ravinia is the longest-running outdoor festival in the United States. As much as I appreciated a paycheck from Ravinia, my heart was simply not in the work. Steppenwolf was up and running in full swing, and my mind was focused fully on our theater company. Charlie, my boss, didn't like me at all. I was still a screwup kid in many ways, and he could sense this. But I made the best of it. One time, when I was supposed to stock the bathrooms with toilet paper, I unlocked the storeroom doors to get my supplies and a bright idea popped into my mind. Toilet paper was expensive—and I thought, *Hey, over at Steppenwolf, we need toilet paper! Paper towels too. A few waste baskets for our bathroom would be great!* So I grabbed the supplies and tossed them over a shady area of Ravinia's fence with a plan to pick them up after work. *Relax,* I told myself. *They've got lots.*

I always felt bad about helping myself to supplies. Years later, after I became better known as an actor, I appeared on *LIVE! with Regis and Kelly* during a week one summer when they shot their show at the Ravinia Festival. I thought, *I want to pay Ravinia back for everything I took.* During the segment, I shared the story of taking the supplies and had them wheel out this huge pallet of toilet paper and paper towels. I nodded to the pallet and said, "Sorry, Ravinia. No hard feelings?"

Suddenly, two police officers jumped out from behind the pallet and arrested me onstage.

Everybody howled.

But in the summer of 1976, not everything was so neatly resolved, as our ensemble was a little wild, trying to get along and learn to work together. In those first months of Steppenwolf, things quickly grew messy and complicated as personal life and theater life intertwined. Moira Harris had particularly caught my eye. She was a brilliant young actor. Beautiful. Passionate. Full of pure fire. I convinced her to date me, and we soon fell in love. She was unlike anyone I'd ever met. But our love affair wasn't without its ups and downs. We were all over the place in our relationship. Two passionate personalities. On again, off again. In love, out of love. Clinging to each other. Mad at each other. Breaking up. Making up. Making out. And it wasn't just the two of us whose relationships were so chaotic.

Laurie and Terry had dated in college, but they broke up right before we started rehearsals. Laurie then started dating John, so John and Terry were at each other's throats. John was set to direct Terry and H. E. and me in *The Indian Wants the Bronx*, and Terry was set to direct Laurie and

Jeff in *The Lover*. After a year, Nancy left and Joan Allen replaced her, and soon Joan and Terry started dating. No one, besides H. E. Baccus, who got married the summer of 1976, had a boyfriend or girlfriend outside the company. We simply didn't have time. The love and the work and the plays and the passion mixed together and complicated everything. Like a family, we would argue our points, agree, disagree, get mad at each other, embrace each other, storm out, laugh, cry—our emotions could be all over the map. We were such an insulated cluster of craziness, and our theater was so small, even the audience members couldn't escape the clutches of us actors. Some of our plays worked well, and some not so well, but there was always an electric charge running through the ensemble members.

We laugh about it now, but occasionally, in those early first days in the basement, Terry would quit and walk out. He's an incredibly passionate and committed artist who sometimes felt he had to leave to make a point. But he'd always come back. Our rehearsals buzzed with craziness and energy and raw desires—and some days we just shook our heads wondering how we were going to get through it. But we felt hopeful too. I think we all quietly saw that as time went by, the passion and insanity going on offstage somehow seemed to be spilling over onto the stage. It was exciting and fun to be performing with these folks.

On opening night of the new Steppenwolf, tension ran high. We were still painting the walls a half hour before the audience started to arrive. We performed two of the one-act plays, one right after the other, and the stage exploded with energy. The next night we planned to do the other two plays and alternate back and forth from night to night. All the craziness in our lives found its target. The first review came out in our local newspaper, praising both the play selection and the acting, and reading it, we all couldn't help but grin.

Our excitement was over-the-top. We were finally starting to rock and roll. And we weren't passing the hubcaps for donations anymore. But at three bucks per seat, three fifty on weekends, the shows were a bargain even in 1976. We had very little money to produce our shows, but somehow we scraped together enough to put on more and more plays. Sometimes the basement was packed. Other times, we had more people onstage than in the audience—maybe a cast of seven and an audience of four. Some nights, no one came at all, so we ordered pizza and bought beer and turned it into our own little basement party. Again, no one was getting paid, but what really mattered was that we were doing our own thing in our own way, and even though our personal lives were chaotic, what happened onstage kept us together and moving forward.

By the time Steppenwolf opened its doors, *Saturday Night Live* had been up and running for a year, and on Saturdays after our shows we'd all go to someone's apartment to watch. Back then, the *SNL* cast included John Belushi, Chevy Chase, Dan Aykroyd, Gilda Radner, Jane Curtin, Laraine Newman, Garrett Morris, and Bill Murray. They were slightly older than we were, yet we identified so much with what they were doing as an ensemble. In general, Steppenwolf performed more serious work than *SNL*, but we approached the craft of being onstage with the same uninhibited passion and craziness.

On nights when no audience showed up, we hosted what we dubbed "Random Nights" in the basement, where we did anything possible to entertain ourselves. The more outrageous and sillier, the better. It turned out to be a good theater exercise, plus it kept our spirits up despite the empty house. John Malkovich had a running gag where he lip-synced to Springsteen's "Blinded by the Light"—the Manfred Mann's Earth Band version—and revved himself up like a deuce, rolling his hips, tripping and sneezing and wheezing with a boulder on his shoulder: the strangest dance moves anyone could imagine. We all hooted and howled and yelled catcalls from the audience. Terry liked to do a mime act, explaining that he was the rare mime who actually speaks. He had a dog named Fifi who did tricks for our entertainment. Terry positioned his hand like he was holding a leash and called out a trick. He ordered Fifi to sit, beg, jump, speak, and r-r-r-r-r-roll over—and we all gasped in astonishment, amazed by Fifi's expertise. Now, we couldn't actually see Fifi or her tricks because . . . she's a mime's dog. Get it? Moira performed as a French singer with the most horrendous French accent you've ever heard. Completely out of tune, she sang songs such as "Fool on the Hill" and "The Way We Were." "The Sound of Silence" was a house favorite. Moira's accent and pitch were so perfectly terrible that Laurie Metcalf had tears in her eyes, she laughed so hard.

Just for fun, I rented a little super 8 film camera with a microphone on it. I put together a short comedy-of-errors film titled *The Audition*, set in the small town of Beason, Illinois. A big-city, out-of-work New York hack is hired to direct *Hamlet* for a Beason community theater production of the play. The director starts with a grandiose speech, then the various citizens of the town try out for the play by giving their best rendition of the famous "To be or not to be" soliloquy.

Everyone in the company was in the movie, so today this is considered everyone's first film performance. Terry starred as the hack director, Dan Ville, who begins to lose his mind as each audition gets worse and worse until finally, after it's all over and he's sitting alone in the empty theater, he closes his eyes in exhaustion and dreams of his perfect Hamlet—which, since he's a terrible director himself, is not all that great. Moira played the assistant director, Cheryl Soul, a Corn Chex–chomping nutcase who crunches on cereal constantly but absolutely loves everyone's audition. Jeff played a character called Billy Guile, a local car dealer with a bad haircut and a hideously ugly plaid jacket. Someone has coaxed him into auditioning, so he walks up with a potbelly and a cigarette hanging out of his mouth and, bored to tears and a bit aggravated at being there, delivers his *Hamlet* speech like he's got some bad indigestion. Then he just quits in the middle of the speech because he's tired and wants to sit down. Al Wilder played a character in a hideously ugly leisure suit who performed the lead role in Beason's most recent musical, so he's overconfident, feeling spunky, and turns the classic speech into a song-and-dance number. Laurie Metcalf danced behind Wilder, dressed up as the self-described "ugliest gal in town," complete with crazy hair, dopey glasses, and no dancing skills whatsoever. When Wilder is asked by the director why Laurie is onstage, he replies, "She's my chorus." H. E. Baccus played Julius Rudell, an eccentric man in very tight shorts with an inflated vision of himself, and Malkovich was the local numbskull called Two-Barrel Wimer.

It was a wonderful experiment in how stupid we could be. We shot the twelve-minute movie in the basement, then realized some of the film

I'd bought wasn't equipped for sound. We had to shoot part of the movie again. Joan Allen was part of the first shoot, cast as a dancing girl with Laurie, but she couldn't be there for the reshoot, so she only appeared in the soundless outtakes I strung together as a blooper reel. We rented a projector and a screen and threw a couple of parties where we showed the film. I still have copies, and one of these days, who knows, maybe it'll show up again.

At one point, Terry decided to leave again. Then he wanted back in again. This time, we held a meeting to decide if Terry could rejoin. We all argued and shouted about "standing on our principles" and "being fully committed." Moira was there, and we were still dating, although our relationship was constantly up and down, on and off. Her father was dying of cancer then, and all the chaos and stress of the meeting prompted Moira to boil over. Her passion turned to fury, and she lost it. I mean, absolutely lost it. She started yelling, "How can we not let our friend back in the company?! My father is dying, and this is all so stupid! If we're a company, then we're a company, and we should stay together no matter what!"

She ran out of the basement into the grassy yard of the school yelling at the top of her lungs. We all ran out into the yard after her. Her logic made sense. Terry was our friend. Moira's dad was dying. Terry wanted back in the company. Why did we care so passionately about something so trivial when life-and-death issues were all around us?

Moira was still screaming and crying. We grabbed hold of her and hung on. Neighbors poked their heads out of doorways. She screamed and screamed, and the commotion grew so loud the police showed up. Moira calmed down. The police left. We all felt bad for Moira, bad for Terry, and we ended the meeting. Of course, Terry was back in the company. He was a founder and our friend. In those early days, the drama wasn't limited to the stage.

I don't think any of us knew exactly what we were doing. The basement cocoon we created gave us a foundation to try anything, do anything, become anything—and the freedom of the space allowed us ultimately to glimpse the world through a wider lens. All of us were committed to becoming better at what we were doing, and we often mixed and mingled our directing and performing, directing one play, acting in the next, sometimes doing both. In those early days, we didn't talk about going to Hollywood or New York or being in the movies. We wanted to do our own thing—there, in Chicagoland—and I think by being in the basement, isolated, we developed the chip on our shoulder necessary to survive. We felt we had a lot of emerging talent and wanted our work to feel real and raw and fearless, and we worked hard to keep it deeply rooted in the sheer grit that we had onstage together. Whether it was true or not, we needed to somehow believe our work was different, unique, and special. It would take some time and effort before anyone tried to branch out beyond our city, but I think in those early days we all felt like we were getting better and stronger and more confident as artists, and that the sky would be the limit—eventually.

What I know today is that our theater benefited from a larger institution—the United States of America. The country of our birth allowed us any number of freedoms that we subconsciously used and enjoyed and benefited from, even though we didn't realize it. We had freedom of speech at Steppenwolf—we could express thoughts and ideas about anything in public or private. The people around us might disagree or debate us or push back when they thought we were being stupid, but by no means were we ever stifled in what we said or thought. We exercised the freedom to assemble. We used a sort of freedom of religion, although nothing we did was religious, which was a freedom all its own. No one forced us to dress a certain way or talk a certain way because of their beliefs. We were free to live or travel anywhere we wanted, and we were free to work any job we wanted—so we played in bands and created our own theater and worked in sewers where we found baby racoons. We were free to educate ourselves by any means possible, formal or practical. And all this freedom led to something. It allowed us to create and innovate. It allowed us to dream big. Gratefully, it allowed us to be *us*. Everyone who stayed with the theater in those early days went on to make their livings as actors and directors. And I think everyone would agree that those days spent in the basement provided the solid foundation for each of our careers. The building of Steppenwolf Theatre is truly an American dream story, a story of starting with nothing but an idea and a passion, and building it into something purposeful, meaningful, and successful. And you know, one of these days I'm going to have to get around to reading the Hermann Hesse novel.

⸎

Moira and I got together as a couple a year after the Vietnam War ended in 1975, and I started to meet her family members who had served in the US Army. Moira's brother, Arthur Harris, was a helicopter pilot, having flown eight hundred combat hours in Vietnam. Moira's oldest brother, Boyd McCanna "Mac" Harris, had been to Vietnam twice, first as a lieutenant and platoon leader, and second as captain and company commander. He'd received the Silver Star for gallantry in combat. Moira's sister, Amy, went through ROTC in college and went into the army herself after graduation. She met and married a great guy, Jack Treese, who'd served as a combat medic with the 101st Airborne Division in Vietnam. Jack earned two Bronze Stars and two Purple Hearts. When Arthur came home from Vietnam, he withdrew from things, and I would see him only on rare occasions when Moira and I would visit her mother. But from time to time, Mac, Jack, and Amy came to visit us in Chicago and would see our plays.

I didn't spend a ton of time with these veterans at first, but anytime we got together, we talked about deeper matters, and as I slowly learned more and more about the people who protected our freedoms, I began to look for ways to give back.

In 1976 and 1977, Mac came to see a few of our basement plays whenever he was on leave from his assignment as a tactical officer at West Point. I was a pretty ragged kid then, with torn-up jeans and a T-shirt and lots of hair. He was spit-shined, strong as Atlas, and had a deep, powerful voice.

"Gary, what are your goals?" Mac asked me one day after a show. He wasn't grilling me. I sensed kindness within his toughness. He was interested in other people's lives and genuinely wanted to know about my goals. But I wasn't sure if he was asking about my goals in life or my designs on his sister. Possibly, he wanted to know where we wanted to go as a theater company. So I described my goals for Steppenwolf, how I wanted to take it as big as possible. We had a conversation, a real conversation. This elite former company commander and me, a long-haired American twenty-one-year-old with big dreams. Of all things, we connected on the subject of leadership.

In high school, at the height of the war, I had been oblivious to so much that was happening in Vietnam. Yet in the early years of Steppenwolf, as I began to form genuine friendships with these military veterans, they began to open my eyes to so much more. I knew the war hadn't gone well. I remembered casualty reports on the news and knew the reports were grim. But now I was meeting actual veterans who'd lived there, served there, fought there, and I knew that many of the Vietnam veterans who'd returned home hadn't been honored for their service.

I didn't know what to do yet about this, if anything. But I felt something stirring inside of me. Honor needed to be granted. Respect was due. A simple "thanks" needed to be said. It would take a few years before I figured out any sort of next step. But in the meantime, I had theater and Moira's family members, and I knew something in our country desperately needed to change. I would start where I could. With Steppenwolf. And without being able to articulate it this way yet, I would begin to do my part to give back.

CHAPTER 4

The Corner of
Hollywood and Love

Moira, sweet Moira. Her story—our story—is intertwined with Steppenwolf and Chicago and Hollywood and the anything-goes culture of the day, as well as hopes and dreams and stops and starts.

In the summer of 1975, Steppenwolf was under way with one final production of the original group of high school kids, a play called *The Effect of Gamma Rays on Man-in-the-Moon Marigolds* by Paul Zindel. My only involvement was writing the music. It would be another year before the fuller ensemble formed, and over the course of the summer, I worked part-time for my dad, played in my bands, and as often as I could I would take a break from all that to visit Terry and Jeff at Illinois State University.

The school had a summer repertory theater for students, and Jeff and Terry took me to see a production of Tennessee Williams's Pulitzer Prize–winning *Cat on a Hot Tin Roof*. The actress playing "Maggie the Cat" absolutely came alive up onstage. Maggie is a desperate character, rejected and scorned, who wears a negligee for the entire first act of the show. She attempts to seduce her estranged husband while trying to coax her dying father-in-law to give them his Mississippi cotton plantation.

I couldn't take my eyes off the actress playing Maggie—long brown hair to the middle of her back, blue eyes and beautifully expressive face, and a dynamic stage presence. She had the raw power of classic Broadway and film actresses like Colleen Dewhurst or Geraldine Page, and her beauty reminded me of Natalie Wood or Sophia Loren.

After the show, Jeff introduced me to her. She was a theater student named Moira Harris, and our initial meeting was quick. Somehow, I found out that she had a crush on Jeff, so I headed back up to Highland Park and continued playing in my bands and working for my dad. I didn't see or hear of her for some time, although later, when she played the role of Blanche DuBois in a production of *A Streetcar Named Desire* at ISU, I hopped in my '69 Camaro and drove down to see that play too. Once again, she was electric. I never knew what she would do next onstage, and every movement she made captivated me. And once again, I couldn't take my eyes off her.

In January 1976, Jeff and Terry and I started holding meetings at Illinois State to put together the Steppenwolf ensemble, and Moira was one of the actresses Jeff and Terry invited to the meetings. We held lots of meetings, and after one I drove Moira back to her dorm. We clicked quickly. She was funny, offbeat, highly intelligent, and sexy. When I stopped in front of her dorm, Moira jumped out, said a quick "see ya," and hurried inside. *Rats.*

It wasn't until the summer of 1976, after Moira had joined Steppenwolf, that she began to show any interest in me. Everybody in our new company who came from Illinois State needed a place to live. I'd already found an apartment in Lake Bluff that Terry and I were going to share, so everybody piled into our apartment at the start, sort of commune-style, and all kinds of things happened in this little apartment until people found other places to rent. Moira and Nancy Evans soon found a rental to split in nearby Highwood, and Moira and I realized our attraction for each other was growing. Pretty soon, we became a couple and soon after decided to live together. Moira's parents were none too happy about our decision. It was the 1970s, the days of "anything goes," and Moira and I squabbled and broke up, got back together, then squabbled some more, then broke up, then got back together. Lather, rinse, repeat.

After our summer season of four one-act plays at Steppenwolf, we opened the fall 1976 season with a play called *Look, We've Come Through,* and it flopped—our first play that really tanked—but as an ensemble we laughed it off. (We should have been tipped off about this play, because the director, H. E. Baccus, found it in a book titled *Broadway's Beautiful Losers.*) After that, we started putting together *The Sea Horse* with Moira and me in main roles and John Malkovich directing. I loved being onstage with Moira. But just before opening night, she developed phlebitis in her leg, a highly painful condition where a vein becomes inflamed. We sought medical help right away, and doctors ordered her to stay off her feet for a while. Moira couldn't go on. Holy cow! It was our opening performance. Tickets were sold, and we even had a few potential donors coming that night. We started to scramble. We asked the few critics who were reviewing us at the time to hold off until Moira was back, and John jumped into action to find a replacement. The show must go on!

Rondi Reed, a classmate of all the ISU folks, had performed the same play the previous year, so Malkovich called her up and promised her fifty bucks for a one-night performance. She drove up from Bloomington-Normal and met me for the first time ever about fifteen minutes before the curtain went up. It's a highly physical play that contains some violent scenes. Moira and I had never choreographed all of our movements, so I explained to Rondi that in rehearsals Moira and I just kind of whaled on each other during those moments. The lights dimmed, the curtain went up, and Rondi and I did the play. She pulled off the performance brilliantly, and thankfully nobody got hurt. The show played well to the audience, and Rondi got her fifty bucks and headed back to Illinois State.

But what about the next night? Laurie Metcalf had returned to ISU that fall to finish her final semester at school, so John called and asked if she would be able to take time off to come back and help. Laurie is an amazingly quick study, so the next day she learned the part in the car on the way up to Highland Park, and when she arrived I also explained to her that for the fight scenes we would just go at each other. Crazy, but it worked. Laurie continued brilliantly in the role for the rest of that weekend. The following week Moira felt better again, came back full force, and was awesome. The critics came, the show, Moira, and I got good reviews, and it did well for us. So, it all worked out in the end. And since Laurie was already in Steppenwolf, we didn't have to pay her. Hey, fifty bucks was fifty bucks.

Steppenwolf put on more plays throughout 1976 and 1977, and from time to time we moved a few shows into the city. In the summer of 1977, we were able to pull some funding together to rent a bigger, more professional space on the North Side of Chicago called the Jane Addams Hull House. This was our first official run in the city of Chicago. We remounted two of our one-acts, *Birdbath* and *The Indian Wants the Bronx*, and, later, another play called *Our Late Night*. I was not in that play, so I took a bass-playing gig in the Quad Cities to back up a vocal group, seven weeks of shows at the John Deere convention. I remember being there on August 16, 1977, when we heard the news that Elvis Presley had died. Sad to see the King go. We played a few Elvis songs that night.

The one-acts did well that summer, the other show flopped, and we tried, as always, to learn from our mistakes in order to make our shows better. In fall 1978, Chicago's St. Nicholas Theater Company, founded by William H. Macy and David Mamet, among others, hired seven out of the nine actors in our ensemble to be in a play called *Fifth of July*, written by the great playwright Lanford Wilson. It was the first time members of our company got paid for acting—eight shows a week for a hundred bucks per person. After taxes, it dropped to eighty-eight bucks a week, and the money didn't go far. We all ate a lot of mac and cheese back then. A can of tuna fish mixed in was a big treat.

Some family location shuffling turned out to have a big impact. My parents decided to move to Los Angeles where Dad opened the West Coast office of his film editing business. Mom, Dad, my brother, and my sister moved out to California while I stayed back in Highwood, living with Moira. Steppenwolf grew stronger all the time, although no one yet made a living from acting. We were into our second season of plays as a full ensemble and growing, yet we were all still working day jobs.

Neither Moira nor I had ever been to California, so in the summer of 1978, we took a break from theater and visited my parents for a couple of weeks. Moira and I were at another tense point in our relationship—so tense we wondered if we should break up for good. We'd broken up a few times before, but a visceral magnetism always pulled us back together. Still, this time we visited my parents with the plan to break up after we returned to Chicago.

California was amazing to us midwestern kids. We did all the touristy things. We drove up the coast from L.A. to San Francisco with my parents, marveling at the ocean the whole way. We stopped in the romantic towns of Monterey and Carmel-by-the-Sea. We headed back to L.A. and toured Universal Studios and Hollywood Boulevard. My mom took us to Beverly Hills to see the stars' homes, then down to Grauman's Chinese Theatre where we put our hands in the handprints and saw the stars on the Hollywood Walk of Fame. Moira and I really enjoyed our trip, even though throughout our travels, the big decision of whether to break up for good still hung over our heads.

When we returned to Chicago, we decided to give it one more go, but our relationship remained rocky. While we were working at the St. Nicholas on *Fifth of July*, Moira's father, who'd been battling lung cancer for some time, was not doing well at all. Moira had a new day job as a receptionist at a law firm in Chicago where one of the attorneys developed a crush on her. Moira's parents and older sister wanted her to break up with me and take up with the attorney. So Moira felt very torn at this time. We loved each other, but our relationship spiked up and plunged down, always confused. During the run of *Fifth of July*, Moira's father passed away. It was hard on her, and I tried my best to help her through.

In January 1979, Chicago experienced a blisteringly cold winter with record amounts of snowfall. Steppenwolf rented the Hull House again and was set to perform the absurdist drama *Exit the King* during one of our hardest winters ever. Snow piled high throughout Chicago, over people's heads in some places, and people literally rode snowmobiles up and down the street in front of the theater. We wondered if anyone would come to the play. In typical Steppenwolf style, we threw everything we had into the show, and after it opened critics reviewed it well. But given the cold nights and frosty streets, and perhaps the nontraditional tone of the play, hardly anyone showed up to see it. After the last show, we got together at someone's apartment. Malkovich looked at me, and I looked at Malkovich, and Jeff looked at Terry, and Terry looked at Jeff. No one knew what to do or say. Steppenwolf was broke, completely flat out of money. It was maybe our lowest point as a company.

The winter ice thawed. In the spring, back in the basement in Highland Park, Steppenwolf somehow scraped up enough cash to put on another play. But in my quietest moments I began to have doubts about what I was doing and I wondered if I should take a break from the theater. Try something else. It was just so difficult to make acting a career. Did I actually have the stuff to make it? I decided not to be a part of the play. Instead, I could take advantage of the opportunity of my parents having a place to stay in California and give Hollywood a try instead. So Moira and I made a decision to take a break from Steppenwolf, move out to Los Angeles, and live with my parents for a while—and we also decided to get married. Mom was thrilled and jumped into wedding planning with Moira, but I could tell something was churning in Moira's mind.

In Los Angeles, I worked with my dad at his editing business and tried to land auditions anywhere I could think of, but everywhere I went, I heard the same thing. Casting directors asked, "Where did you study?" And I said, "Well, I didn't study. I started a theater company in Chicago." And they said, "Go get some acting lessons and come back."

Dad knew someone at the daytime soap *General Hospital*, so I landed a job for one day as an extra. It was a disco scene with the two stars, Luke and Laura, one of my first brushes with being on set. I danced in the background at a club while Luke and Laura played their scene. This was my first experience in Hollywood, just one of a dozen extras shaking my hips in the background. I felt like an idiot, and afterward I wasn't sure what to make of it all, but at least it put a few bucks in my pocket.

A tiny Hollywood theater called the Met had placed an ad in the newspaper. They were looking for an actor to step into the role of the son in a play called *Curse of the Starving Class* by Sam Shepard. Malkovich had performed the same show a year earlier in Chicago—not with Steppenwolf—and I'd seen it, so I was already familiar with the play. They were auditioning actors because the guy playing the son had been in the role awhile. It was an "equity waiver" production in a theater with only fifty-five seats. *Equity* is the term given to the theater actors' union, and under an equity waiver contract, in theaters with under ninety-nine seats, equity actors can work basically for free and do four performances a week, a total of eighty shows of the same production, before a regular union contract needs to be negotiated. The Met theater wanted to keep the show running without going union. If you act in an equity show, you waive a salary, but you get paid gas money, with the chance that agents, casting directors, and film producers will wander into the show and see you. So I auditioned and landed the role of the young son named Wesley. Sally Kirkland and James Gammon, two well-known Hollywood staples, played the mom and dad. Wesley was a great part, a wild kid who is cursed and ends up going completely crazy. There is a live lamb onstage throughout the show, and toward the end of the play the wild kid walks onstage stark naked, picks up the lamb, and carries it offstage. My parents came to my opening night. *Look, Mom! It's me in my birthday suit.* Yikes! We started doing four shows a week.

It was hilarious how poor we all were, how desperately we all wanted to make it into the movie business. Gammon lived across the alley from the theater in a tiny shoebox of a walk-up, and he'd done more than one of these equity shows. He'd become so used to doing the play that he simply hung out in his living room watching TV until his scene came up. He would then pop across the alley, do the scene, then amble off home again. I wasn't quite this industry-weary yet. I was thrilled to be part of the show, and lo and behold, an agent actually came to see me and even landed me a few auditions. They were all busts.

But I had the play. Meanwhile, Mom was planning the wedding, and I was trying to figure out what Moira was thinking. One day, shortly before the wedding date, Moira told me she planned to fly home to Illinois to spend some time with her mom before coming back in time for the wedding. A couple days after she landed in Chicago, the phone rang.

"Gary, I don't want to get married," Moira said. "I'm not coming back."

"Wh-what?" I said.

She paused, then added, "I can't do it."

"Wait! Invitations have gone out. We've got all this food ordered."

"I know, but I'm not going to do it. I can't. I just can't."

We were both young. We'd been through our good times and some difficult times, and looking back I'm not surprised at her reluctance to get married. Deep down, I think we both had some fear about making lifelong vows.

I hung up and told my parents the wedding was off. I didn't say much more than that, and let my parents deal with the mess of cancellations and everything else. Moira stayed in Chicago, and I stayed in Hollywood and kept doing the play. Eventually I found out that Moira had returned to California with her mother. Reflecting on the death of her father, Moira had decided to become a nurse, so while taking acting classes at the Lee Strasberg Institute, she also was going to nursing school. But we didn't see each other. We didn't connect. We didn't talk.

In late summer 1979, I found out that Robert Redford was making a big movie called *Ordinary People*, and I landed an audition but didn't get called back. How could that be?! I was perfect for this role, I thought. Mr. Redford didn't know what he was missing. The story takes place in Lake Forest, Illinois, right next to Highland Park where I grew up. *This is me! I already know this character inside and out! I should be playing this part!* I'd heard all these Hollywood urban myths, like the one where Steven Spielberg climbs over the fence at Universal Studios and gets his start in the film industry. I thought, *Hey, I can do that too. As soon as he sees me, Mr. Redford will cast me. All I need is for him to see me face-to-face!*

So I sneaked into the Warner Bros. lot, planted myself down on the couch in the office of casting director Penny Perry, and informed the receptionist that I wouldn't leave until I could have an audition with Mr. Redford himself. The receptionist asked if I had an appointment. I said no, but explained the story. The receptionist went and told Penny Perry, and Penny came out and asked in a kind, but very flat voice: "Gary, what are you doing?"

"I know I wasn't cast," I said. "But I grew up in Highland Park. I'm perfect for this movie! I need to see Robert Redford."

She sighed. "Sorry. You are *not* going to see Robert Redford."

"Well, I'm not leaving. I'm going to sit right on this couch until I do."

She crossed her arms. "Gary, don't do this. If you don't get off the couch, I'm going to have to call security."

"Please! I grew up right there!"

Penny's eyebrows lowered. "You auditioned. You didn't get called back. Leave the building, or I will have you taken off the lot."

I stared back at her. Silent. Hangdog. Reluctantly, I accepted the fact that Robert Redford would not be meeting Gary Sinise that afternoon. I slowly got up, utterly defeated, left the office, and walked out the front gate of the studios. I wasn't doing very well in this town. The thought of heading back to Chicago sounded better and better. On the way home I came to the conclusion that had been brewing in me for a while now: *Hollywood hates me.*

Timothy Hutton landed the part. It was his first acting gig since playing a bit role in a movie when he was a kid plus a few small TV slots on *Disney*. Tim had never lived anywhere close to Highland Park, but for his performance in *Ordinary People*, he ended up winning an Oscar. He was only twenty when he won, the youngest male actor to win an Academy Award for Best Supporting Actor. And I had to admit, he was really good.

That's how it goes in Hollywood.

And, nope, to this day I've never met Robert Redford.

Having decided Hollywood hated me, I started packing up to go home. A week before I left Los Angeles and headed back to Chicago, I called Moira and asked her to dinner at a jazz club on Cahuenga Boulevard called the Baked Potato. She agreed, perhaps only to say goodbye to me, and in the true spirit of the first few years of our relationship, we had dinner and sparks flew again. She was stunningly beautiful, as usual. We hadn't seen each other or talked for a year, but we talked for a long time and sorted out a bunch of things. The electricity was palpable—and then during dinner I dumped my hot baked potato on my lap. Thankfully, nothing important was scalded.

I still needed to head back to Chicago. Hollywood might have offered no place for me, but Steppenwolf had made some good progress in my absence. While I was gone, they'd put on several successful shows, including a revival of *The Glass Menagerie*, which would be our final production in the Catholic school basement, the summer of 1979. In the fall, the theater would do productions of *Waiting for Lefty* and *Say Goodnight Gracie* at different theaters in Chicago. Then in early 1980, we were able to rent the larger space in the Hull House to make official the big move from Highland Park into the city. Steppenwolf had added some new members to the company too: Francis Guinan, Tom Irwin, Rondi Reed, Mary Copple, Mike Sassone, Glenne Headly, and John Mahoney. Mary and Mike would stay for only a few years.

Just before I left Hollywood, my agent landed me an audition for a bit part on the prime-time evening soap opera, *Knots Landing*, playing a teenager doing some underage drinking at a party on a beach. I got the part! My character's name was Lee Maddox, and I had a couple of lines and a make-out scene with a girl while sitting beside a campfire. My very first time acting on film. Let's just say it wasn't *From Here to Eternity*. Certainly not enough to keep me in Los Angeles any longer.

Steppenwolf opened the 1980 season in March. I moved back with no place to live. I just showed up with my bags and said, "Hi, I'm back. What can I do?" Steppenwolf folded me back into the company immediately, although our current season was already under way, so I had no formal roles in plays for a while. Meanwhile, I did whatever I could to help. Park cars, mostly—splitting the ten-dollar-per-car parking fee between Steppenwolf and me. I also stepped back into Steppenwolf as a "substitute" actor—if someone needed to miss a performance for a night or a few weeks, I jumped into their role. I performed in *Death of a Salesman* and also *Say Goodnight Gracie* for a weekend, which turned out to be one of our biggest hits up to that point. We added a midnight series of plays, and I performed in one, *The Collection* by Harold Pinter. Steppenwolf wasn't rolling in dough, but we could finally pay our actors a bit. Francis Guinan offered me space to sleep on the floor of his apartment. After a while, I found a small studio apartment a block away from the theater. Mice had moved in before me, and every night I heard the patter of tiny feet scamper across the countertops. Moira was still in California, finishing nursing school, but we talked regularly on the phone and wrote letters back and forth. The embers underneath the charred wood of our relationship roused to life and burned ever more brightly as time went on.

With no roles yet available in Steppenwolf, I heard about an audition for a role with another company called the Wisdom Bridge Theatre. The role was a paying gig, in a play called *Getting Out*. I landed the larger supporting role, playing a drug-addicted pimp named Carl. For playing Carl, I received my first award nomination, called the Joseph Jefferson Award. The nomination was for Best Supporting Actor, and I won.

I loved Chicago. In Hollywood, I was a dopey disco dancer in the background with Luke and Laura. I was a loser guy on the beach. And I'd been thrown off the lot at Warner Bros. and was told by a casting director to come back when I'd had some acting lessons. I couldn't get ahead no matter how hard I tried. But back in Chicago, I went to work as an actor almost right away, got paid for it, and won a recognized award—all within six months.

Steppenwolf remained superbusy, moving at a tornado's pace. In the fall of 1980 we did a great production of *Balm in Gilead*. It was a huge hit with a huge cast—twenty-eight characters in all—and did so well we did it again the following summer, this time at a larger theater in Chicago called the Apollo.

Balm in Gilead is about misfits who hang out in a street corner diner in New York City. Every character is a hooker, pimp, drug addict, or alcoholic, and I played a junkie-druggie stage manager. Malkovich directed and used some cool music—Rickie Lee Jones and Bruce Springsteen and Tom Waits—to backdrop the whole show. I'd grown my hair out long, so I could really get into my character, and most days I walked around wearing old ripped jeans, a T-shirt, a red bandanna, and sunglasses.

Moira finished nursing school in California, yet she never worked as a nurse. She moved back to Chicago in 1981 and rejoined the company, and we formally rekindled our relationship. Somewhere in the middle of the revival production of *Balm in Gilead,* Moira and I took a good look at each other, shrugged, and said to each other: "Hey, let's get married."

So we did. We'd been dating for five years. The morning of July 21, 1981, we got a quick blood test because you needed one in those days to get a license, then made an appointment with a judge for later that same day. This time, there were no invitations or appetizers or monogrammed napkins. It was the total opposite of the kind of wedding that had been planned a couple of years earlier in California.

Moira and I didn't even have any rings. We'd been living together in a basement apartment on Montana Street, not far from the Apollo Theater where *Balm in Gilead* was playing and right down the street from the Biograph Theater (gangster John Dillinger was shot and killed in the alley there). Just before we went to the judge, I dashed down the street from our apartment to a Woolworth's five-and-dime store. I found two small rings in a plastic bag—a buck sixty-nine for both rings—and ran back to Moira. We invited a few friends to join us—Laurie Metcalf, Jeff Perry, Jeanine Morick, Moira's sister Lois, and one of Lois's good friends. We jumped into a cab and headed to the courthouse.

The judge was a diminutive African American woman. Maybe five feet tall. Moira and I stood before her desk and she asked, "Okay, you ready?" We both nodded. I'd taken off my bandanna and sunglasses and slipped into slacks, a light-blue shirt, and a blazer. Moira wore a black blouse and a short skirt. The judge pulled out a little music box and wound it up. The Carpenters' "Close to You" drifted out of the music box and we all grinned and hummed along. When the song finished, the judge walked us through our vows. We took our rings from the plastic bag and put them on each other's fingers. (Within three weeks, our fingers turned green, and we never wore those rings again.) I kissed the bride. We were married. The ceremony lasted maybe two minutes, tops. We took a few photos; everyone hugged and headed out of the judge's office for an early wedding celebration meal at Carson's barbecue joint. After dinner, I went home, changed clothes, and headed off to do the play that evening, while Moira left with her sister and friends for a little more celebrating.

Later that evening, after *Balm* finished, I told the cast that Moira and I had tied the knot, and I invited everybody to come on over to our apartment for a party. Everybody was always up for a party, so I brought the whole cast and crew back. Only one problem: Moira wasn't home yet—and it was late. I started calling around, trying to find her. A lot of theater folks hung out in a nearby bar called the Old Town Ale House, so I called them up, and sure enough, Moira and her sister were there—and they'd been there for a while.

"Honey," I said into the phone, "I brought the cast over. Let's have a party. It's our wedding night!"

Moira, sounding slightly tipsy, said, "Okay. I'll be home soon."

Cast members were drinking heavily in our apartment, doing all sorts of party stuff, when Moira returned half an hour later. Everybody was tipsy by then. As soon as she came through the door, Moira's emotions slid all over the place. She laughed hysterically one minute, cried like a baby the next. I have a photo of Moira, Malkovich, and me hugging while Moira sits on John's lap on a chair in our kitchen, laughing with mascara running down her face. Very passionate, very drunk, like everyone else there. That was our wedding night.

Despite the general insanity of our lives, I was later able to see and be grateful for the many positive things that happened during those early years of Steppenwolf. We faced many challenges and made many messes, yet those years set the table for so much good to happen later on. A lot of party stuff happened back then: beer, booze, pot, coke, magic mushrooms. And while not everybody we knew participated heavily, it seemed that every night, after every performance, someone threw a party. This wasn't just happening at Steppenwolf. Less than a year later, on March 5, 1982, *Saturday Night Live*'s John Belushi was found dead of a heroin overdose at the Chateau Marmont Hotel in Los Angeles. It felt like nearly everybody in those days—my whole generation—was going a bit crazy as we tried to find our way, grow up, and figure out our stuff. But onstage, we were serious and committed, and we left the partying for after our work was done. For Steppenwolf, this jumble of emotional childishness and passion infused its way into a lot of our early work, coming together in such a way that over-the-top emotion, commitment, and passion became signature characteristics of Steppenwolf.

In the early 1980s, our theater grew, and we began to raise more money. We started to sell subscriptions and developed a stronger board of directors. We scored some hits at the box office, enabling us to extend the run of our plays. Eventually, as we started to have enough work as actors, we all were able to quit our day jobs and focus completely on building the theater, all the while getting better as actors and directors and theater artists.

And Moira and me? After forty years of being together, through all our ups and downs, all our confusion, all our passion, all our mistakes, all our successes—we are still married and still in love.

CHAPTER 5

When We Started to Look Beyond Ourselves

H. E. Baccus had been the artistic director of Steppenwolf from our beginnings when we were in the basement of the Catholic school in 1976. Four years later, in the fall of 1980 and about six months after I'd come back from Hollywood, *Balm in Gilead* became a huge hit for us, and we were on a roll. For the next production, H.E. had selected a comedy called *Absent Friends* that he was going to direct. During rehearsals, everything was going smoothly, or so we thought. One morning H.E. called us out of the blue and announced he wasn't coming back in. He was a musician, he insisted, and he wanted to focus his energy there. So he quit the theater for good. We were caught completely off guard, but we wished him well and then scrambled to find another director. Malkovich stepped in and finished the production, which turned out to be a hit.

Once we got through opening night and the play was up and running, we met to decide on the next permanent AD. Malkovich and I were both suggested. John reluctantly said okay to being considered, but his tone didn't suggest he really wanted to do it. He'd filled in as AD a few years earlier when H.E. had taken a summer off, and under his leadership we'd done a controversial dark comedy by Wallace Shawn, *Our Late Night*. Edgy and sexually explicit, it received terrible reviews. We had thought it was kind of funny, but audience members walked out in droves. Being artistic director is a tough job with a lot of pressure. You pick all the plays. Some of them work; some don't. So while John accepted putting his name in for a vote, I don't think his heart was in it. The ensemble voted, and I landed the position. I think John was relieved. He liked his flexibility and the ability to work at Steppenwolf or other theaters if parts came along. As for me, I jumped into the role as artistic director, ready to go. I proved a much different type of leader than H.E. I was convinced we needed to approach our work more like a business. The following Monday morning, I came in with a new set of rules. High on the list was the following: "All staff members in by 9:00 a.m. every day." I made several other changes, and even fired someone. Good Lord! The new rules and approach came as a shock to the ensemble, sort of like General Patton had just walked in. While we still maintained our collaborative approach to the direction we wanted to go as a company, as AD I felt it was time to approach things a bit differently, to step up our game and allow the artistic director to lead in a new way.

One rule I implemented was the now-infamous—at least among the company—"no pot" rule. No pot could be smoked (or eaten) anywhere around the theater until after showtime. No beer either. Everyone thought the "No Pot" rule was hilarious coming from a guy who openly partook from time to time. But for the most part, everyone went along with it.

On a few occasions, the new rules were broken, and I made my disapproval known. Once, during a performance of a play I directed, I sneaked into the theater to check on the play and watched from the back of the house. During one scene I saw that a bunch of lighting cues I'd set for the play had been screwed up—totally off. After the show, I went up to the light booth to talk to the crew and found open beer cans. They'd been drinking during the show and had messed up the cues. I hit the ceiling, threw their beer into the garbage, and shouted at them to shape up. They never messed up again. Another time I went out to lunch with our board president and afterward brought her back to the theater, only to find a friend of the company who we'd worked with a few times sitting there calmly rolling a doobie. I quickly turned the president around before she noticed him and walked her out to her car. I then came back and chewed him out. After a while, I calmed down and explained to him, and to others who had gathered around, that I was serious about our theater and wanted folks to get on board with the new way of operating. We had such amazing talent in our group, and I was simply trying to focus our energies on getting better, saving the partying for after hours.

I felt confident in Steppenwolf. We all felt confident in Steppenwolf. Perhaps too confident. We had great faith in the chemistry and energy of our ensemble. But I believed we needed to get more serious about how we approached our work and built our company. And we did. And after a while, the "no pot" rule became a funny Steppenwolf legend that we still laugh about today.

Yet even with a little bit of chaos in our business approach to things, onstage we were dynamite, and by that time we were brash and even a bit arrogant about our work. We felt we had one of the best companies anywhere and as actors we could do anything we set our minds to. When Malkovich had directed *Balm in Gilead*, the success of the show had fueled those feelings of invincibility. John was ready to tackle his next big challenge.

One of my primary responsibilities as the new AD was to figure out what to put on the stage. But when I began as AD, I inherited a season that had already been planned by our previous AD. One production already in the works was *Savages*, by British playwright Christopher Hampton, with Malkovich set to direct. The plot centers around a historical atrocity that happened in the early 1960s: the systematic removal from the rain forest and the eventual slaughter of a single tribe of South American Indians. The play was an ambitious undertaking for our company—not only because of the calamitous subject matter, but also due to the simple logistics of assembling the needed cast.

The show was written for five or six South American tribespeople, but John wanted an epic. He envisioned twenty-five tribespeople in the cast, and he wanted them all naked for the whole show. We didn't have anything close to South American tribespeople in our ensemble, so we hired mostly Caucasian actors from all over Chicago. We held rehearsals with our big, naked cast, put Moe wigs on their heads (we called them Moe wigs because they looked like the hair of the Three Stooges character), and painted them up with full body makeup. Looking back, this entire idea was totally misguided, of course. But we did it. We were a risk-taking kind of company, right? Sometimes those risks work. Sometimes they misfire. The wigs and the body paint were just of few of many misfires for this production.

We did our tech rehearsals, adding the lights and a set that had these long drapes hanging on the back wall that looked like five strips of turkey bacon. Another misfire. The show began. Malkovich thought it was great to have a big group of fleshy people onstage, and I thought, why not? But since the Hull House Theater had only 134 seats, twenty-five naked people onstage felt sweaty and cramped—and not in a nice way. Attendance was low, and having a huge group of unclothed people sitting everywhere backstage before each show created a surreal vibe in the company. One day I wandered backstage and Jeff Perry, my best buddy, whom I'd known since high school days, was sitting with his Moe wig on. He was wearing his glasses, smoking a cigarette, legs crossed, and playing backgammon, as naked as the day he was born. He casually nodded at me, and I casually nodded back. What else were we supposed to do?

Critics hated the show. Absolutely despised it. *Savages* went down in history as an infamous Steppenwolf failure. Today, it gives us all endless pleasure to sit around, fully clothed (thankfully), telling stories about all the nakedness, wondering what could have possibly gone wrong.

As AD, I searched for all kinds of plays—and my radar was definitely tuned for plays about Vietnam. In 1981, we were only about six years removed from the American withdrawal from Saigon.

I'd been talking with Moira's two brothers, Mac Harris and Arthur Harris, and to Jack Treese, the husband of Moira's sister Amy, about their days in combat. The more we talked, the more I received a personal education about how bravely our country's veterans had fought and how poorly they were treated when they returned home. I came to see how our country had turned its back on the returning warriors and how that war still divided us. It was a shameful period in our nation's history, and many Vietnam veterans had simply disappeared into the shadows, not wanting to talk.

Jack, the combat medic, was nineteen years old when he served as a member of the Second Battalion 502nd Airborne Infantry. From July 3, 1967, to March 12, 1968, he saw 245 days of combat and survived some extremely difficult battles. He told me how he'd been so happy to be coming home before landing in San Francisco and seeing protests right in the airport. Glancing down at his uniform, he realized he was in hostile territory on American soil, so he went into the airport bathroom, took off his uniform, and put on civilian clothes for fear of being spit on or screamed at. Like so many of our Vietnam veterans, there was no "welcome home" for him.

Jack would go on to stay in the army for twenty-two years. He came from a difficult family environment, and joining the army as a young man gave him structure, discipline, and a home. It was always tough for him to recall the hostile reception our veterans received when returning from Vietnam, although I think for Jack and others who continued their service post-Vietnam, their transition was less difficult than for those who came home and immediately went back to civilian life. Somehow the culture shock wasn't as severe for those who continued to serve alongside fellow combat veterans. Years later, on a gray and misty September morning, he and I would travel to Washington, DC, where he would visit the Vietnam Veterans Memorial Wall for the first time. I watched him trace the names of two of his fallen comrades with a pencil and a thin piece of paper. It was a quiet and somber moment of reflection for Jack that I'll always remember.

Arthur told me he'd come back from Vietnam a changed man. Before he deployed, he had trained at helicopter school at Fort Wolters in Texas. He was an excellent pilot who survived many combat missions in Vietnam as well as a crash during training that gave him a banged-up hip that troubles him to this day. From 1971 to 1972 he served as a warrant officer second class with Delta Company and Bravo Company, 229th Assault Helicopter Battalion, First Cavalry Division out of Bien Hoa, Vietnam, enduring more than eight hundred combat hours as a helicopter pilot. He'd seen and experienced terrible moments during the war, one hot zone after another, and when he returned from Vietnam, for many years he had difficulty shaking away the memories. In fact, even today, talk to Arthur about Vietnam and it's as if it were yesterday; even the smallest details are burned into his memory—his mind totally sharp regarding his days in the war zone. After Vietnam, he went back to college and flew for the Illinois National Guard for a while. But adjusting to life outside combat did not come easy. He married, but as time went on he struggled, he drank more and more, and eventually he became estranged from his wife and daughters.

Years later, Arthur was living in a small place in Florida and, like so many of our Vietnam veterans, was having a tough time. Our home in California had a small guesthouse, and my wife and I invited him to come stay with us. He had served our country, and we wanted to try to help him get back on his feet. Arthur accepted the invitation, and once he settled in he started to attend AA meetings. He responded well to the AA program and also started to see a therapist. Over time, a trust grew between them. He started to share some of the things he'd witnessed in Vietnam, and healing began. Arthur also described to her trying to get his benefits when he returned home and how he eventually gave up as the VA had dragged its feet for too long. So, the therapist began to take him to the VA to fight for those benefits. After three years fighting red tape, he was eventually able to secure his long-overdue disability payments. Arthur planned to stay with us for six months, but with all that was going on, he ended up staying in California for five years. After that, he was able to use his back benefits to purchase his own place in Florida, where he lives quietly today.

Overall, Arthur helped me understand the challenges that many of our Vietnam veterans and their families have gone through, challenges very similar to those of Lieutenant Dan. Arthur's experience of falling into the shadows upon returning from war, struggling not only with the memories of combat, but with the alienation he felt from a divided nation and a government that had let the Vietnam veteran down, is part of what fuels my mission today, and I will always be grateful for his service to our country.

Moira's oldest brother, Mac Harris, made a big impression on me. He was a highly decorated officer and received the Silver Star, Bronze Star (with two Oak Leaf Clusters), Purple Heart, Army Commendation Medal, and Vietnamese Cross of Gallantry. From 1975 to 1978 he taught at West Point. He was promoted to major, served as a tactical officer, and was on the faculty of the Department of Behavioral Sciences and Leadership. He then attended Command and General Staff College at Fort Leavenworth, Kansas, as a postgraduate student. Upon his completion of the course in June 1981, because of his extensive knowledge, experience, and army-wide reputation as the authority on creative leadership, he was promoted to lieutenant colonel and selected to head the Center of Leadership and Ethics at Fort Leavenworth. There, one of his larger accomplishments was to write the new United States Army manual on leadership, known as Field Manual 22-100. He spent eighteen months researching, writing, and creating a manual that represented a positive and practical philosophy of leadership. His work soon became used as standard doctrine throughout the entire United States Army, and for his exceptional work on FM 22-100, Mac received the Legion of Merit Medal, given for outstanding service and achievement.

Years later, I met General Vincent Brooks, who would eventually rise in rank to become a four-star general and the commander of the United States Forces Korea. A one-star when we first met at a fund-raiser for a 9/11 memorial we were building at the Pentagon, General Brooks told me he'd gone to West Point in the late '70s, graduating class of 1980. I asked him if he knew Mac, and his face lit up, beaming with admiration. Mac had been one of his teachers. I also met General Curtis "Mike" Scaparrotti, who also became a four-star general and was Supreme Allied Commander Europe of NATO Allied Command Operations. He had gone to West Point as well, class of 1978, and he too knew Mac. Both of these incredible leaders told me how much they loved, respected, and admired him.

I learned so much about the Vietnam experience from Jack, Arthur, and Mac. In 1981, as a result of the new perspective I was gaining, I looked for a play to direct about Vietnam. I pored over all the theater magazines that described plays in various cities around the United States, and all the while continued to talk about the war with these family members whose wartime service and coming home had inspired me to tell our veterans' stories. I subscribed to *Drama-Logue*, the unofficial newsletter of the Los Angeles theater scene, and I stumbled across an ad for a play called *Tracers*, written and performed by Vietnam veterans about their experiences before, during, and after the war. A light bulb clicked on. This was exactly what I was looking for.

I flew to Los Angeles and saw the play at the Odyssey Theatre. The play was foulmouthed and blunt, darkly hilarious and grim, but powerful. Much of the play consisted of oral history, with characters pouring their hearts out, describing and reenacting the things they went through overseas. In one horrific scene, in pantomime, the veterans tried to reassemble the pieces of fellow soldiers who'd been blown apart. Torsos were matched to legs. Hands were matched to arms. The play brimmed with passion and tragedy, and I was deeply moved by it. *Tracers* made me trace the years of my life when I didn't think about Vietnam and I didn't understand. The next night I returned and saw the play again.

On February 20, 1981, I typed a two-page letter addressed to the entire "*Tracers* Ensemble" in care of director John DiFusco, the Vietnam vet who conceived the play, cowrote it, and owned the rights to it. The letter ended with this plea: "I feel the play should be seen. It should be seen and experienced by others like myself. I want Chicago to understand. It would be a great achievement for our ensemble of non-veterans to bring to *Tracers* what you all did. It would educate the actors as well as the audience. If and when you are ready, please consider Steppenwolf. Thank you for bringing *Tracers* to us."

John DiFusco had never heard of Steppenwolf. He wrote back and said, "No, sorry; it's a play both written and performed by veterans, and we feel it should always be done by veterans, so we're not letting anybody else do it."

So I waited. Time passed, and the show finally closed in Los Angeles. I called again and repeated my request for Steppenwolf to do the show in Chicago, but the answer stayed no. Every so often I reached out and asked for any updates on the play. I didn't press hard. I simply asked, particularly because the play wasn't being done anymore. It was just sitting, waiting, unused. John still felt very reluctant to let anyone else do the play. He insisted that it was a play by veterans, and only to be done by veterans. Still, I kept calling.

In the summer of 1981, our revival production of *Balm in Gilead* was running at the Apollo Theater, so I asked John DiFusco if he'd like to come to Chicago and see our work. We flew him out on our dime, and he saw the play. It was filled with rawness and craziness too, and after seeing *Balm*, John changed his mind. *Balm* had given us credibility in his eyes, and convinced him that we would put everything we had into *Tracers*. At last, he decided to take a chance with Steppenwolf. In late 1982, he granted me the rights, and I started assembling the cast for our 1983–1984 season.

I talked to my brother-in-law Mac about what he thought about our putting on the play. He liked the idea and informed me about certain details I needed to make sure I got right. More than anything, I wanted him to come see the play. But in August 1983, he was diagnosed with terminal cancer. Mac's manual for the army was published in October 1983, and that same month his promising career and life were cut short. He passed away at age thirty-nine, leaving behind his wife, Anne, and three-year-old daughter, Katie. The eulogy at his funeral in Pontiac, Illinois, was given by a dear friend of Mac's who had also served in Vietnam. I had never been to a military funeral before. It was very somber. There was the honor guard. The flag-draped coffin. The twenty-one-gun salute. I have never forgotten it. Mac was laid to rest beside his father in the cemetery across the street from where he grew up. Lieutenant Colonel Boyd McCanna "Mac" Harris had truly lived a life of service to others, and his passing only put the cap on my commitment to do the play right. I wanted *Tracers* to honor Vietnam veterans such as Mac Harris and help tell their stories.

Something else happened in the month of October that also strength-ened my commitment to tell the stories of our service members. President Reagan had sent a peacekeeping force to Beirut, Lebanon. On October 23, 1983, a suicide bomber drove a truck into the building that was used as a barracks for our service members, killing 220 marines, eighteen sail-ors, and three soldiers. I saw television reports about that horror a month before I was going to start work on *Tracers*. I had already assembled my cast, and I got calls from several members, asking if I'd heard about the devastating attack on our troops. It was a terrible day, and it reinforced my desire to honor our veterans with a great production.

Five weeks before we started rehearsals for *Tracers*, I gathered the ensemble to begin diving into the preparatory work. I knew we couldn't do this play in any kind of half-hearted way. We had to fully empathize with and care about the content of this play, about what the veterans truly went through.

As a cast, we read books about Vietnam and discussed what we'd read. A thirteen-part series called *Vietnam: A Television History* aired on PBS, so we watched it together as a cast. We took Tai Chi classes to get physically fit. We traveled an hour outside of Chicago to meet with veterans who taught us about firearms, which we then fired so we understood what a loaded rifle felt like in our hands. On a few occasions, we visited the North Chicago Veterans Administration near Naval Station Great Lakes to meet with a group of Vietnam veterans, patients at the VA, who were struggling with post-traumatic stress, undergoing any number of challenges because of their service. As we sat with them, they told us about what they'd done and seen, and they spoke very openly. They shared their stories with us, their heartache and their pain. They shared the horror of seeing their friends die in combat, and the horror of coming back to an America that had rejected them and often treated them as pariahs. Many of the vets told us it was healing for them to talk. For us, it reaffirmed our commitment to get things right.

One of the final things we did in preparation for the play was head to a summer camp that was closed for the winter in the small town of Sawyer, Michigan. A staff member at Steppenwolf had a connection there and was able to arrange for us to use it. I wanted to create a "boot camp" experience for the cast, and we were able to sequester ourselves as an ensemble for six days, out in the middle of nowhere, to focus completely on building our platoon. As it was dead of winter, the camp was frozen, knee-deep in snow, and it would be tough on the cast, doing all that training outside. But it was going to be a great ensemble-building exercise, and as director I was going to do everything that I required the actors to do.

I asked Dennis Farina (who later became known for playing Ray "Bones" Barboni in *Get Shorty*) to be our drill instructor at the camp. He was also going to play Sergeant Williams, the drill instructor in the play. Before becoming an actor, Dennis had served in the army for three years and done a tour in Vietnam, and later served for eighteen years in the Chicago Police Department, burglary division. The toughest of the tough, Dennis woke us up at three o'clock every morning by banging garbage can lids. He ordered us outside to do push-ups and jumping jacks in the snow until we thought we'd pass out. We wore our fatigues everywhere and went on long hikes and marches in the snow. For most of that week, Dennis did his best to make our lives a living hell. Just what I wanted.

We were fortunate to have two actual Vietnam veterans in our cast: Dennis and a fabulous African American actor named Greg Williams. On our final day at the camp, New Year's Eve 1983, we hosted war games. One of the ensemble members, Gary Cole (later known for his role as Bill Lumbergh, the nightmarish boss in *Office Space*), became our enemy. He donned white camo, hiked into the wilderness, and hid in the snowy forest, and we needed to hunt him down. We tried to simulate the quietness we'd need to maintain in the forest, not knowing where the enemy was hiding. Instead of paintball guns, we carried model rifles that looked like real M16s and little bags of flour. If we saw the enemy, we were to throw a bag of flour at him. Two of our guys became lost and wandered too close to a neighbor's house. The owner ran out, alarmed, and demanded to know why our guys were sneaking around in the snow, carrying rifles. He phoned the sheriff, who came quickly, and I explained (somewhat frantically) that the guns were fake and this was just play practice. Eventually it all got straightened out.

On the last night of the camp we threw a party, one over-the-top New Year's Eve bash. All the guys went a little bonkers after a week in the snow. Next morning we ate breakfast, did a workout, then read the play for the first time. This was the first time the cast had even picked up the script, and the first reading crackled with energy. It was awesome to hear it come alive. Our platoon was ready, and as a director I was ready. We headed back to Chicago, and for the next four weeks we rehearsed the play, my cast ever-investing themselves in the lives of these characters. Then we opened the doors to the show.

The play begins with a Vietnam veteran in a bar. People are asking him to describe his experiences. "What was it like? Did you kill anyone?" The veteran loses it, and things spiral out from there. The crowd was hooked from moment one.

John DiFusco came to Chicago to see the show. I stood offstage, watching him on and off throughout the entire performance. The play ends with a powerful percussive scene that turns into a sort of tribal chant, a song with all the actors shouting, singing, dancing a war dance, hollering the same one line, over and over again.

How does it feel to kill somebody?!
How does it feel to kill somebody?!
How does it feel to kill somebody?!

It was the central question our returning Vietnam veterans were asked. The image that sticks in my mind forever is of John during this song. He was sitting in the audience, his head slightly bowed, and when the cast started to chant, his hand raised in a quiet fist.

After each performance, we received a standing ovation. The crowd cheered wildly. The reviews all came back positive. We decided to provide a free performance on Tuesday nights to any veteran who wanted to attend—a tradition that continues to this day, in slightly altered form, at Steppenwolf.

At first, veterans who came to the Tuesday shows were skeptical that we could re-create anything that represented their experiences. But word got out to the veteran community, and our Tuesday night crowds grew bigger and bigger. We performed in the 220-seat, former St. Nicholas Theater on North Halsted Street, and at the end of each show, vets in the audience got up out of their seats and swarmed the stage to shake hands and hug us actors. After each Tuesday-night performance, we hosted Q&A sessions with the veterans, often very emotional, and a lot of the same veterans came back week after week. Their stamp of approval felt life-changing for us, more important than any review we could ever get. That's when I knew we were on to something good and lasting. A few veterans got together and made us plaques—one for each member of the cast—thanking us for telling their stories. The plaques read:

WE, THE VETERANS OF THE POST TRAUMATIC STRESS DISORDER UNIT, BUILDING 135 G, NORTH CHICAGO V.A.M.C., WISH TO EXPRESS OUR HEARTFELT THANKS FOR YOUR KINDNESS, CARING, AND UNDERSTANDING. YOUR UNSELFISH ENDEAVORS TO MAKE THE VIETNAM COMBAT VETERAN FEEL WELCOME IN A SOCIETY THAT HAS REJECTED HIM ARE GREATLY APPRECIATED.

WE APPRECIATE YOUR EFFORTS MORE THAN WORDS CAN EXPRESS.

AGAIN, THANK YOU, OUR FRIENDS.

Today, people often ask me about the highlights of my career. *Tracers* is one, an incredibly meaningful, absolutely extraordinary experience. As we did this play, I could see that the veterans felt like something was happening— for *them*. They'd been stuck in the shadows, discredited, abused, or simply ignored, and now they were watching these actors honor them and bring their stories out of the shadows.

I will always be grateful to John DiFusco and the cast of *Tracers* for the opportunity to work on this life-changing play. For the first time, I felt like I was giving back by honoring our veterans, by not letting them fall through the cracks, by not letting them feel unappreciated or forgotten.

I met many Vietnam veterans who had attended our free performances, and in the early 1990s I was asked to help raise funds to build the Lansing Veterans Memorial in Lansing, Illinois. A Vietnam veteran who had seen *Tracers*, Tom Luberda, organized the creation of the memorial. It features the names of our fallen heroes on a black granite wall with a giant UH-1 Huey helicopter mounted overhead, while a statue of a soldier carrying a wounded comrade to the awaiting chopper stands as a reminder to never leave anyone behind. I was honored to play some small part in helping Tom and the veterans realize their dream.

And to say thanks for my involvement, they put my brother-in-law's name on the wall.

LTC BOYD MCCANNA HARRIS.
US ARMY NINTH INF. DIV.
AMERICAL DIVISION, VIETNAM.

CHAPTER 6

Glimpses of Glory

As artistic director of Steppenwolf, it was my job to read plays, and read plays, and read plays. Sam Shepard, the Pulitzer-winning playwright who often delved into the darker side of American family life, became one of my favorites, and in 1981 I sought the rights to Shepard's *True West*. I dressed up in a nerdy corduroy jacket, slacks, and paisley tie, looking as official as I knew how, and flew to New York to meet with Sam's agent, Lois Berman. At twenty-five, I still had crazy hair, and Steppenwolf could barely pay for my plane ticket, let alone a hotel, so I slept on the apartment floor of a friend, *Saturday Night Live*'s Tim Kazurinsky. My corduroy jacket didn't impress Lois, who told me she'd never heard of Steppenwolf and wanted the better-established Goodman Theatre in Chicago to do the play. I took off my jacket, pulled off my tie, and flew back to Chicago, out of luck.

The play wouldn't leave me. I *had* to direct this play, and I knew it would be great for the company, so every so often I phoned up Lois and asked if the Goodman had given *True West* any love yet. Now, at the time, I had an unusual office arrangement. Steppenwolf rented an always-cramped space at the Hull House, but I needed something just for me. So I climbed a metal ladder attached to a sidewall of the theater and created my own office space in the lighting booth, high above the theater's floor. Somehow I lugged a tiny desk up the ladder, and I had a phone put in.

That's where I sat the day I answered the phone to hear Lois finally say, "Well, we haven't had much luck with the Goodman. I guess you can have the rights." I scrambled down the ladder, ran into the back office where everybody else shared space, and shouted, "We got the rights to *True West!*" Everybody cheered.

Little did we know then how big this play would become for Steppenwolf.

We opened *True West* in spring 1982. The play received great reviews and did so well that we moved it to the larger Apollo Theater in Chicago. Malkovich in particular was fantastic in his role and received all kinds of press attention. I knew we had to do something bigger—much, much bigger—with *True West*. We needed to take it to New York.

Theater success happens all around the country, but a success in New York can draw national recognition quickly, raising a theater's profile. To have a hit show running in New York could only help us back in Chicago. So I called up Wayne Adams, a New Yorker who'd produced *Say Goodnight Gracie* for us in Chicago, and asked him to come see *True West*. He flew out, loved it, and returned with investor Hal Thau, who also loved it. Wayne and Hal raised $120,000, a lot of cash back then, for us to produce the show in New York. The opening was slated for October 1982. I flew to New York to scout theaters and found the Cherry Lane, a beautiful, older, 180-seat theater downtown near Sheridan Square. It was perfect.

Not everybody was happy.

Steppenwolf was in the middle of a move into a different theater in Chicago. The Hull House had proved too small for us, so we'd agreed to renovate the former St. Nicholas Theater space. Our board needed to raise extra money to make this possible, and the board, as well as a number of our actors, didn't think the timing was right to take a Steppenwolf show to New York. And they didn't think that I, the artistic director, should be spending so much time away from Chicago during the renovation and move. I disagreed. I felt we had to jump at this opportunity. We needed to find a way to make both situations work—opening the new theater, and moving the show to New York. I knew that the artistic director leaving town at the same time we were renovating a new theater was not exactly the best timing. But I wanted us to do both things simultaneously. The majority of the company did not agree with me and thought that by going to New York I was abandoning the theater just before all the construction had to be done. So right before I left for New York, I went to the St. Nicholas Theater. Some old risers needed to be chopped up and removed. I went in early one morning, fired up a chain saw, and buzzed through the risers like cordwood. Company members filed into the theater, one by one, to see what I was up to. I must have looked like an angry nutcase, attacking the risers with the chain saw, but I didn't want anyone to think I didn't care. And besides, I needed to relieve a little stress with that chain saw.

Complicating matters, the New York producers wanted us to switch up some members of the cast of *True West*. Laurie Metcalf, a terrific actress then in her twenties, had performed the show in Chicago, playing the mother, a character in her sixties. The producers wanted us to recast the part with a New York actress of actual age. Additionally, Francis Guinan and Jeff Perry, who were also in the cast, decided not to go to New York, siding with the members of the ensemble who didn't think the time was right to move the show. So I needed to recast their parts as well. John was still up for it, but he was going to be directing our opening play at the new St. Nicholas, so I needed to figure out how to rehearse *True West* in New York with the new actors and without Malkovich being there in the beginning. I was definitely pushing a big boulder up a hill on my own, and as there were now only a few of us involved, the ensemble got so ticked off with me that they decided that the New York production could not be billed as a Steppenwolf show because it wasn't going to be a total Steppenwolf cast. So there was no mention of the company anywhere on any of the posters or newspaper ads for the show.

Perhaps most difficult of all was the situation with Tom Irwin. Tom is a fantastic actor who today has appeared in dozens of plays, movies, and TV shows, including his role as the soft-spoken father in the hit TV series, *My So-Called Life*. Tom had stepped into the role of the younger brother for a few weeks in our Chicago production of *True West*, and when Jeff told me he wasn't going to New York, I'd asked Tom to come and do the play there. Tom had agreed. But after we started rehearsals in New York, one of our producers took me aside and said I needed to play Tom's role. The year before, the producer had seen Malkovich and me acting together in our production of *Of Mice and Men*, and he felt that John and I acted very well together. Over the course of the next several days both producers kept encouraging me to make the change. This was a really tough moment. It was the first time we'd taken a show to New York, and everything was new. The pressure was building. It had been a stressful summer just getting the show to New York in the first place.

I don't want to sound like I'm dumping this decision about Tom all on the producers. I knew it was going to be controversial within the company, and there had already been tension about whether we should take *True West* to New York at all. But no matter how much I tried to avoid making this decision, I felt I could do a good job in the role, and the producers kept urging me to make the change. So I did. The difficult job of telling Tom what I'd decided fell to me, and the decision didn't go over well with either Tom or Steppenwolf, unsurprisingly. Not only had I gone off on my own and produced the show in New York against the wishes of the theater, now I'd just let one of our actors go and replaced him with— myself. *Sheesh.* The company was not happy with me, and since they were in Chicago focusing on our work there, and as there was a possibility that I may be staying in New York for a while if the show did well, they voted to remove me as artistic director. I was crushed. But I understood. Jeff Perry became the new AD. And me? I needed to focus on getting *True West* opened. Thankfully, down the road, there were no hard feelings between Tom and me, and he appeared in three out of the next four shows that I would direct in Chicago, including *Tracers*.

Here's the good news. After *True West* opened in New York, the cast and producers held an opening-night party down the block at Chumley's, an old speakeasy turned into a hamburger joint. Malkovich was married to actress Glenne Headly at the time, and she and John were there, along with Moira and me. In classic New York tradition, the reviews came out on opening night. The *New York Times* was delivered to the restaurant; someone handed the paper to Wayne, and he stood up on a table and read it out loud:

[True West] is an exhilarating confluence of writing, acting, and staging. As performed by John Malkovich and Gary Sinise, two members of Chicago's Steppenwolf Theatre Company making their New York debuts, and as directed by Mr. Sinise, this is the true "True West." The compass needle is unwavering . . .

The review was a rave. We went nuts. A single review from the *Times* can make or break a show. Early the next morning, the box office phone started ringing off the hook with people trying to get tickets. Other reviewers loved us too.

Here's how forgiveness can work. When the programs for *True West* were printed, they didn't mention Steppenwolf in any official capacity, because the ensemble back in Chicago didn't want it. But the programs contained the bios of Malkovich and me, and pretty much all John and I had ever done were Steppenwolf shows. So the media picked this up, and the company started getting great publicity about these two actors from this little-known theater in Chicago who night after night were kicking butt at the downtown Cherry Lane. Steppenwolf started being mentioned all over the New York and national press, which of course was a positive thing for us back at home. As difficult as it all was getting there, the doors had been opened for our company in New York. Some of the fears and reservations held by many of the folks in the company started to melt away, and the board of directors and ensemble members of Steppenwolf began to soften their stance toward me. All would soon be forgiven.

John's performance was especially getting a lot of attention, and his star began to rise during the run. He was doing media interviews and photo sessions for magazine covers. He had recently hired a manager and was meeting a lot of very famous people who were coming to see the show. This of course was all brand-new to us. Two guys from Chicago had come to New York as unknowns, and suddenly celebrities such as Jackie O, John F. Kennedy Jr., Robert Duvall, Bernardo Bertolucci, Susan Sarandon, and others were sitting in the front row and coming backstage afterward to meet us. I say "us," but really it was mostly to meet John, who was so powerful in the show and getting press comparing him to Marlon Brando.

The week after we opened, John told me he'd been approached by William Morris talent agent Johnnie Planco and had signed with him. Planco was a very powerful agent back then, and he had wasted no time in signing John. I hoped this might happen to me as well, so I waited for the phone to ring. But after two or three months of running the show, no agents had approached me. I decided to go to the box office and ask which agents had come to see the show. I got the list and made phone calls to them myself. Although I'd heard from no one, they were happy to set up meetings, and after a while another agent at William Morris signed on to represent me. Perhaps it would lead to something, I thought, but nothing much changed immediately after.

John, on the other hand, was riding high. He was enjoying his new-found celebrity, and things were going great for him on that front. Many nights we would come into the theater to get ready for the show, and John would fill me in on who he'd had dinner with after the show the night before. It was always at a great New York restaurant with someone very well-known in our business. I would listen, nod my head, and then fill him in on what I'd done after the show, scoring over 100,000 on the Asteroids video game at the little Greek diner near my apartment. The gyros were wonderful there.

I was happy for my friend. He's a great actor, and it was clear to me that he was going to launch into the movie business after we concluded our run of the show. And I couldn't help wondering if a movie role might be in the cards for me also.

True West ended up running for almost two years, albeit recast with different actors after John and I finished our sixth-month run, as is often done. As soon as we finished we went into a television studio and shot the play for a PBS production on *American Playhouse.* The play continued at the Cherry Lane with other actors in the roles, among them Jim Belushi and Gary Cole, and then the brothers Randy and Dennis Quaid, both very well-known by then. I continued to direct each new cast, and Randy and Dennis liked their roles so much that later we took the show to Los Angeles, opening at the LA Stage Company. Then Daniel Stern and Tim Matheson played the roles back in New York. Toward the end of its New

York run in 1984, Erik Estrada came in. Erik was very kind, always good-natured, and although his fame was already high from playing Ponch on *CHiPs*, he hadn't done much theater. "Just show me what to do," Erik said, the first time we met. So I worked with Erik to help him understand the role, and he did great. After nearly two years and 762 performances, *True West* closed, a very good run for an Off-Broadway show.

From the time *True West* opened in October 1982, everything ran non-stop. The morning after we finished shooting the PBS version, John was indeed off to film his first big movie, *The Killing Fields*, which was shot in Thailand. His film career was off to the races, and within a few years he would receive his first Oscar nomination as Best Supporting Actor for *Places in the Heart*. As soon as I finished my specific involvement as an actor with the run of *True West*, I was back at Steppenwolf directing *The Miss Firecracker Contest*. Then the winter of 1984, I directed *Tracers*, and that spring we brought our production of *Balm in Gilead* to New York, running eight months Off Broadway, another big hit for us. Right after that, I directed a production of *Orphans* in the winter-spring of 1985, a play about two brothers who kidnap a stranger. It had a tremendous cast of company members Terry Kinney, Kevin Anderson, and John Mahoney. The actors were awesome, and wanting to push it over the edge in tone and style, I scored the play entirely with Pat Metheny music, cranked up loud. It got great reviews in Chicago, and that summer we moved the play to Off Broadway, where acclaim from the *New York Times* opened even more doors for us.

The great British actor Albert Finney came to see *Orphan*s and liked it so much he asked if I'd direct him in a London production of the show. He wanted the role of Harold, played by John Mahoney in my original production. Albert was a legend, and I was knocked out by the magnitude of his request. So we made a deal to bring Kevin Anderson from the original cast as the younger brother, and as Terry was caught up with developing another play he was going to direct, we brought in Jeff Fahey to play the older brother. In March of 1986, *Orphans* opened for a limited engagement at the 173-seat Hampstead Theatre before moving to the larger Apollo Theatre in the West End of London. Albert was in the finest form imaginable, winning the Olivier Award for his performance. During rehearsals, I stayed in an extra room in Albert's house. Although Albert was about twenty years older than I was, we went out every night, and I could not keep up. We'd wine and dine and party until 2:00 a.m., and I'd be conked out the next morning when Albert would stop by my room at seven, bright-eyed and clearheaded, hollering, "C'mon, Gary, we're going for coffee!"

Many top British actors came to see Albert in the show, including Sean Connery, Anthony Hopkins, and Vanessa Redgrave. Very gracious and extremely smart, Vanessa took Moira and me out to dinner one evening and talked about international things we knew nothing about. We just nodded whenever it seemed appropriate and said, "*Yeah? . . . Yeah.*" Or . . . "*Yeah!*"

From 1982 to 1987, we produced even more shows back in Chicago, moving a total of six of those shows to New York—*True West, And a Nightingale Sang, Balm in Gilead, Orphans, The Caretaker*, and *Educating Rita*. With the exception of *The Caretaker*, which was produced in midtown Manhattan at the Circle in the Square Theatre, these were all Off-Broadway productions, and all of them did well. In early 1985, I was appointed artistic director again, taking back the reins from my buddy Jeff Perry.

More good things were coming. That summer, Steppenwolf won the Tony Award for Regional Theatre Excellence. A Tony is the highest honor you can receive in the New York theater. A bunch of teenagers had stayed true to their dreams, created their own fiercely independent theater company in a basement in Highland Park, given it everything they had, and emerged on the other side with the top honors in the country. It had taken us just over a decade to be recognized nationally for our work.

We hatched more big plans. In summer 1986, I directed the production of a play written by musician Tom Waits and his wife, Kathleen Brennan, titled *Franks Wild Years*. Terry Kinney started out directing the play, but Tom and Terry didn't see eye to eye, and at one point they came into my office to try to talk things out. There was a lot of tension, and for a while Tom just sat and rocked back and forth, clearly feeling a lot of anxiety. I was worried. Steppenwolf had brought in some outside investors who had put some big money into the show in hopes of moving it to New York, and as artistic director it was my job to sort things out.

After trying our best to work through the problems, it was clear that Terry, Tom, and Kathleen were not going to be able to get on the same page, so I had no choice but to step in to take over directing the play. We were only days before the first audience, and we needed to get something up onstage quickly. It was important immediately to make Tom comfortable with working with me, so I started the new rehearsals by asking him simply to perform for our ensemble all the songs he'd written for the play. We put a single spotlight on the darkened stage, and while the band played, he stood under the light and entered the spirit of each song, relaxing more and more as he played and sang for us. I gave everyone the next day off so I could go through the script to figure out what I wanted to do. We had to work fast. I decided I needed kind of a clean slate so I could come up with a new staging. I removed most of the set that had been built, choosing instead to go with very simple and movable set pieces. We came back together with a reworked script, and over the next few days restaged the show, did our technical rehearsals, and added the lights and sound. It all began to gel, but the clock was ticking and the end of the first act was still not right. I woke up early one morning with an idea and came into rehearsals that day asking Tom for a new song. I felt we needed a big Vegas show tune to take us into intermission, so Tom went off with his band and came back in ten minutes. Right there on the spot, he'd written the song "Straight to the Top," a classic Sinatra-styled up-tempo show tune. We decided Tom should wear a red velvet tuxedo and black Elvis wig, and he infused the song with a passionate clown-like tap dance. It was hilarious, and a great way to end the first half of the show.

In the end, the show came together great. And while our hopes of moving the show to New York did not materialize, the investors made some of their money back, and the summer turned out to be peaceful, joyful, productive, and fun for the cast of *Franks Wild Years*.

During this period in the mid-1980s, other doors opened, and at one point, the summer of 1985, we simultaneously ran shows in three different cities. We did *Miss Julie* in Chicago, *Orphans* in New York, and two shows in Washington, DC: *Coyote Ugly*, which Malkovich directed, and *Streamers*, another play set during the Vietnam War that Terry directed and I acted in. Then, a few years later, in 1990, we opened *The Grapes of Wrath* on Broadway. That production won us another Tony, this time the award for Best Play. Director Frank Galati, who also adapted the script, won the Tony for Best Director. Lois Smith and I received nominations for featured actress and actor in a play: Lois for her role as Ma Joad, and me for my part as Tom Joad, the iconic role played by Henry Fonda in the 1940s film version directed by John Ford. These accolades all helped cement Steppenwolf's reputation—both nationally and internationally.

Those were amazingly fruitful years for Steppenwolf. The New York productions helped many Steppenwolf actors break into the movies all while we continued to strengthen our theater in Chicago. We added more actors to our ensemble; our board of directors grew stronger as our growing reputation drew interest from more high-profile Chicago businesspeople; and we were able to raise more funds, increasing our ability to grow. In 1990, we realized another dream when Steppenwolf broke ground at 1650 North Halsted Street and built our own multimillion-dollar building. We designed our theater from the ground up and opened the doors not long afterward. The land of our birth had allowed us to pursue our dreams. Steppenwolf had truly arrived.

In theater, as in so many other areas of life, people's lives intersect in unexpected, even amazing ways. Who you know can become just as important as the work you do. *The Grapes of Wrath* is a good example. In 1985, when I was artistic director, I asked director Frank Galati to come direct the company in a production of the 1930s Kaufman and Hart comedy *You Can't Take It with You*. During rehearsals, it became clear the ensemble absolutely loved working with Frank, so I invited him to join the company. He enthusiastically accepted, and in that same meeting I asked him if he had future projects he wanted to work on. Frank told me he'd always thought that John Steinbeck's *The Grapes of Wrath* would make a great stage play. I loved the idea, and we went to work to get the stage rights. Three years later, in 1988, we finally opened the play in Chicago, one of the most ambitious projects we'd ever done. It was so big, that it could not be staged in our current theater, so we rented the larger Royal George down the street. *The Grapes of Wrath* is a long, epic novel, and Frank worked and reworked the script to get it right. It was a huge undertaking. When it first opened, each performance stretched a whopping four hours. We did eight shows a week, and on Saturdays and Sundays we did two shows each day. Those weekends we barely had time to eat between shows before we were back out onstage. After closing in Chicago, we worked on the script some more, reducing the runtime to about three hours. In the spring of 1989, we moved the show to the La Jolla Playhouse in San Diego before taking it to London for two weeks, performing at the National Theatre. Reviews were strong. Due to the success in London, we attracted New York producers, and in the spring of 1990, after more reworking, we opened the show on Broadway at the Cort Theatre with a very tight two-and-a-half-hour production. The show received great reviews and won a Tony for Best Play and for Best Director for Frank Galati. At the end of its run, we performed it on PBS for *American Playhouse*. Elaine Steinbeck, John Steinbeck's widow, was a wonderful woman and had granted us the rights to adapt the play. She knew and loved Steppenwolf's work, and she and I had become friends over the years.

During this same period—after closing *The Grapes of Wrath* in Chicago—I went back to California, and over the next few years directed television episodes of *Thirtysomething* and *China Beach*. I also acted in a bigger TV movie with James Woods and James Garner called *My Name Is Bill W.*, about the founding of Alcoholics Anonymous.

In 1984, I had switched from the William Morris Agency to a high-profile New York agent at International Creative Management (ICM), Sam Cohn, who also represented Meryl Streep and director Mike Nichols. Sam really wanted me to focus on directing. By then, I'd directed some acclaimed productions—*True West*, *Tracers*, and *Orphans*—and picked up some TV work, acting and directing in Chicago with Michael Mann's *Crime Story*. The relationships with Elaine Steinbeck and Sam Cohn became pivotal in my life. Sam ushered me into Hollywood, and Elaine was the key to two projects that turned into career-shifting opportunities.

In 1986, Sam introduced me to a Hollywood producer named David Puttnam, who came to see *Orphans*. He'd produced *Chariots of Fire*, *The Mission*, and *The Killing Fields* (Malkovich's first movie, done right after *True West*), and had recently been hired by Columbia Pictures to run the studio. Sam called me and said that David wanted to offer me a directing deal in Hollywood at Columbia. David would pay me to move to California (I said "wow" to that), set me up with an assistant and an office (an actual office, not an office that you needed to climb up a ladder to reach), and pay me an actual salary for two years (I said double "wow" to that). The deal was for what they termed a "first look," which meant my job was to look for movies I wanted to direct, and then offer anything I might find to Columbia first. If Columbia didn't want the movie, then I would be free to do it somewhere else.

How green I was. Sam asked me, "How much do you need for two years?"

I tried to imagine what a first look deal might yield and asked, "How about sixty thousand dollars per year? Do you think that would be okay?"

Sam chuckled. He called David, then called me back and said, "David thinks you should get seventy-five thousand per year. Okay by you?"

I was speechless. Sixty thousand sounded like a fortune to me, much less seventy-five. They gave me an office on the back lot of Warner Bros., where Columbia Pictures was based at the time—the same lot, incidentally, that I'd been thrown out of a few years earlier when I'd tried so hard to see Robert Redford. At the time I made the deal I was still artistic director at Steppenwolf. I turned over the reins to Jeff Perry and Randy Arney, invited my assistant Kate Richie to come be my assistant at Columbia, and in 1987, Moira and I moved to California where we rented a little two-bedroom house in Sherman Oaks. Life was changing. I had a pay increase from what I was making at Steppenwolf and a movie deal, and wouldn't you know it, Moira and I were pregnant within a year.

That spring, I pitched a few projects, but Columbia passed on all my ideas. Then I found a script titled *The Farm of the Year* about two brothers in Iowa. Their father dies, and the brothers inherit the family's successful farm. But after running it for a few years, the farm fails, and the bank moves in to take it over. David Puttnam at Columbia liked the script, but another company, Cinecom Pictures, owned the rights and wanted to produce it. David, ever affable, told me, "Go, make it great."

Cinecom pledged $5 million to make the movie and hired me to direct it. I started tweaking the script, scouting locations, and working on preproduction. Richard Gere signed on to star, along with Penelope Ann Miller, Brian Dennehy, Kevin Anderson from Steppenwolf, and a young Helen Hunt, who later went on to win an Oscar for Best Actress in her role in *As Good as It Gets*. I brought over several other actors from Steppenwolf to round out the cast: Terry Kinney, Bob Breuler, Francis Guinan, Laurie Metcalf, Randy Arney, and Malkovich. I also cast Moira to play Richard Gere's girlfriend, and in a small roll I cast a then-unknown actress named Laura San Giacomo (who later became known for her role as Maya Gallo in the sitcom *Just Shoot Me!*).

We shot the film in Cedar Rapids, Iowa, and I found my transition from theater directing to film directing a little more difficult than I'd anticipated. I was just thirty-two years old and often felt unsure of my decisions. Moira and I rented an apartment in Cedar Rapids, across the street from the production offices we'd set up, and I spent so much time in our apartment tweaking the script that the production manager walked across the street one afternoon and urged me to spend more time in the offices— the production folks were all convinced I was hiding out from them. We began shooting. The days were long, and I kept cutting and adding things to the script. Laura San Giacomo had just the one small part in the movie, a few scenes, but the day she arrived I decided to cut her character. It just wasn't working in the script, and I didn't want to shoot something that would end up on the cutting room floor. Just as I had experienced with Tom Irwin and *True West*, one of the hardest parts of being a director is making decisions for the sake of the project that may disappoint people. Fortunately, Laura responded sweetly and didn't hold it against me.

Meanwhile, the production manager was set to receive a bonus from the studio if he brought the movie in under budget, so he continually sliced and diced where I wanted more. In one major scene, the brothers burn down their farm. I'd envisioned the Great Chicago Fire or Atlanta burning in *Gone with the Wind*, but we ended up with what looked like three candles on a birthday cake. Not enough money had been spent on the scene. So I scheduled a reshoot with lots of fire everywhere, spent a lot more money with multiple cameras rolling, and got what I wanted—so much so that we scorched the rented farmhouse and had to repair it afterward. I also decided to have the writer, Chris Gerolmo, rewrite the end of the movie. The script had originally ended with a big chase scene. An Iowa cop chases Richard Gere's character, Frank Roberts, on dirt roads through the cornfields. We started shooting it with actor Daniel Roebuck in the role of the cop, but a big chase at the end wasn't feeling right for the film that I'd been shooting for the past six weeks. I decided I wanted the movie to wind up with something more poetic, more heartbreaking, so I asked Chris to rewrite it and had to tell Daniel that his scene was out. He and I have remained friends, and he never fails to remind me that I fired him from my first movie. Chris came up with a beautiful scene between the two brothers as they are forced to go their separate ways and say goodbye. The producer, Fred Zollo, introduced me to the great composer John Barry, who wanted to write the score for the film. But by the time we started shooting, Barry had become sick and had to drop out. We needed to hire another composer, and fortunately we got Robert Folk. But with this aspect of the film, too, I would also second-guess which way to go. All the music I'd ever done for plays was hard-hitting rock and roll, but because Barry had wanted to write the score, I'd shifted my thinking to an orchestral score, so that's what Folk wrote. It was beautiful, but I still wasn't sure.

To add to the pressure, in the middle of all this confusion, I received a call from the producers who said the selection committee at the Cannes Film Festival wanted to see a cut of the movie.

Cannes! Holy crap! Cannes means red carpet and paparazzi, big movie stars chauffeured to the front door in limousines. Every filmmaker dreams of being in competition at Cannes. A great reception there can really help a movie out.

The pressure was on to get the film ready for the festival. I cranked up my editing pace. The studio execs then decided to fiddle with the title of the film, changing it from *The Farm of the Year* to *Miles from Home*. I kept editing, right up to the point when Richard Gere, a pregnant Moira, and I all hopped on the plane for Cannes. Richard and I carried canisters of the 35-millimeter print with us. Richard had been there before, but it was an exciting and totally new experience for me. All the craziness of Cannes was a real shock to the system. *Miles from Home* didn't win any awards and received mixed reviews, but it was fun to be at the festival.

Once we got home, I went back into the editing room and kept making changes. The movie needed to be shorter, and I changed the music all around. I decided the scenes with Moira and Richard Gere were unnecessary, so I cut my very own wife out of the film. Ever the consummate professional, Moira told me not to worry.

Miles from Home opened at the World Playhouse in Chicago on September 12, 1988, the same month Steppenwolf opened the inaugural production of *The Grapes of Wrath*. Richard Gere came into town for the movie's premiere and we held a party. Some critics liked the film, including the great Roger Ebert, but publicity was limited, and I think a total of only five theaters ever showed the film. It never found its audience and fell flat, earning a grand total of $188,964.

The experience wasn't all bad—for me, anyway, although I'm sure the studio wasn't thrilled. I learned many great lessons about filmmaking, including things that I would do differently next time. And I vowed there would be a next time. I just needed to find the right movie.

Our first baby was due just after *Miles from Home* closed in theaters. The due date was November 8, 1988, election day the year George H. W. Bush ran against Michael Dukakis. That morning we got up early, walked up the street to vote, then went for a bite to eat at McDonald's, after which we planned to see a movie. But Moira started feeling funny. At first we wondered if it was the double cheeseburger and fries she'd been craving and had just downed. But then we realized she was having contractions, so we went home to wait for them to quicken. I had a little plastic drum and started beating on that, doing what I called a "labor dance," singing and chanting in hopes the baby would hear and be motivated to come out. We kept the TV on, and by late in the day Bush appeared to be winning. Moira wanted to wash her hair before we went to the hospital, and when she emerged from the shower, wrapped in a towel, she stood at the sink brushing her teeth, watching the election results on TV. Just then a huge contraction hit. She moaned, still with toothpaste in her mouth, and uttered, absolutely deadpan, "The Dukakises must be sad." It set me to laughing, despite our circumstances. Her contraction passed; she finished brushing her teeth. Then she said it was time. I started running around like a nut.

We jumped in the car, heading for Valley Presbyterian Hospital in Van Nuys. In the car, Moira's water broke. I was a nervous wreck, but Moira was amazing, breathing through each contraction. We reached the hospital, and Moira stuck with her commitment to give birth naturally. It was very clearly painful for her, but she got in her room and began to push, entering an incredible, tranquil zone where she pressed through the pain. Our beautiful baby girl was born just after midnight, the early moments of November 9. We named her Sophia Ana Sinise and called her Sophie.

When we brought our new baby home from the hospital, we laid her on the bed and just stared at her. I looked at Moira, and Moira looked at me. So much had happened that year, 1988. We'd opened my first film, *Miles from Home*, and opened a great play in Chicago, *The Grapes of Wrath*. We'd been to Cannes. We'd had our first child. Together, we both looked back at Sophie.

Nothing compared to her.

In early 1990, Moira discovered she was pregnant again, this time with a boy. That summer I was acting on Broadway in *The Grapes of Wrath*, and Moira, now six months pregnant, was in Chicago doing a play with Steppenwolf called *Love Letters*. In multiple phone calls we discussed what we should name our son. One day the name became clear to me. I called up Moira: "We should call him Mac, after your brother!"

Moira was thrilled. Boyd McCanna "Mac" Harris—the Vietnam vet, Silver Star recipient, and West Point instructor—had passed away in 1983 of cancer, and we all thought of him regularly. When our son was born on November 10, 1990—almost two years to the day after Sophie—we named him McCanna Anthony Sinise—Mac for short. The Irish and Italian influences together sounded very American to us.

One of my favorite films at the time was the American Civil War epic *Glory*, starring Denzel Washington, Matthew Broderick, Cary Elwes, and Morgan Freeman. The movie had opened the year before, and I loved its soundtrack. Moira had labored throughout the night with Mac, and he'd been born early in the morning, about five thirty. I'd been up all night with Moira, so I left the hospital about seven o'clock to go home, grab a shower, and change. As I drove out of the hospital's campus, I put on the soundtrack to *Glory*. Stopped at a traffic light and thinking about my new son while the sun came up in the distance, everything hit me. My son was healthy. Moira was healthy. My family was beautiful. The magnificent music filled the air.

I choked up. Tears came into my eyes.

Grateful didn't begin to describe how I felt. I was so much more than grateful. Already I'd made so many mistakes in my life and so many times I'd chosen the wrong path, yet somehow a mercy was still being shown to me. Why did I deserve all this goodness? I wasn't a believer in Providence. I never really thought about God. Yet something beyond me was so clearly involved in my story. Something unseen was pulling me along, never giving up on me, helping me find and fulfill my purposes in life. If all this blessing was an act of Providence, then that was okay by me, even if I still had a long way to go toward understanding what I was only then beginning to glimpse.

As I brushed away tears at the stoplight, I think I whispered a semblance of my first prayer. The prayer was hazy, but the intention was clear. Call it a longing perhaps. The first twinges of belief. Two words, layered with more than one meaning . . .

Thank you.

CHAPTER 7

Steinbeck Country

Long before the images ever became a reality, I visualized this:

A journey starts inside a boxcar, and you hear the *clackity clack* of the train going across the tracks. It's night, and you see lights from outside coming through the boxcar slats. Opening credits roll as the camera moves across the slats of the car. Then the light breaks through the slats, and slowly it reveals something huddled in the corner.

It's George, sitting in the boxcar in the dark corner by himself. Why is he there alone?

The camera cuts quickly to a young woman in a torn red dress, brightly lit by the California sun as she runs through a field of barley. Then it cuts again. George and Lennie are on the run, because Lennie has become too excited around the woman in the red dress. Lennie is a gentle giant, mentally challenged, who has the mind of a five-year-old. As an adult he's harmless, but he's a big puppy who can't control his own emotions. And he's always been taken care of by George. The girl has run away from Lennie, because she doesn't understand. Frightened from the encounter, she runs, screaming and yelling, toward a group of migrant workers in the fields. Then we cut away from her, and see that George and Lennie are running in the opposite direction to get away as fast as possible.

That's how I envisioned the movie would start.

Hold that thought.

During *Miles from Home*, I'd struck up a friendship with John Barry, the Oscar-winning composer who'd originally been hired to do the music. He'd recovered from his illness, and one day in 1990, while I was performing in *The Grapes of Wrath* on Broadway, he invited me over to a private screening of a rough cut of a new movie he'd just scored. He hadn't told me beforehand that it was *Dances with Wolves*, a huge, three-hour epic, starring, produced by, and directed by Kevin Costner. The movie went on to win multiple Oscars, including one for John for Best Score, yet the thing that stunned me most was this: although Kevin had never directed before, there he was, performing three vital functions in this movie. He inspired me to do the same.

My agent, Sam, wanted me to focus on directing. But I knew I wanted to keep acting. I'd never produced a film, but I'd been around enough producers to know a little bit about it. I knew also that unless you take matters into your own hands, you can only have whatever comes to you. I'd always been a person who dreamed something up, then made it happen. So my goal became finding a project where I could produce, direct, and act.

When *The Grapes of Wrath* finished, I searched for what to do next. I knew I wanted to do something epic, something that moved people, and preferably another movie. But what? Then Elaine Steinbeck reentered my story. Elaine had become a real champion of Steppenwolf. She'd seen that we could take her husband's novels and handle the stories really well. On the last day of shooting the PBS version of *The Grapes of Wrath*, I stood with Elaine during a break out by the theater's back steps. I thought about the boxcar image, swallowed, sucked up my courage, and said, "Elaine, would you give me the rights to *Of Mice and Men*? I'd like to try to make a movie out of it." I paused and added tentatively, "I'd need your help, too, because I don't have any money."

She chuckled quietly, smiled her beautiful, dignified smile, and said, "Well, honey, it's already been a film. Three times."

She was referring to its first adaptation in 1939 starring Lon Chaney Jr. as Lennie and Burgess Meredith as George, and its second adaptation in 1968 starring George Segal and Nicol Williamson, plus Will Geer, the grandpa from *The Waltons*. It had also been made into a TV movie in 1981 starring Randy Quaid and Robert Blake.

I explained to Elaine that from the time I first saw it onstage at the Guthrie Theater in high school I'd loved the story, one of the first that had excited me about acting. I hadn't known anything about John Steinbeck then, but the story had moved me greatly, and this was exactly the type of story I wanted to tell on film. Elaine smiled again and said she'd think about it. She was so gracious. Within a short time, I was able to make a deal with the Steinbeck estate for the rights to *Of Mice and Men* for one year—completely free of charge. Suddenly I was a producer with a project. I could direct it and act in it. We'd already done a production at Steppenwolf where I had played George, and I knew the story forward and backward. I just needed to make a movie happen.

That's all.

Having been focused on Steppenwolf and my work there for so long, I had made a decision that this project was going to be a new challenge for me, separate from theater. While I would end up working with a few pals from the company, unlike *Miles from Home*, which included several Steppenwolf company members, this project would be a distinct effort altogether. So before going forward I wanted to let my two best friends, Terry and Jeff, know that I was striking out on my own with this one. It was a difficult thing to do, but I felt it was time to try something else. This created a bit of tension and distance between us cofounders at the time. Terry had directed me in the Steppenwolf production of the play back in 1980, and Jeff had played a pivotal role in that production. But now, I was going to make the movie on my own, and because of this, we parted company for a while.

So, how do you create a movie from the ground up? Earlier, my agent had set up a dinner between Alan Ladd Jr., the head of Metro-Goldwyn-Mayer (MGM), and me, and I'd worked on a couple of development projects with MGM in the past, although nothing had come of them. So I met again with Alan and explained how I wanted to make *Of Mice and Men*. Alan loved the idea and jumped on board. The studio made a deal with Elaine (my rights were only to pitch it; the studio still had to pay for the rights to use it), and suddenly we were in business.

I reached out to a producer buddy of mine, Russ Smith, and asked him to coproduce with me. MGM gave us $8.8 million to put the production together, a relatively small budget but definitely workable. Malkovich and I had done the play together ten years earlier, so he was the obvious choice for the role of Lennie. The fact that he'd been nominated for an Oscar for *Places in the Heart* was a definite plus with MGM. I signed on to play George, and Russ and I started searching for the right screenwriter.

A movie isn't made overnight, and I couldn't sit around and wait while things came together, so in the meantime I auditioned for a role in a small-budget World War II movie titled *A Midnight Clear*. The great cast included Ethan Hawke and Kevin Dillon, and I landed the role of Vance "Mother" Wilkins, my first major role in a feature film. The story is set during the Battle of the Bulge, so we needed a location with lots of snow, mountains, and trees. We ended up shooting in Park City, Utah, in winter. The character I play is very fragile, a soldier experiencing shell shock who's been in the fight for some time, so I needed to lose some weight for the role. Just before shooting began, Moira and I visited her mother in Florida. I spent much of my time running on the beach, drinking SlimFast shakes, trying to get myself to look thin and gaunt.

While in Florida, Russ and I talked on the phone about finding a screenwriter for our film. He recommended the legendary Oscar-winner Horton Foote, who'd written the screenplays for *To Kill a Mockingbird* with Gregory Peck and *Tender Mercies* with Robert Duvall. I called Horton at his home outside Wharton, Texas, and told him he'd be perfect to write our script. He wanted to know why we possibly wanted to make another version of *Of Mice and Men*. Considering how I might persuade him, I thought of one of my favorite films of all time: 1973's *Scarecrow*, starring Al Pacino and Gene Hackman, about two misfit loners who develop an unlikely friendship. The acting is edgy, powerful, and moving, and I said to Horton, "I want to make a movie just like *Scarecrow*. Have you ever seen it?" He hadn't, but I mailed him a copy; he watched it, called me back immediately, and gushed, "I love that movie! Now I understand what you're talking about." He signed on that day to write our script for *Of Mice and Men*. Russ and Horton flew up to Utah while I was filming *A Midnight Clear*, and in between takes we went through the first draft of the script for *Of Mice and Men*.

I had my family with me in Utah: Moira, Sophie, Mac, plus Moira's older sister, Lois, and her son, Boyd. One night Moira received a phone call from her twin sister, Amy, that their mother had passed away. Moira was devastated, and the following months were very hard on her and her sisters. They'd now lost both parents, as well as their older brother.

I finished shooting, came back to California, and landed the role of the villain in a movie called *Jack the Bear*, featuring Danny DeVito and in a small supporting role a fifteen-year-old standout named Reese Witherspoon. MGM approved Horton's script while I was working on *Jack the Bear*, so we started pre-production of *Of Mice and Men* while I was still filming with Danny. I got my first cell phone, a Motorola flip, and worked the phone between every take on *Jack the Bear*.

Our date to begin shooting *Of Mice and Men* was slated for September 1991. Yet we had a problem. The story is set in California, and we needed a big field of barley. Where were we going to find a big field of barley in California in September? We searched in Montana—the first time I'd been there—and although it was past harvest and we didn't find our growing barley field, something else caught me that would impact my future. Near Great Falls, out in the middle of nowhere, I was startled every so often to see huge concrete slabs surrounded by fencing. In the center of these slabs sat a giant iron cap, and underneath that cap were housed nuclear missiles, pointed in those days at the USSR. In later years, I would play a bunch of concerts at bases in Montana, Wyoming, North Dakota, and Missouri. These bases are part of Air Force Global Strike Command, the guys who take care of our nuclear arsenals. I would always have mixed feelings when seeing nuclear weapons up close. The weapons protect us, yet they're horrific, and we can never forget both facts of their existence. I hoped, then and now, as so many people do the world over, that they would never need to be used again.

We continued our location scout and finally found a ranch just outside the Santa Ynez Valley near Santa Barbara, California, that had an old barn out back where we could build some bunkhouses and the other sets we'd need for a movie. The folks said that within six weeks they could grow us a wheat field that would work for all the barley scenes. We needed a river, so we scouted Acton, California, where an old movie ranch sits atop artesian wells. Ranch owners said they could dig down, water would come up, and they could flood the area to create a river effect. We decided to do all our interior shots on a sound stage in L.A. We cast the movie with a wonderful group of actors, including the great Ray Walston as Candy, Sherilyn Fenn as Curley's wife, John Terry as Slim, Joe Morton as the ranch's stable buck, Crooks, and my own dear Moira as the woman in the red dress.

We started shooting, telling the story with simple, elegant, poetic shots, letting the actors do the work in front of the camera. I hired my dad to edit the film, and during shooting we had an editing room set up in the town of Solvang, California, near where we shot. At the end of each day, I'd head over to the editing room and watch the dailies, all the film we'd shot the day before. Dad would show me the material, and I'd give him some notes. Going back and forth from directing to acting felt challenging, but I knew the project well from Steppenwolf, and I felt confident with the material. While shooting, I hardly had to look at the script. We wrapped principal photography just before Thanksgiving 1991, and for the next several months we were in postproduction at offices we'd rented at CBS Studios in Studio City, California.

Similar to what had happened with *Miles from Home*, the committee that selects movies for Cannes wanted to see this film for their May 1992 festival. I knew *Of Mice and Men* wouldn't be a summer blockbuster, but I had high hopes that it would be well received and was thrilled when the festival called. It's an artistic film, an acting movie, an American classic. Perfect for Cannes. They accepted it into competition. And just like last time, we edited and tweaked the movie right up to the moment we flew to France. Moira was pregnant with our third child when we went to Cannes this time, and I wondered with a chuckle what the French thought. *Mon Dieu! Every time we see that Sinise fellow, his wife is pregnant.*

It wasn't all fun and games. On April 29, 1992, not too long before we left for Cannes, jurors in Simi Valley delivered the verdict in the trial of the four white policemen accused of beating motorist Rodney King, an African American. Three of the accused were acquitted, while a mistrial was declared for the fourth. Racial tensions ran very high and exploded.

The day the L.A. riots touched off, I was mixing the sound for *Of Mice and Men* at Sony Studios in Culver City. One of the technicians called me into the office, and there on his TV all hell was breaking loose. A helicopter was circling above a street where a truck driver named Reginald Denny had been pulled out of his vehicle and was being beaten by a mob at the intersection of Florence and Normandie. The cameras cut to other areas of the city, and stores were being looted and burned. Several other innocent motorists were attacked and beaten.

The images were deeply frightening—and all this violence was happening not too far from where we were working. I told everyone we were shutting down and they should go home immediately. As I drove home, my eyes darted from left to right as I wondered if I, too, would be pulled from my vehicle and beaten. Anarchy reigned in Los Angeles, and police raced here and there. I wondered how I was going to protect my family if the violence reached our home. I was scared.

For the next five days while the riots raged, I tried to work at home while watching the city burn on television. The California Army National Guard, the Seventh Infantry Division, and the First Marine Division were called in to help restore order, but for some time, mobs still roamed. In the end, sixty-three people were killed, 2,383 were injured, and more than 12,000 people were arrested. Property damage was estimated as high as $1 billion. Los Angeles would never be the same. I admit I was so consumed with my own work that year—directing, producing, and acting in my film—that I did not even know when the verdict was coming in the Rodney King case. What a shock. It was a tough time for our city and our country, and I'll never forget what Rodney King himself asked during those terrible days of rage: "Can we all get along?"

A week after the riots ended, we were finally able to go back to work to get the movie ready for the festival. We finished things up by adding the beautiful score written by Mark Isham. We left for Cannes a few days later. *Of Mice and Men* was screened toward the end of the festival, so by then everybody had viewed many films and had a lot to compare my movie with. My coproducer, Russ Smith, attended our screening, along with Malkovich and many of the MGM executives, including Alan Ladd Jr., the top guy at MGM. Moira was there. My mom and dad were there. The movie was screened in Palais des Festivals et des Congrès, a giant movie theater with a seating capacity of twenty-three hundred seats, all filled. On the way from the hotel to the theater, the streets were lined with cheering people. At the theater, the red carpet was packed with paparazzi and journalists. Everybody wore tuxedos or ball gowns. Flashbulbs popped everywhere. As a filmmaker, when your movie is being shown, you can't stand in the back and pace, which is what I nervously felt like doing. You must sit in the middle of the theater, along with the production team, in the middle of the gigantic crowd. You hope the crowd enjoys the show. If they don't, then you sit there and take your punishment, even if you get booed. And this was my first film as a producer. My second as a director. Only my third as an actor.

The crowd and I watched the movie. It started just as I had envisioned it, on a train, inside a boxcar. We heard the *clackity clack* of the train going across the tracks. The story progressed, the movie finished, and the credits rolled, with the lights still down. The plot concludes tragically, not triumphantly, and it's not a movie where you walk away feeling happy. Still, the story is deeply moving and powerful, and my hope was that after seeing the film, viewers might be motivated to do a little more to make sure people aren't alone, abandoned, marginalized, or left on the fringes.

When the credits began to roll, a little lull crept into the auditorium, a tense moment of silence. Sometimes the audience waits until the very end of the credits to show their feelings. Sometimes they make their decision with credits still rolling. I felt my skin crawl. *Will the audience clap? Will they boo?* I held my breath, waiting for the response.

And then it happened.

A dam burst. The entire room erupted into applause. Huge applause. With the credits still rolling, the audience clapped and clapped. One person stood. Then another. The entire theater rose to their feet. A standing ovation. The team and I stayed sitting in the middle of the crowd, and they brought the house lights up and shined a spotlight on us. The crowd continued to clap wildly. They cheered through the entire credits. Malkovich and I stood, took a bow, and waved. The credits ended, and nothing appeared on the screen. The audience continued to clap and cheer. Malkovich and I sat down and took a few moments, the audience continued to clap and cheer, then Russ, John, and I stood. I saw Tom Selleck standing off to one side in the crowd, clapping, cheering. I didn't know him personally, but I could pick out his familiar face anywhere. He wore a white tux, and as I glanced over, Tom caught my eye and smiled and nodded as only Magnum, P.I., could do. The standing ovation went on and on. The noise in the room was deafening. Someone said later that the ovation lasted a full ten minutes. Finally, the clapping wound down, and I stood again and called to the crowd, "Thank you! Thank you! Thank you so much!" Tears filled my eyes, and a wave of emotion nearly choked me. We had worked hard, and this was our moment of truth. It felt spectacular.

You would think a huge standing ovation at Cannes would mean a studio would really get behind a picture, publicity-wise. At one point during the ovation, I'd looked over at Russ and quipped, "Wow, I'm so glad the MGM executives are here to see this. It will be really good for the film." And Russ had quipped back, "Either that, or I think we just made a French film." By that, he meant it was going to play well only in art houses. We both laughed ruefully.

Sure enough, the movie opened October 2, 1992, in America and saw a small release, just 398 theaters total. I did a lot of press in the States, and then another promotional tour overseas where I went to Paris and London and other European cities where it was shown, but it never really took off, although the movie received excellent reviews wherever it went. The studio had made a marketing decision prior to the movie's release. Whereas I thought we should have full-page ads for five weeks, they took out only one full-page ad on opening day. After that, nothing. To be sure, the studio executives were gracious. One of the main execs at MGM at the time (and daughter of the great filmmaker Sydney Pollack), Rebecca Pollack, was particularly kind toward the film. The execs considered it an artistic success, but I think they suspected the movie wasn't going to make much money, so they weren't going to spend much to market it. Columbia's *A River Runs Through It*, starring Brad Pitt and directed by Robert Redford, came out seven days after *Of Mice and Men*, and although the stories were different, the heartland tone was similar. Both were considered rural movies with beautiful scenery, and conventional wisdom said both movies would fight for the same audience dollar. I thought our reviews were just as good as the reviews for *A River Runs Through It*, and I mentioned this to the studio executives, but a marketing decision had been made. *A River Runs Through It* went on to win an Oscar and earn $43 million. *Of Mice and Men* received a ten-minute standing ovation at Cannes but grossed just over $5 million.

I don't hold this against anybody. MGM was never "against" the movie. For MGM, it made sense to get a good artistic creation in the pipeline, but they knew Steinbeck's *Of Mice and Men* wasn't going to be a blockbuster and make a bundle. Still, they were happy with the strong performances and exemplary reviews, and in the end, I've always been so grateful that they allowed me to make the movie that I wanted to make.

The story of *Of Mice and Men* is universal. George and Lennie are two lonely souls who befriend each other in a harsh world. They have a dream of someday owning their own place to call home. We all want companionship. We all have a dream. We all deal with loneliness. These are timeless themes that move people; that's what I wanted to be a part of. We succeeded in delivering that message.

And I am happy to say that while it took a little time for us to reconnect, two of the first people I wanted to show the film to were my buddies Terry and Jeff. After exchanging messages that discussed our feelings about my making the film, I screened it for both of them, and they were supportive and proud. Any hurt feelings were set aside, and getting their thumbs-up was a great boost for me. I love these guys like brothers. But sometimes choices are made that send us in different directions. And I had decided to do that. Our work together has always been the greatest gift to me creatively. And our friendship, even more.

The film has proved to have great staying power. Today, more than twenty-five years later, more people have seen our production of *Of Mice and Men* on DVD in high schools around the country than ever saw it in theaters. I still get letters from high school students thanking me for making the film. They've studied it in school, where Steinbeck's great novel is still taught. *Of Mice and Men* is still a powerful and moving story and a film I'm proud of.

I considered it a personal success too. On my first movie, I had made decisions tentatively, but with *Of Mice and Men*, it was the opposite. I felt very confident and knew exactly what I wanted to see on the screen. I'd succeeded in one of my main objectives—to act in a larger role in a movie that I also produced and directed. I'd followed my dreams, intuition, and heart, and worked hard to make my dreams a reality. It was a tremendous artistic challenge, and I'll always be thankful for what I learned and for the self-confidence I gained spending that year in Steinbeck country.

∞∞∞

Six weeks before the opening of *Of Mice and Men*, our third child was due. Sophie had been born naturally, but Moira wanted epidurals after that. Mac came so quickly the epidural didn't work. For the third child, the anesthesiologist was in the middle of putting the epidural in Moira's back, when Baby announced that *now* was the time—and Baby would not wait.

And there she was. Ella Jane Sinise. Beautiful.

Born August 20, 1992, Ella was our smallest baby, and two weeks after her birth, we sat at an appointment with our pediatrician. She listened to Ella's little heart and said, "I want you to go see a cardiologist right away. There's something odd in Ella's heartbeat." I tell you, when a pediatrician says that, your life clouds with fear.

We took Ella to the cardiologist, who ran all kinds of tests. We learned she'd been born with three holes in her heart, which frightened us greatly, but the cardiologist said sometimes these holes close on their own, so he wanted to wait awhile—a few *years*, in fact—before deciding whether any surgeries would be required. We lived on pins and needles the next several years.

At five, Ella was small for her age. She didn't seem to be growing as fast as our other children had. We then learned that two of the holes in Ella's heart had closed on their own, but the third was too big and surgery was needed.

We called everybody we knew. All the doctors. All the friends. Everybody who'd ever experienced anything like this. My agent even put me in touch with Sylvester Stallone, whose daughter had needed heart surgery when she was young. Sly said his daughter was doing very well, and he described the procedure for me. Ella's condition wasn't as complicated as his daughter's, and that gave us some peace of mind. Still, our concerns continued. Dr. Alfredo Trento, the very gifted head of cardio-thoracic surgery at Cedars-Sinai, agreed to do the procedure.

Early in the morning of the day of the operation, Moira, Ella, and I sat in the waiting room, waiting for the staff to come and get our little girl and take her back for the surgery. Ella sat on my lap and I held her closely, smoothing her blonde curls.

"Daddy," she said in a small voice. "When are they going to fix my heart?"

"Soon," I murmured. "Very soon, honey. You'll be all better."

The nurse opened the doors to the waiting room and nodded to us. I carried Ella to the nurse and placed Ella in her arms and watched as they disappeared through the doors of the operating room. Moira and I stood there, stunned. I can still feel that moment of emptiness. When you hand your child to someone else, and she isn't near you anymore, everything is out of your hands. Moira and I held each other. We paced. Then we sat on the couch again, trying to keep it together.

Dr. Trento is a tall, highly educated man with a hearty smile and a grayish shock of hair—the best specialist in his profession, with a list of medical accomplishments on his bio that literally continues for more than forty-three pages. After Ella's open-heart surgery, when Dr. Trento personally delivered the news that all went well, I wanted to hug him and give him effusive thanks. Instead, I choked up, very emotional, and all I could do was whisper, "You have amazing hands."

Dr. Trento looked at me intently and answered in his Italian accent, "Gary, it's God. God puts his hands on me, and then I touch my patients with God's hands."

Moira and I crept into the Intensive Care Unit where our little daughter lay. Ella had a tube in her neck and another tube in her chest. Machines surrounded her with blinking red lights. Lying in the hospital bed with a thin blanket to cover her, she looked so small, so vulnerable. She was sleeping, still groggy with anesthesia, and all we could do at first was stare at her while the fact sank in:

She was going to be just fine.

It would be an understatement to say we were grateful at that moment. On the outside, we simply took three steps forward in the hospital room and sat, our hands clasped in each other's hands, our bodies huddled close around Ella's bedside. But on the inside, we were kneeling before an altar, wordless in our gratitude, cheering far harder than any ten-minute standing ovation, our arms upstretched to heaven in thanks.

Within a few days, we were able to take Ella home. She was in a lot of pain at first. Anytime she coughed or sneezed, her chest expanded, and she cried. A slew of appointments followed. Gradually she healed. She started to grow faster. When she was ten, we took her to the cardiologist and he said to Ella, "Well, we have good news and bad news. The good news is you're all healed. The bad news is I won't get to see you anymore, and I've really enjoyed getting to know you."

In 1992, Moira and I had three wonderful little children, and after *Of Mice and Men* came out, I said to Moira, "I'm really going to go for this film business thing. I'm going to put all my energy into it." Moira agreed. She started to audition less and less and focus more on the kids. I parted peacefully with my New York agent and signed with Bryan Lourd at Creative Artists Agency (CAA), a global powerhouse of a company and one of the top agencies in Los Angeles, and I hired a publicist and personal managers at Brillstein-Grey Entertainment. I wanted to surround myself with a team of people who could get me to the right folks in the movie business.

In fall 1992, my agents set up a general meeting for me to sit down with Steven Spielberg. As a director and producer, Steven was already legendary, having pulled off a string of blockbusters including *Jaws*, *Close Encounters of the Third Kind*, *Raiders of the Lost Ark*, and *E.T. the Extra-Terrestrial*. Steven asked me what I was doing, and I told him about *Of Mice and Men*, and he said, "Oh, I'd love to see it. Will you show it to me? Just bring it over to my house. I've got a screening room there. We'll watch it together."

And I said, "Uh . . . uh . . . uh . . . of course."

We set up the screening. Just outside the theater in Steven's house, he had a little lobby with a popcorn machine and a candy counter. His wife, Kate Capshaw, joined us, and we all grabbed some popcorn and sodas and sat down to watch *Of Mice and Men* together. It was surreal. Steven and Kate were both very gracious, and they loved the movie. Afterward, we stood outside their home, saying our goodbyes. Kate gave me a little hug, and Steven turned to me while I wracked my brain. *Think, Gary, think.* I was desperate to ask Steven one brilliant question. But all I could muster was, "Steven, how do you know where to put the camera?"

He chuckled and said, "I just watch a lot of movies."

So simple. So profound. To become a great filmmaker, you must study the greats. You learn and steal from people you admire. Over the years I had endlessly studied the actors I admired: Al Pacino, Jack Nicholson, Gene Hackman, Robert De Niro, Jon Voight, Robert Duvall, Dustin Hoffman, Marlon Brando, and many others. Steven took the last sip of his soda and added, "Oh, and, Gary, based on what I just saw in *Of Mice and Men*, you should definitely keep directing."

Directing.

Hmmm.

Driving away from Steven Spielberg's house, I mulled over his advice and couldn't help but notice my mixed feelings. I felt so thankful for my time with Steven and Kate, yet I thought back to those early days in high school when I was hanging out in the Glass Hall with my bandmates, trying so hard to fit in and look cool. As a grown-up, I knew that directing held many more possibilities for me. But I also knew my real love had always been acting. Acting had pulled me up out of that difficult time in high school. It had given me a direction and purpose, and acting had held my close attention for so many years. As I headed home to Moira and the kids, I held out hope that acting—not directing—would come through again, even though no acting opportunities were anywhere in view.

Of course, I couldn't have known that just over the horizon was an amazing opportunity, one that would open a new world for me—and not only in acting.

Incidentally, after completing *Of Mice and Men*, I haven't directed a movie since.

CHAPTER 8

Big Movie Years

In 1993, my agents called with an offer to play the lead role in a big ABC miniseries titled *The Stand*, based on Stephen King's epic postapocalyptic novel. I jumped at the chance. Stephen had originally wanted to turn his novel into a movie, but his book was so long, with so many characters, that in the end a four-day television miniseries (eight hours total) proved the best way forward. The miniseries format ruled the networks then.

The project would involve a huge, one-hundred-day shoot—twenty-five days per two-hour episode (to put that in perspective, years later when we did *CSI: NY*, we shot each one-hour episode in eight days). Shooting for *The Stand* would be like shooting four back-to-back movies. Dozens of actors would be involved, many well-known, including Rob Lowe, Molly Ringwald, Ed Harris, Kathy Bates, and even basketball legend Kareem Abdul-Jabbar. It felt great to get offered something this big right after *Of Mice and Men*.

We shot the miniseries mostly in Utah. Stephen King was on the set from time to time, and even played a small part in the movie. I didn't get to know him well, but anytime we talked, he was very encouraging. Laura San Giacomo played a role in the movie. I remembered uneasily how I'd cut her part completely out of *Miles from Home*, but it was good to see her again, and she held no hard feelings.

Molly Ringwald was very sweet and we worked well together. Several of her well-known John Hughes movies were made in Chicago, so we often talked about my home city. In 1993, email was just beginning to become popular, and Molly introduced me to it. Every day, Molly emailed her father, who was blind, and his computer would read back her words to him. This fascinated me.

Rob Lowe and I share a birthdate—March 17, St. Patrick's Day—so during the shoot we celebrated our birthdays together at a restaurant in Salt Lake City. Rob is hilarious. He did many dead-ringer impersonations, including a perfect nervous-looking Christopher Walken. Rob had worked with Chris onstage, and he told me how Chris would constantly look out at the audience while he delivered his lines, instead of looking at the other actors. When Rob asked him why he did that, Chris replied (and here Rob delivered his best impersonation complete with head bobs), "Well, they know I'm here. And I know they're there. I think it would be rude to ignore them." It was hysterical.

The Stand cost more than $28 million to produce, and it was well promoted, received good reviews, and ended up winning a few Emmy Awards. I was nominated for a Screen Actors Guild Award. We finished shooting in June, and I returned to California, where another call came, this one for an audition in a Paramount picture to play the part of a wounded Vietnam veteran. The movie's working title was simply the name of the main character: *Forrest Gump*.

From the start, I wanted this role. Any project that dealt with the Vietnam War interested me, due to the work I'd done in the 1980s with Vietnam vets, in addition to my close connection with the Vietnam vets in my family. The innovative director Robert Zemeckis, who'd had a string of hits, including the *Back to the Future* movies, *Romancing the Stone*, and *Who Framed Roger Rabbit*, would helm the film. The project, based on a 1986 novel by Vietnam veteran Winston Groom, was already set to star Tom Hanks, and the screenplay was adapted by Eric Roth, another wonderful writer. I knew it stood a chance of being a terrific project all around.

But I didn't get the role at first. I auditioned in a conference room at Paramount Studios. Wendy Finerman was producing the movie, along with Steve Tisch, Steve Starkey, and Charles Newirth. Wendy had secured the rights, and it had taken her a long, nine-year-journey to make the film a reality. Wendy was present at my audition, and she'll tell you today that she knew immediately I was the right actor to play Lieutenant Dan Taylor. But the wheels of Hollywood can turn slowly, and after I auditioned it took some time before I heard anything.

In the meantime, I kept auditioning for other movies. That's what you need to do in Hollywood—always keep going. You never know what will or won't materialize. I auditioned for *Little Buddha* with Keanu Reeves and for the Western epic *Wyatt Earp* with Kevin Costner. Both movies were big, expensive projects. Keanu was coming off a string of hot hits, including the *Bill & Ted* franchise and the action thriller *Point Break*. Kevin had exploded in popularity with *Field of Dreams*, *Dances with Wolves*, *Bull Durham*, *Robin Hood*, *JFK*, and *The Bodyguard*. I kept phoning my agents, asking if anything was happening with *Forrest Gump*, but they'd say things like, "Well, they're considering a lot of different things right now. You're still on the list, but it isn't finalized yet."

I would have been happy to land the roles in either *Little Buddha* or *Wyatt Earp*, and I kept my fingers crossed, hoping something would happen. Meanwhile, Moira and I both auditioned for *Tall Tale*, a Disney movie starring Patrick Swayze. They offered Moira and me the roles of the mother and father, and the idea of acting with Moira in a movie was really appealing. Simultaneously, I learned I hadn't gotten the part in *Little Buddha*. They'd liked my screen test a lot, but the part ended up going to singer Chris Isaak, who was just starting to break into the movies. I also learned I'd been passed over for *Wyatt Earp*, although I was told I'd been in the final mix.

I was all set to say yes to *Tall Tale* when the phone rang. I'd landed the role of Lieutenant Dan Taylor in *Forrest Gump*. It would mean I'd need to turn down the Disney movie. Did I still want *Forrest Gump*?

It's a funny thing about movies—how do you ever know what's going to be a hit? Disney has been known to produce some wildly popular movies, and *Tall Tale* featured Patrick Swayze, who'd done very well. Would working with Tom Hanks in *Forrest Gump* prove a better choice? Moira and I talked it over. We decided I needed to place my bets with *Forrest*

Gump—plus, I really wanted to play the role of the Vietnam veteran— while she took the role of the mother in *Tall Tale*. So Moira took the kids to Colorado to shoot the Disney movie, while I flew to Beaufort, South Carolina, to work on *Forrest Gump*.

Life is full of ironies. If I had landed the roles in *Little Buddha* or *Wyatt Earp*—roles I had desperately hoped for at the time—then I wouldn't have been able to do *Forrest Gump*. *Little Buddha* turned out to be a box-office disappointment. *Wyatt Earp* received mixed reviews and floundered in the wake of the similarly themed movie *Tombstone*, released six months earlier. *Tall Tale* was fun, but didn't earn back its budget (although Moira was great in her role) and has largely been forgotten today.

And then there was *Forrest Gump*.

Beaufort, South Carolina, is near Parris Island, where the East Coast Marine Corps boot camp is located. It's hot, humid country known for its bayous, shrimping industry, and antebellum architecture. I arrived in early September 1993, to prepare to begin shooting. Before leaving Los Angeles, I was fitted for a long-haired wig for Lieutenant Dan's "lost and angry" phase, and I needed to come to the set with scruffy facial hair. In Beaufort, we did all the makeup tests and wardrobe fittings first, getting our looks down for each section of the film. To prepare for shrimping scenes, we took a day trip out to sea on a shrimp boat to watch the deck-hands drag their nets for shrimp. We did some work with a dialect coach to get the accents right and also went to Marine Corps Recruit Depot at Parris Island to do a little weapons training for the Vietnam scenes.

I wanted to give my all to the character of the wounded Vietnam veteran, so I began reading the 1992 Pulitzer Prize–winning autobiography *Fortunate Son* by Lewis Puller Jr., a United States Marine Corps officer who had been severely injured when he stepped on a booby trap bomb. Both his legs were vaporized, and he lost his left hand and nearly all of the fingers on his right. Puller was the son of the most decorated marine officer in the history of the Corps, Lieutenant General Lewis "Chesty"

Puller. Like Lieutenant Dan, Lewis Puller returned from Vietnam and struggled with many demons, including alcohol abuse, the difficulties of living with his injury, and the isolation he felt as a veteran of an unpopular war. He worked hard to overcome his challenges, became a lawyer for the VA, and even ran for Congress at one point. But just a few months before *Forrest Gump* opened, Lewis lost his battle with those demons, taking his own life on May 11, 1994. I was very sad to hear of his passing. Reading his remarkable book and knowing his story helped motivate me. They became important parts of my preparation for the character.

Prior to shooting, Bob Zemeckis, Eric Roth, and the cast had two or three sessions where we read through the script. The actors Bob had assembled were terrific: Sally Field as Mama Gump, Robin Wright as Jenny, and Mykelti Williamson as Bubba. During these sessions, we would read the script and Bob and Eric would fine-tune as we went along. At one point we got to the section in the script where Forrest says he's going to start a shrimping business. In this version of the script we were reading, Bubba had only mentioned his fascination with shrimp one time. So Bob stopped the reading and asked Eric, "Why does Forrest decide to go shrimping? Bubba's barely said anything about it." The two of them looked at each other, and that's when they decided that all Bubba should ever talk about is shrimp. So whenever you see Bubba in the movie, what is he talking about? Shrimp! And of course, Forrest Gump, in honor of his friend Bubba and his love for shrimp, carries out Bubba's dream of starting a shrimping business.

Later, just before we began shooting, Bob and I were at a restaurant, and it popped into my head that during the scene where Forrest Gump pushes Lieutenant Dan across a busy New York City street and they almost get run down by a yellow cab, Lieutenant Dan should stop and bang on the hood of the car and shout, "Hey, are you blind?! I'm walking here! I'm walking here!" This was a funny homage to Dustin Hoffman in *Midnight Cowboy*, Oscar winner for Best Picture in 1970. Bob loved the idea, and even took it a step further by underscoring the scene with *Everybody's Talkin'*, the iconic song from the movie.

The first scene we shot was the scene were Forrest comes piloting into the harbor in his shrimp boat. When he sees Lieutenant Dan waiting for him on the pier, Forrest gets so excited he jumps off the boat and swims for his former platoon leader. The shrimp boat runs in circles by itself and eventually crashes into the dock. All went well during that day's shoot, and we rounded out the week by shooting some of the other long-hair scenes, the rest of the shrimping scenes, and Lieutenant Dan screaming at the heavens during the hurricane. For that I was stuck up in the rigging of the shrimp boat all night. To create the hurricane, the boat was docked with crew members pulling it up and down with ropes on either side to make it rock back and forth. Heavy water cannons were positioned in different areas around the boat that shot water up at me while giant Ritter Max fans were turned up full blast to create wind. On top of that, they had a DC-9 jet engine set up to blow like crazy while I hung on for dear life and screamed, "You call this a storm?! Blow, you son of a b**h! Blow! You'll never sink this boat!" Luckily, I didn't have to shoot the next day. After a night of that, my voice was shot.

I then shaved and took a short break from shooting in order to head into the woods for four days with other actors in Lieutenant Dan's platoon to train with a technical advisor named Dale Dye, a decorated Vietnam veteran. Captain Dye had served in the United States Marine Corps, and he'd trained the actors for *Platoon*, as well as serving as technical advisor for many other military-themed films over the years. He put us through our paces. I'd pictured Lieutenant Dan much like my brother-in-law Mac Harris. Both Mac and Lieutenant Dan focused tightly on their military careers, and both wanted to be the best platoon leaders they could be. While Mac had gone to West Point, I wanted Lieutenant Dan to have a slight southern accent, so I decided that he had gone to the Virginia Military Institute (VMI).

For four days we lived in the woods. At night, we needed to maintain silence. It grew pitch black, and we couldn't have lights. We slept in the dirt and maintained a constant guard. Days were hot and muggy. Snakes slithered by us. Rats scuttled past. Mosquitoes were relentless. We couldn't bathe. It rained on us, we stayed wet, we stunk. All this was designed to give us a taste of how it felt to be in a platoon in the jungle. It also gave me the opportunity to lead my men. I learned how to navigate, read maps, plan missions, and take care of my platoon.

On the last day in the woods, Captain Dye sent us on a mission. I needed to quietly lead my platoon several kilometers to another part of the forest where we were ordered to attack a base they'd set up. The maps tell you where there's a hill or water or trail. We started the mission, and everything progressed fine. Then we came out of a tree line into an open area, and everything suddenly erupted. *Boom! Boom! Boom!* We all hit the dirt. I went down right on top of an anthill. Captain Dye and his crew from Warriors, Inc. had planted a bunch of charges in secret to simulate mortar explosions and artillery. We carried real rifles, loaded with blanks, and my platoon started firing back. It was my job to get them under control and move them out of the open into the cover of the forest. We did that, but as a result my navigation plan got out of whack. I was lost in the woods, which was exactly what Captain Dye wanted, since real missions seldom go exactly as planned. We ended up traversing a waist-deep creek, and eventually we made it to the area we were supposed to attack. There, Captain Dye and his crew were waiting in ambush for us, poised as the enemy. We got the snot knocked out of us. On our way back to base camp, Dale and I walked together, and he gave me an evaluation. Even though some things had gone wrong, he gave me a pretty good grade. And years later, he gave me a good pat on the back, saying I could have made a fine soldier. The shower I took my first night out of the woods was one of the best showers I ever had.

The next morning we were back on the set, filming the Vietnam sequences. We shot all the marching scenes, all the rain scenes, and then the scene on the base where Forrest Gump and his good friend Bubba first meet Lieutenant Dan. Forrest and Bubba are "replacements"—soldiers sent into an established unit to take the place of others who've been wounded or killed. Lieutenant Dan meets Bubba and Forrest and gives them a few terse lessons on how to behave in the field. The meeting is the first image viewers see of Lieutenant Dan. He's on his way to the outhouse, toilet paper in hand, wearing only boxer shorts and flip-flops. The shot was made strategically, because we wanted viewers first to see Lieutenant Dan standing on two good legs. Those legs would soon be gone.

During the shooting of the Vietnam scenes, I invited on the set my brother-in-law Jack Treese, who'd been a combat medic in Vietnam. The costume designer had issued me a set of dog tags. But when Jack was in Vietnam, he'd made a set of rosary beads out of string and rope and hung his dog tags on it. Jack let me wear his actual dog tags and rosary in the movie. Jack wasn't Catholic, but he told me that in Vietnam he wanted all the help he could get.

We shot the battle scenes on Fripp Island in a forest near a golf course. The greensmen brought in all kinds of jungle foliage to make it look more like Vietnam. It was almost comical. On one side of a tree line, golfers were teeing off, and on the other side, we were staging a battle and blowing things up.

When we shot the main battle sequence where all hell breaks loose, everyone was tense on set. The special effects team spent the whole day setting up charges and squibs (the little explosions you see when bullets hit the ground). The pressure's really on an actor in this type of scene, because you need to nail it in one take. If you mess up, another entire day is required to get it all set up again.

Everything was choreographed and rehearsed. At least eight cameras were set up and running. Bob Zemeckis called for action. The charges started to explode. We were supposed to wait for a cue, but with so many bombs going off we couldn't hear our signal. Bubba went for it anyway and screamed, "Run, Forrest, run!" And Lieutenant Dan yelled at everybody to pull back. Explosions burst everywhere. *Kaboom! Kaboom! Kaboom!* We played along and kept going. But we were slightly off on our timing. Bob was ticked at us because we almost missed our cue. Fortunately, the scene worked anyway, so in the end Bob was happy.

During the main battle scene, Lieutenant Dan is blown up and his legs are severely mangled. Several of his soldiers are killed. With his platoon under fire, Lieutenant Dan is on the radio trying to call in an air strike. Forrest runs in, trips over him, and sees the lieutenant is badly wounded. Forrest picks him up and carries him to safety out of the jungle. As Tom

Hanks is running with me slung over his shoulder, a rocket-propelled grenade is fired toward us. It blows up the tree next to us, and we fall. Tom grabs me by the scruff of my fatigues and drags me the rest of the way out of the jungle while I fire a .45 revolver at the enemy. While I'm firing, the .45 jams, so we need to do another take. Captain Dye started giving me crap about it, saying it was my fault. I was hot and tired and beat up and not in the mood, so we got in each other's faces. My brother-in-law Jack was filming with a little handheld camera, and he caught some of the hullabaloo on tape. Captain Dye and I were both just releasing tension, so however it looked we held no hard feelings between us.

Several times we needed to reshoot the scene where Tom carries me out of the jungle. As Tom ran, my inner thigh bounced up and down, up and down, up and down, on top of his shoulder. We shot take after take, and when the day's shooting was over, I started to stand up and suddenly collapsed. All that bouncing on Tom's shoulder resulted in a football-sized bruise on my leg. I could barely walk. Fortunately, all the Vietnam scenes were finished, so I headed back to Los Angeles (where all the rest of my scenes were scheduled to be shot) and had three weeks off while others went to shoot in Savannah and elsewhere before my shooting resumed. This was good because up next were the scenes where Lieutenant Dan's legs are gone.

The special effects team had designed several ingenious ways of making the camera see me as if my legs were no longer there. In a hospital scene, my legs are covered in a blanket. Forrest comes in with an ice-cream cone for me, and I toss it in a bedpan. A medical guy comes in and says, "Time for your bath." He pulls the sheet off where my legs should be, but my legs are gone. He then picks me up and sets me in a wheelchair. People often ask me if my legs were down inside the gurney—and they were. But when I'm lifted out of there, the rest of that scene was shot using an old technology known as blue screen. I wore stockings made out of blue screen material on my legs; then the special effects guys in postproduction removed my legs and painted in the background, frame by frame.

For the wheelchair scenes, the special effects guys had created a wheelchair that I could sit in while bending my legs underneath me. I needed to be limber for those scenes. But I still had this huge welt on my thigh.

I could hardly move my leg, much less bend it underneath me. For those three weeks in L.A., I went for physical therapy every day, trying to get my leg limber again. Fortunately, by the end of the three weeks, my leg was back in shape.

I finished shooting my scenes earlier than some of the other actors. Then, right before principal photography ended in December 1993, I was called back to the set to reshoot one of my scenes. Lieutenant Dan's ancestors are shown fighting and dying in every major war America has ever fought in between the Revolutionary War and World War II. I'm dressed up differently to play each "ancestor," and the scene plays out like a montage, with the camera never cutting away and getting closer and closer to my face as the scene progresses. For the scene of World War II, I die on a little sandy beach (made to look something like Iwo Jima), and they'd discovered that when I'd fallen over during the initial shoot, the set had shaken underneath me, ruining the shot. On the very last day of shooting, actress Robin Wright was shooting her final sequences on the roof of an apartment building on Wilshire Boulevard in the Westwood area of Los Angeles. It's the scene where Forrest's love interest, Jenny, contemplates suicide, and they were shooting at night. They called me in about midnight to reshoot my sandy-beach death scene. They had built a little beach set on the apartment building's rooftop. About two in the morning, we shot the final scene with my falling down on the sandy beach again. That was the last shot of *Forrest Gump*. We held a celebration, and all was a wrap.

Paramount held a small screening right before the release for all the cast and insiders. There are a lot of scenes that don't feature Lieutenant Dan, so I was able to sit there almost like an audience member, watching it in its entirety for the first time. At the end, the credits rolled, and we all had big smiles on our faces. We didn't know exactly how it would play to audiences, but I think we all knew we'd put together an excellent movie. I told Bob and Tom how great it was, how fortunate I felt to be a part of it. The movie felt satisfying. Moving. Inspiring. It just sat right in our guts.

Before the movie opened, we started the press junkets. That's when you plant yourself in a hotel for a couple of days, and all the press from around the world flies in and stays at the hotel. Each actor stays put in an individual room, and you do interview after interview, saying similar things in each. It can get repetitive, but on June 17, 1994, something broke up the monotony. Bob Zemeckis, Tom Hanks, and I, along with some others, sat in a conference room of the Four Seasons Hotel in Beverly Hills and watched on TV as O. J. Simpson's white Bronco rolled through Los Angeles. Just before the movie came out, Paramount had put up billboards all over Los Angeles, all saying a single word—*GUMP*. It was a brilliant promotional gimmick, and got people all over town wondering, *What's a GUMP?* I wondered if O. J. had driven by any of those billboards and asked himself that same question.

Forrest Gump came out on July 6, 1994, and was an instant box-office smash hit. I couldn't tell you exactly *why* the film worked to the degree it did, but it played to a lot of different emotions, covered a lot of territory, and had lovable characters at the center of it, anchored by Tom as Forrest and Sally Field as his mom.

Right after the movie opened, Mykelti Williamson and I went overseas to help promote the movie in Munich, London, Vienna, and other cities. He and I had become good friends during the filming, and in our free time we'd played a lot of golf on Fripp Island. Alligators had crawled out to sun themselves on that course, but no alligators were on the courses in Europe. We headed up to Scotland from London one evening to play at the famed Turnberry course. The idea was we'd play three rounds at Turnberry, two the next day, and one the following morning before heading back that afternoon to continue more press engagements. It was a couple of hours' drive from London to Turnberry, and we had a driver, so Mykelti and I drank champagne in the back of the Rolls-Royce, and I eventually nodded off. Next thing I knew, Bubba was screaming at the driver, "Watch out! You're going into the ditch!" The driver had nodded off too. I stayed awake for the rest of that drive. We played a couple great rounds in Scotland and finished up the press junket. Everywhere we went, people seemed to love the movie.

About three weeks after the movie's release, I was back in America and took my family up to a waterpark in Big Bear for vacation. As we splashed around in the pool, a bunch of older kids splashed near us. Suddenly one yelled, "Hey! Lieutenant Dan!" The kids had seen the movie and swarmed me, asking questions and wanting autographs. I wasn't used to being recognized, but from then on, it seemed like anywhere I went—from grocery stores to restaurants to waiting in line at Starbucks—people called out, "Lieutenant Dan!" I started to sense that something big had transpired in my career. People didn't know my real name yet, but I'd crossed a line from "actor" to "recognized actor." That would require adjustment.

One day I came out of our house in Pasadena to get the newspaper. A speed bump lay in front of our house with a sign that read "bump." Somebody had painted the *b* into a *g* so it now read "gump." That felt a little strange—the idea that strangers knew who I was and where I lived.

One day a policeman knocked on our front door. "Mr. Sinise," he said when I answered. "We've had some break-ins in the neighborhood lately. I'm just checking to see if you've had any problems." When I said everything was fine, he pulled from behind his back a screenplay he'd written, held it out, and added, "Um, I was wondering if you could read this. I think it would make a great movie." I tell ya, when the police are bringing scripts to your front door, it's time to move. Moira and I soon found a house to rent in Malibu.

When *Forrest Gump* crossed the $100 million mark, Paramount sent gifts to the cast and producers, an Apple computer each—a nod to the scene where Forrest invests in "some kind of fruit company." When the movie crossed the $200 million mark, Paramount sent another gift. I've forgotten what it was now. When it crossed the $300 million mark, Bob Zemeckis called and said Steven Spielberg wanted to take Moira, me, Tom, and Tom's wife, Rita Wilson, out to dinner to celebrate. I wasn't typically palling around with high-powered Hollywood rollers, so it felt good to be included. A couple of days later, Paramount sent another gift—a giant replica of the park bench featured in the film. The base was made from concrete, and it must have weighed 450 pounds. Luckily, my front porch was strong enough to accommodate it.

Forrest Gump garnered a long list of awards, including thirteen Academy Award nominations and six wins, including a win for Best Picture. I received an Oscar nomination for Best Supporting Actor.

The film won three Golden Globes, three People's Choice Awards, and three wins from the National Board of Review of Motion Pictures, including one for me for Best Supporting Actor. It received one win at the Screen Actors Guild Awards and three nominations, including another one for me.

The film also received a Writers Guild of America Award, and two Saturn Awards. And that's only scratching the surface. Today, the film is preserved by the Library of Congress in the United States National Film Registry for being deemed "culturally, historically, or aesthetically significant." Any number of phrases and quotes from the movie have found their way into today's cultural lexicon, from "Life's like a box of chocolates. You never know what you're gonna get" to "Run, Forrest, run!"

Personally, *Forrest Gump* proved to be more than just a big award winner. The next few years became an incredibly energizing and fruitful period in my career, thanks in big part to *Forrest Gump*—although not solely. In 1994, *The Stand* ended up as the highest-rated miniseries on TV. It came out two months before *Forrest Gump* came out, and then *Forrest Gump* was the top movie of the year—and I'd had prominent roles in both, so my agents were now calling me with more and more film possibilities. Significantly, the role of Lieutenant Dan introduced me to the Disabled American Veterans organization, and I began volunteering and doing public service announcements for them, along with volunteering for a few other military charities from time to time. Little did I know how Lieutenant Dan would resonate with our veteran community, but in the 1990s, my volunteer work was still scattered. Mostly, I focused on my acting career—and it was running strong.

Right after *Forrest Gump* wrapped, Ron Howard was set to shoot a movie titled *Apollo 13* about the historic 1970 explosion on the NASA spacecraft headed for the moon and the subsequent mission to get the astronauts safely home. I read the script and loved it. Tom Hanks was set to play Commander James Lovell, and I was called in to audition for whichever of the other three astronaut roles I wanted.

The role that appealed to me most was of astronaut Ken Mattingly. Ken was initially supposed to be in the spacecraft, but a week before launch, one of the backup pilots contracted the measles from one of his kids. Ken hadn't had the vaccination, so they didn't want him in space with the possibility of contracting the disease, and he was replaced by astronaut Jack Swigert, ultimately played by Kevin Bacon. In real life, Ken became a big part of the rescue mission in the control room, trying to figure out how to get the guys back from space, and I liked that twist. Usually I'd need to get a callback from an audition, but Tom had vouched for me, and when Ron came to the premier of *Forrest Gump*, he met me in the lobby and said, "Really great job. I'm glad I cast you." And just like that, I was set to be in *Apollo 13*.

To prep for the movie, Ron, Tom, Kevin, Bill Paxton (who played astronaut Fred Haise), and I went to space camp in Huntsville, Alabama. We spent time with astronauts Jim Lovell and Dave Scott (commander of a later space mission to the moon) to absorb the story of the doomed flight. Then we went to NASA's mission control center in Houston and flew on the Boeing KC-135 Stratotanker training plane to simulate zero-gravity conditions. The plane flies up to forty-five thousand feet, then quickly drops for twenty-five seconds before leveling off and climbing again. For those twenty-five seconds, everything floats inside the aircraft.

They call these climb-and-drop maneuvers "parabolas"—and we were set to do forty of them, one right after another. We all wore flight suits with two pockets on the chest. In each pocket was a little plastic barf bag. When the time came for the first parabola, the plane plunged, and we unstrapped ourselves from our seats. Sure enough, we all flew around inside the padded walls of the plane, gliding through the air like we were swimming in space. Ron Howard experienced these parabolas along with us. Everything was going well, but by the time we got to forty, Ron piped up and asked if we could do another ten. Unfortunately for me, at forty-two I needed my barf bag. I rode out the remaining eight parabolas with a green face.

The extra ten parabolas weren't all about fun and games. Ron was sincerely trying to determine if he could put cameras and a set inside the plane and shoot the weightless scenes in the zero-gravity conditions. Our ten extra maneuvers convinced him it could be done. NASA supported the project and approved the request. So for two weeks, the astronaut-actors shot all their weightless scenes up inside the plane in twenty-five-second intervals, incredibly difficult to do. All my scenes happened down on the ground with the final moments shot with NASA flight director Gene Kranz (played by Ed Harris) in Mission Control, which was re-created back at Universal Studios.

Apollo 13 came out on June 30, 1995, and it was a big hit, garnering stellar reviews and eventually bringing in more than $350 million worldwide. It was nominated for nine Oscars, including Best Picture, and won two, along with a host of other awards. Kevin, Tom, Ed, Bill, Kathleen Quinlan (who played Jim Lovell's wife), and I won a SAG together with the rest of the actors for Outstanding Performance by a Cast.

When we finished shooting *Apollo 13*, it was an explosive time in my career, and I was asked to play the lead role in *Truman* for HBO. I didn't know much about Harry Truman before the project, but the script was based on the Pulitzer-winning book by David McCullough, so I read that, then started poring over source material, reading more books, and watching documentary film footage. I spent hours in the archives of the Truman Library in Kansas City, studying his speeches.

After Franklin Delano Roosevelt died in office toward the end of World War II, Harry Truman took over as president. He made the difficult decision to use the first atomic bomb, the only world leader ever to use nuclear weapons in war. Truman later desegregated the military, implemented the Marshall Plan to rebuild Western Europe after World War II, recognized Israel as a state in 1948, and created the Truman Doctrine—a major policy designed to counter the rise of communist Russia's ideology and expansion (in many ways marking the start of the Cold War). He led the nation during the Korean War.

Two big questions I had were how was I ever going to look like Harry Truman, and how could I age from early thirties to late sixties within the scope of a movie? I needed to create a believable impression of a historical figure, and plenty of pictures of Truman still exist. The producers hired

Gordon Smith, a Canadian makeup artist, to design a full prosthetic, silicon-gel face for me—from scalp to chin—as well as hiring Benjamin Robin and Russell Cate to apply the hair and makeup. (Ben would go on to do several movies and TV shows for me in the coming years and became a dear friend.) For this production, special wigs were made, and I needed to shave my head because Truman had little on top. (Right after *Truman*, I shot a part in *Albino Alligator*, starring Matt Dillon and Faye Dunaway. If you look closely, you see my hair is barely coming in from when I shaved it last for *Truman*.) It took four hours each morning to get me into the prosthetic, hair, and makeup, and another hour each night to remove it all. We'd shoot for twelve to thirteen hours in between, six days a week, for thirty-five days total. At one point, well into the shooting schedule, we were shooting in the replica of the Oval Office at the Truman Library. It was nearly seven o'clock on a Sunday morning, and after weeks of such long days, I looked around the room and saw the crew was dead tired. I was exhausted myself. In the makeup trailer, while getting my prosthetic makeup removed, the producers came in to discuss the call for Monday. I stopped them and said, "I think we are going to take a day off tomorrow. Everyone is completely out of gas. These hours are killing us. Time out. I'll be taking a break tomorrow." The producers left immediately to stop printing the call sheet for the next day. When I eventually emerged from the makeup trailer to go home, the crew was standing outside and broke into applause. Word had gotten out that we were taking a day off. Yes, *Truman* proved a grueling project, but it was a great story and well worth it.

In the end, I felt I fully inhabited the character. The movie ended up garnering strong reviews and winning a slew of awards, including an Emmy for Best Miniseries or Motion Picture Made for Television. I was nominated for an Emmy and won the Golden Globe for Best Actor and the Screen Actors Guild Award. I felt overwhelmed by how my life had changed. Certainly I was grateful for how things were going.

Ron Howard's next movie was a crime thriller called *Ransom* starring Mel Gibson, Rene Russo, Liev Schreiber, and Donnie Wahlberg. Ron asked me to play the villain—a detective gone bad named Jimmy Shaker who kidnaps Mel's young son and holds him for ransom. I read the script and despised this character so much I turned down the part. My children were little at the time; the villain is a psychopath, and I hated the idea of anyone stealing children. He was also written as older than me, so I had trouble seeing myself doing it. I auditioned for a couple of other projects, then started second-guessing myself. Ron Howard specifically asked me to play this part. How could I turn down Ron Howard? But I'd already said no. Was it too late?

In October 1995, I went to the Halloween parade at my children's school and ran into Brian Grazer, Ron's producing partner. Brian's children went to the same school as mine, and I'd worked with Brian on *Apollo 13*, so I asked how everything was going with *Ransom*. Brian said Ron hadn't cast the role of the villain yet, and Brian wondered if I was rethinking my decision. I admitted I was.

When I got home, I called my agents and mentioned I'd run into Brian and we'd discussed *Ransom*. My agents told me that the role had not been cast yet, but Ron was in discussions with another actor. I indicated that if the part was still available, I'd like to do it. My agents hung up the phone. Fifteen minutes later, my phone rang. It was Ron Howard, who asked, "Now, is this just good agenting, or are you really second-guessing doing this part?" I laughed and said, "Well, Ron, my agents are good, but yes, I'd be interested if the role is still available." Luckily for me, Ron gave me the part.

I'd played a villain before in *Jack the Bear*, but the villain in *Ransom* was creepier. It was a major role, too, with the story arc cutting back and forth between Mel's character and mine. At first I didn't like absorbing the thoughts of such a dark character, but after a while I started to really get into it and gave the role my all. Some moments of accidental slapstick during shooting helped me get through it. In one scene, I was supposed to knee Mel in the stomach, but I landed too low. Luckily, Mel had performed these types of scenes before and was prepared: he wore a cup. Later in the week, I had a gift basket with an assortment of pecans, almonds, and pistachios sent to Mel's room with a note saying, "Sorry about your nuts. Maybe you can use these. Enjoy the basket."

We shot *Ransom* in New York City during awards season. On the morning the Oscar nominations were announced, Mel received a nomination for his outstanding work directing *Braveheart*, but Ron Howard was passed over for his work directing *Apollo 13*. We were all happy for Mel, but I was disappointed for Ron, because he'd really poured his heart into *Apollo 13*. The movie received a lot of other nominations, just not for Best Director. There wasn't exactly tension on the set that morning, but there was definitely a strange vibe. I decided we needed to get the elephant out of the room. That same morning, Ron was directing both Mel and me in a scene, giving both of us instructions, and there was some discussion about what should happen. I stopped Ron cold, pointed at Mel, and said, "Hey, maybe we should listen to the guy who just got the nomination for Best Director." Everybody laughed, including Ron, and we patted Ron on the back. We all knew how hard Ron had worked on *Apollo 13*.

In the end, *Ransom* was a big hit. Critics liked the movie, a very different film for Ron Howard, a tense, suspenseful drama. It ended up earning more than $309 million at the box office.

The SAG awards were held during the filming of *Ransom*, and I was up for an award for *Truman*, but I couldn't fly to the West Coast and back to New York in time to be back on set. When they announced that I'd won, I was watching the show on TV. "Gary Sinise couldn't be here tonight, so we accept this award on his behalf." Eating a lonely dinner in my hotel room, I had to chuckle.

So many other things were happening during this time. I was here, there, and everywhere. In addition to the film work, in the fall of 1995 I had directed Sam Shepard's Pulitzer-winning play *Buried Child* for Steppenwolf, and in the spring of 1996 we moved it to Broadway. The play was nominated for five Tony Awards, including Best Play. The 1990s were proving to be a very productive period. Overall, I felt tremendously thankful for the opportunities.

But it wasn't all success.

In 1996, director John Frankenheimer asked me to play the lead role in a made-for-TV movie about controversial Alabama governor George Wallace. Frankenheimer was already legendary by then for directing *Birdman of Alcatraz*, *The Manchurian Candidate*, *Grand Prix*, and *French Connection II*, and I read the script and liked it. But I'd recently played

Truman, so I wanted to do a feature film next, always trying to move from supporting roles into leading roles. When I turned him down, John became emphatic over the phone and said, "No—you can't do that! Let me come out to your house right now and bring you some material." He drove out right away, and he showed me books, and we watched a video of George Wallace, and John talked me into it.

I'm so glad I said yes. John was a strong, sure-handed, master director, and playing the lead in this movie was going to be a great challenge. George Wallace was a complex, contentious character who was steeped in controversy throughout his political career. He became sucked into a backdoor allegiance with the Klan and made a series of wrong decisions, famously stating at his inauguration for governor, "Segregation now. Segregation tomorrow. Segregation forever." He stood in the schoolhouse doorway to block African American students Vivian Malone and James Hood from registering for classes at the University of Alabama. Yet he finally experienced a redemptive moment in real life, shown at the end of the film, where he apologizes to the African American community for all the wrongs he'd done. While I certainly didn't agree with the bulk of George Wallace's actions, this was a big movie role, Shakespearean in depth and power, and as challenging as anything I could imagine.

The wonderful Mare Winningham played George Wallace's first wife, Lurleen, and Angelina Jolie, only twenty-one at the time, played Wallace's second wife, Cornelia. My old pals from Steppenwolf, Terry Kinney and Francis Guinan, were also in the film, along with a terrific supporting cast. In the end, Angelina won a Golden Globe. I was nominated for a Golden Globe and won an Emmy, a SAG, and a CableACE Award.

So many great things were happening—all these wonderful projects with terrific actors, directors, and writers involved, many awards and accolades, year after year after year. But here's what wasn't successful: if you could peer underneath the surface of my life, you'd see a slightly different story.

Bit by bit, our family was facing some very difficult challenges—and they all came to a head during the filming of *George Wallace*. During this intense, crazy era, some harmful habits caught up with us, and into my family's life would come more pain than we'd ever known.

CHAPTER 9

Darkness and Light

At four thirty in the morning on January 17, 1994, our home in Encino rattled and shook for what seemed like an eternity. Books tumbled off shelves. Lamps and vases toppled over and crashed onto the floor. Moira and I were both up in a wink. Ella, seventeen months old, was sleeping in a little bed in our bedroom. Moira grabbed her and rushed outside, while I sprinted into Mac's room. Sophie was staying the night at her grandparents' house not far away. The power was out, leaving our house totally black, and as I ran to Mac, I stepped on something flat and slick that shattered underneath my bare foot. A glass-framed picture had fallen off the wall. Luckily, my bare foot wasn't cut, and I kept right on running. The house was still shaking when I grabbed Mac and raced with him outside. Moira and the baby met us on the driveway. Car alarms blared all over the neighborhood. Neighbors shouted. Our house continued to crackle and groan.

A huge earthquake was shaking Los Angeles. Later termed the "Northridge Earthquake," it registered 6.7 on the Richter scale, killing fifty-seven people and injuring another eighty-seven hundred. Our rental house in Encino was up in the hills of the San Fernando Valley, and as we stood on our driveway in the pitch black of night, we looked across the vastness of the valley and every light was out. A total blackout. All we saw were electrical transformers exploding here and there—just random spots of fire amid the darkness. Normally, the valley at night was awash in color from thousands of streetlights, but this night the valley looked eerie, spooky, like the end of the world was upon us. We didn't know what to do or where to go, so we huddled in our car, waiting for the sun to come up so we could see better, while listening to news updates on the radio. My parents soon drove over to our house with Sophie, and when the sun came up I went back into the house to examine the damage. The house was livable, fortunately, but the walls were cracked, household items were strewn everywhere, furniture was toppled, and we needed to do a lot of cleaning up.

Even then, I didn't trust the structure, particularly after two large aftershocks hit that same day, with many smaller ones following. My brother-in-law Jack Treese and my wife's sister Amy lived not far from us, so we drove over to their house to check on them. Streets looked like war zones. Shattered glass lay everywhere. Gas lines blazed. Commercial buildings were reduced to rubble. A multistory concrete parking lot at one of the malls had pancaked on top of itself. An entire section of Interstate 5—the main north-south freeway along the West Coast—had collapsed. For the next three days, we camped out in my parents' backyard in tents, afraid to go back into our houses, wondering what the future would hold.

As horrible as that earthquake was, our family thankfully emerged relatively unscathed. Yet something else would shake us even more deeply over the next few years, causing us to wonder at times if we were going to make it.

⚬⚬⚬

Back in the mid-1970s, a young, incredibly talented theater student joined us at those early meetings held at Illinois State University to discuss the creation of Steppenwolf. As one of the meetings was winding down, she pulled a fifth of Scotch out of her purse and announced, "C'mon, everybody, let's go!"

Everybody laughed. We were all into partying. Pot and booze were always available on college campuses, and the fact that this young theater student kept a bottle of whiskey in her purse didn't seem unusual to any of us.

That student was Moira before I knew her very well, and I drank and partied right along with her and the rest of our friends in those days. Everyone drank, it seemed, yet in the coming years, the challenges with alcohol became more difficult for Moira, to the point where in the mid-1990s, alcohol held a strong grip on her.

Moira was the youngest of five children in the Harris family. Born first was her oldest sister, Lois. Then came two older brothers, Boyd and Arthur. Then came a fraternal twin sister, Amy. Moira was actually the baby of the family because she was the second of the twins. As a young child she loved to be at home with the family. She studied hard in school and for the most part stayed out of trouble. In her high school years in Pontiac, Illinois, the party scene began to unfold, although unlike me—the wild nut in high school, always boozing around with my buddies and skipping school to smoke pot—Moira was the good girl in high school. She attended a few high school parties and had a little taste here and there to fit in, but she never got drunk then. She was smart and pretty and always got good grades. Her freshman and sophomore classes named her homecoming queen, and first runner-up in her junior and senior years.

Moira and Amy, known around their high school as "the Harris twins," were both popular, yet they were very different in personality. Amy was more confident and adventurous, Moira more reserved. Amy signed up for ROTC in college and after graduation went off to see the world by serving our country in the US Army. Moira stayed closer to home, pursuing theater and acting.

Moira always felt close to her family, and even though Illinois State University was less than an hour's drive from home, being away was hard for her. In high school, the twins had been together constantly, doing many of the same things together and always looking out for each other. But in college, they slowly started going in different directions, moving in different circles. Moira was never a person to go against the grain, which usually meant she followed someone else's lead and didn't rock the boat.

When she got to college, she saw that "going with the grain" included a fair amount of partying—and she fell into it right along with all her new friends. It wasn't necessarily a part of her nature to be wild, nor did she drink all the time, but joining the crowd at those parties became her way of coping. She wanted to fit in. Yet even at the parties, Moira was trying to escape. You wouldn't have known that if you met her. She was a great theater student. Onstage she was dynamite, a real powerhouse, and at those parties she was always fun. But offstage, inside her soul, she was wrestling with her fears. When she had a drink, the alcohol boosted her confidence, allowed her to feel more a part of things, and helped her to mask that fear. Over the years I have known many wonderful performers who are explosive and funny onstage, but who are shy, fearful, reserved, and even a bit awkward in daily life. Performing gives them confidence and a feeling of self-worth. Sometimes they will add a little alcohol on top of that. And Moira wrestled with self-confidence and fear. Performing and alcohol helped quiet those feelings.

Our paths crossed because of our mutual friends and our love of theater. In the early days of Steppenwolf, Moira and I certainly shared many a party together. But as we began to grow up, I was able to minimize my partying ways, particularly after I became a father. But alcohol gripped Moira tighter and tighter as the years rolled on, and it wouldn't let go.

A few danger signs were visible early on. One night sometime in the 1980s, we had dinner at a restaurant with some Steppenwolf friends. All of us were drinking wine. When the meal was over, everybody got up to leave, but some half-full glasses of wine still sat on the table. Moira sort of scoffed and said, "Hey, we can't leave all this good wine here." Moira emptied everybody's glass. No one batted an eye. *That's just Moi. Everyone loves wine. She just loves it a little more.* This type of thing occurred more than once. Most of our friends from that era seemed to grow out of their partying, although a few didn't. One college friend's life shattered from alcohol in the mid-1980s. He went to rehab, quit drinking, and pieced his life back together. But again, the way we all saw Moira—me and others close to her—was to tell ourselves things like, "Well, she just likes her wine. It's no big deal."

As time went on, I began to see that it *was* a big deal, as life with Moira's drinking got scarier and scarier. At one point, about 1995 or so, I simply stopped drinking with her. I figured if she didn't have me as her drinking buddy anymore then that would help and maybe she would stop. But that was wishful thinking. Alcohol was consuming Moira by then, and sometimes she would drink so much she'd pass out. As time went on, I had to be careful what I said and how I said it, because when she drank she would react unpredictably and act kind of crazy. She started to hide her drinking from me and the family. I'd get rid of all the booze in the house, but then I'd open a top cabinet and find a bottle tucked far away in the back. I'd even sometimes find a bottle hidden in the tank of the toilet. At times when she came home, she'd reek of perfume and mouthwash, an effort to hide her drinking from me.

By the time I signed on to do *George Wallace* toward the end of 1996, alcohol had taken control of Moira. It was as if she had two personalities. When she wasn't drinking, she was her beautiful self, the respectable Dr. Jekyll. But when she drank, she turned into the out-of-control and scary Mr. Hyde. Sophie was about nine years old at the worst of Moira's drinking, Mac was six, and Ella was five. Moira was always a great mom and tried her best, but because of her drinking, at times I felt afraid for our children. Each night Moira would drink. Then each morning she'd feel guilty and apologize. I'd tell her she simply couldn't keep doing this, and she'd say, "Yes, you're right, I'll stop," but the next night she would do it again. She couldn't help it. So many good things were happening in my acting career. I had started rehearsing *George Wallace* with John Frankenheimer, and I was trying to focus on my role. But night after night, when I came home from rehearsals, our home turned into a battlefield.

Of all our children, Sophie knew something was wrong. She often needed to adopt a parental role with her younger brother and sister, which wasn't fair to her. One night I came home from rehearsal, and Moira had been drinking again. The kids were in the back of the house playing, and Moira and I got in a huge fight in the kitchen. At one point during the argument Sophie came marching in with Mac and Ella, singing and dancing and jumping around in hopes of trying to distract us by making us laugh. They knew trouble was in the air and were trying to help. Sophie especially. Moira and I stopped yelling at each other. I walked them back to play in the bedroom, then came back to the kitchen and after a while was able to calm Moira down. While it hurt to see the kids trying to act as peacemakers, their interruption actually helped to defuse the tension in that moment. But it was only a momentary calm in a gathering storm. We had a wonderful housekeeper, Lulu, who had become part of the family by then, and she always tried to take care of the kids while also helping Moira. Yet every night proved difficult. Finally, it became clear that Moira had no ability to stop her drinking.

I didn't know where to turn. I started going to Al-Anon Family Groups, for people worried about someone with a drinking problem. I started seeing a psychologist who specialized in alcoholism and helping families through difficult challenges. I learned that family members must become tough in their love. I needed to become ruthless in combating this addiction—for the sake of my wife. But it was very hard to do. You want to plead and beg and appeal to the wonderful, loving person you know is there deep down inside. But that person has been consumed, swallowed up, and cannot hear you.

One evening in January 1997, I came home from rehearsal and found Moira drunk, and we got into a massive fight. It was just before shooting began on *George Wallace*, the biggest movie role I'd ever had, and it was hard for me to stay focused on the movie with so much turmoil happening at home each evening. I called John Frankenheimer and finally told him everything. John had been very open with me when we first met. At one point in his life he'd been on top of the world as a director, but he'd become insane with alcohol, and it ruined large pieces of his career and family life. He'd now been sober for more than twenty-five years and was a serious attendee of Alcoholics Anonymous meetings. He was a hard-core AA warrior and told me what I needed to do. I needed to take Moira to rehab—and I needed to do it *right away*!

The next morning, Moira became very apologetic. She promised she'd never get drunk again, but I explained that when I got home that evening, she needed to go to rehab. I called the psychologist, and he recommended a place in Port Hueneme, just north of us, called Anacapa by the Sea. That night when I arrived home, Moira was drunk again. I packed a bag for her and helped her into the passenger seat of our black Ford Mustang. She was on edge, resistant, but got into the car anyway. We started the ninety-minute drive north on the Pacific Coast Highway to the rehab facility. Twenty minutes up the road, Moira started freaking out—screaming, going crazy. I thought of Linda Blair in *The Exorcist* when confronted by the priest. I was so scared. At one point Moira started fiddling with the door handle as if trying to open the door to throw herself out of the car. I reached over, grabbed her, and held on, wondering, *Who is this person? What the hell is happening?!* It was the longest drive of my life.

When we finally reached the rehab facility, the therapists took Moira into their care and ordered me to leave. As I shut the door to the lobby, Moira looked back at me through the window, staring daggers. Her face was so startling. So not *her*. Normally, Moira is the most beautiful and wonderful spirit. But this was not my wife. The Moira I knew was lost, and I wanted to help find her again. She truly didn't have control over her life.

When I returned home that night, I sat, exhausted, on a large landscaping rock that sat outside our front door. I stared up into the night sky. The kids were safe inside with my parents, and I couldn't go into the house just yet. I needed to be alone for a moment. I'd just left Moira with people I didn't know, and I desperately hoped I'd done the right thing. As I sat on the rock, a shooting star streaked across the sky. The brilliance of light startled me to stillness. *There are greater things at work in the universe,* I reminded myself, and I almost relaxed. At least I felt a measure of peace within my despair. I was able to put one foot in front of the other, go into the house, say hello to my family, hug the kids, climb into bed, then get up the next day to begin work on *George Wallace* again.

An average stay in rehab is twenty-eight days. My wife stayed in rehab for seven weeks. She was there the entire time I was shooting the movie. I received a call from the facility at one point, and a rehab supervisor indicated they were having a hard time getting Moira to admit she had a problem. She thought she was fine and that everybody there was messed up. That meant trouble. If you never admit you have a problem, then you'll never get better.

Moira's mom was a very funny lady. She reminded me of the eccentric and endearing character of Aunt Clara played by actress Marion Lorne in the 1960s television show *Bewitched*. But when Moira's mother drank, and she drank regularly, a different personality would emerge. She had lost both her husband and her firstborn son to cancer, and as time went on, alcohol became more and more of a companion. Once, Moira and I were staying at her home, sleeping on the floor near the kitchen, and I saw Moira's mother get up at 7:00 a.m., shuffle to the fridge, put ice in a coffee cup, and fill it with vodka. Plus, she had some health problems for which she took medications, and she often mixed her medications with booze. One night in 1991 she went to sleep on the couch and didn't wake up. Her heart had simply stopped beating. The loss of Moira's mom was very difficult for everyone—and very tough on Moira. They were very close and much alike. And neither one thought she had a problem with alcohol.

The counselors at rehab asked me to get letters from Moira's friends, writing her honestly, telling her what they had observed about her drinking. I gathered those letters and sent them to her. They were difficult for her to read. She became troubled and thoughtful, but also indignant. At one point, we'd both partied with these people—and now they were telling her she had a drinking problem?! She concluded they were all nuts.

The pressures at work began to overtake me. Each night I needed to learn a lot of lines for the next day. At one point I asked my parents to stay with our children, and I moved out of our house into a hotel, the Chateau Marmont on Sunset Boulevard, so I could focus on the part. I worried constantly about Moira. Worried constantly about my kids. Worried constantly about doing a good job on *George Wallace*. I received another call from the rehab center saying that they wanted to increase Moira's stay because she still was not admitting the problem. The first step to healing is admitting that you are powerless over alcohol. I put John Frankenheimer on the phone with the folks at rehab. and John told them to be tougher with her and not to let up. He remembered what he had been like at his worst, and he explained that if people hadn't been supertough with him then, he never would have gotten sober.

When the seven weeks were up, I traveled to Anacapa by the Sea again and brought Moira home, hoping this challenge was all behind us. On the road back to Malibu, Moira looked out across the ocean, turned to me, and said, "You mean to tell me I can never have a nice glass of champagne ever again—even while sitting on the beach watching a sunset? Never? Again? In my life?"

I wasn't sure how to respond, but I thought, *Oh boy. I'm not sure rehab has done the trick.*

<hr />

When *George Wallace* finished, I was set to play Stanley Kowalski in *A Streetcar Named Desire* at Steppenwolf in Chicago. Moira started to go to AA meetings in Malibu. I flew to Chicago and began rehearsals on the play, and once the show was up and running, the plan was for Moira and the kids to come out for a visit.

In those days you could go straight to an airport's gate to meet an arriving party. The kids came off the plane first. Moira came last. She'd been out of rehab for about six weeks, but as soon as I locked eyes with her I knew she'd been drinking again. You get to a point where you can spot it a mile away. I thought, *Oh boy, what now?* I didn't want to fight or argue while they were visiting me, so I rationalized. I gave her the benefit of the doubt. *Maybe this was a onetime thing. She's going to be all right. Maybe it was just one little drink on the plane to calm her nerves.*

Moira and the kids stayed with me in Chicago for ten days. She was okay the entire time, so I kept rationalizing, thinking her drinking on the plane was a onetime thing. They flew back to California, and I continued with the play until it finished a few weeks later. When I came home, I started to find alcohol around the house again. The amount I found wasn't as much as before she'd gone into rehab, so again I rationalized, hoping things were going to clear up and get better.

I was still talking with the psychologist, and he warned me to be careful. I was just about to start my next part, a costarring role with Nic Cage in the movie *Snake Eyes*. Part of the movie was to be shot in Atlantic City, another part in Montreal. I flew to Atlantic City, and later Moira joined me for a few days—without the kids, who were with my folks. Moira and I stayed in a casino hotel. There were shows and booze everywhere. On one of my nights off we saw the great Patti LaBelle, a fantastic show, and we had a great time. Moira drank a little on the visit, but she never got drunk and everything stayed under control. It was a wonderful visit, and I hoped the worst was behind us. Perhaps, I thought, she was now able to have a glass of wine without drinking until she passed out. She flew home and all seemed well.

Right before Labor Day weekend 1997, the *Snake Eyes* production moved to Montreal. Moira and the children went to Lake Tahoe to visit friends. Late one afternoon my phone rang. It was nine-year-old Sophie, crying. "Daddy—Mommy's drunk again. She keeps drinking vodka and telling me it's water." We were both silent for a moment. Sophie loved her mom so much, and her heart was breaking. Choking through her tears, Sophie whispered, "Daddy—I don't know what to do. I just want to be a kid." I got the picture—Sophie was taking care of Mac and Ella because Mommy was too drunk. I never doubted that Moira always tried to be a good mother with our children. She was never anything but a loving mother. But when just Moira and the kids were traveling and Moira had been drinking, well, it was hard to know what would happen—and that felt very scary. I wanted to be the loving husband, the gentle husband. I wanted to ask Moira nicely, "Please don't drink again." But with the vicious enemy of alcohol taking over the life of the woman I loved, I learned you could show no mercy fighting this enemy.

Moira and the children were scheduled to return to Malibu from Tahoe the next day. I reassured my daughter, then called Moira and calmly told her I had a few days off, and as it was Labor Day weekend, I was coming home tomorrow. She was drunk on the phone and said, "Oh great, yay. I'm so happy."

I called John Frankenheimer and said, "Moira has relapsed, John. I'm heading back to Los Angeles, but I don't know what I'm going to do."

John said, "It's time to take the gloves off." And then he told me what I needed to do.

When I arrived home the next day, Moira opened the door and I spotted it right away: she'd been drinking again. I came into the house, gave her and the kids a hug, and acted as if everything were normal and fine. After a short while I said to Moira, "Honey, you look tired. Why don't you go lie down and take a nap?"

She said, "You know, I *am* kinda tired. I think I will." She went to lie down in the back bedroom. Twenty minutes later I checked on her. She was out like a light.

I packed three suitcases, called a car to pick us up, and wrote Moira the hardest letter I've ever had to write. I explained we'd reached a point of decision. She couldn't have our family and still have alcohol. She needed to choose between us, and she needed to get serious about her choice, because I was finished. I told her I loved her so much, and I wanted her to be okay. What I wanted most in life was for her to be sober and happy, and for us to be together again as a family. But we couldn't do that if she continued to drink. I was taking the kids.

The car arrived, and I loaded everybody in as Moira continued to sleep in the back bedroom. I still had shooting to do in Montreal. The kids were in school, and I didn't know where we were going, but I knew I needed to get them out of the house. We checked into the Chateau Marmont that night so we could regroup and I could figure out the next step. My parents were living near my sister in Idaho Falls, so I called them from the hotel and explained what was happening. They said they'd help any way they could. My thoughts swirled, and I was torn between taking the kids to Idaho or with me to Montreal. Either way, I had to get out of Los Angeles. It was a few days before I needed to be back on set, so I called John Terry, an actor friend who'd played Slim in *Of Mice and Men*, and asked him if we could come spend the night. He lived in Park City, Utah, and in case I decided to take the kids to my parents' I could get to Idaho Falls easily from there. I just needed time to think, and I knew I could make my decision from John's house. The following morning, we checked out of the hotel, flew to Salt Lake, rented a car, and drove up to

Park City. John and his family were very supportive, even though there was still so much to figure out—schooling in Montreal, finding someone to help with the kids while I was shooting. After considering everything, I decided I wanted the kids with me. I simply did not want to be away from them.

After a night in Park City, we headed to Montreal. On the way to the airport, I discovered all three children had head lice. I got them to Montreal, placed them in the bathtub, and scrubbed their heads with special shampoo while picking out the nits. My youngest daughter, Ella, almost five, still sucked on a pacifier a lot. She was crying, and I looked into her mouth. It was filled with tiny sores. I threw away the pacifier and took her to a doctor, who prescribed some medicine for her. Being the sole parent was not going to be easy.

Moira called us in Montreal. She was sober on the phone, and we had a very frank discussion. I told her she wasn't going to be able to see the children for a while. I would keep the kids, they would be fine, and all I wanted was for her to focus on getting this thing under control: getting, and staying, sober, once and for all. There would be no more begging or pleading from me. This was it.

She said, "I know. I know."

Perhaps it was the tough love talking or the hard reality that I had taken the children away from her. I didn't trust her words fully yet, but I thought maybe, just maybe, she wasn't simply saying those words this time. Maybe she finally *did* know that she was powerless over alcohol and needed help.

The next day, she checked into the Betty Ford Clinic in Palm Springs. This time, I didn't drive her. This time, she got herself there.

The children stayed with me in Montreal, and after shooting wrapped, I took them to Idaho to stay with my parents. They finished out the first half of the school year with their cousins.

Moira didn't see the children for three months. She went to Betty Ford for twenty-eight days and then to a halfway house in Texas for a while. I encouraged her to do this, fearing the twenty-eight days were not enough, and she agreed to go. It was tough for her there, and after staying for a while and doing their program, she promised me she felt strong and was ready to go home. I supported her decision, but still kept my distance, and stayed in Idaho with my parents and kids for most of that time. Back home in Malibu, for the next ninety days after being released, of her own choice, Moira attended ninety AA meetings. One each day.

During this season, I spent a lot of time in Idaho with the kids and stayed in touch with Moira by phone. She worked hard to attend the meetings and missed all of us. We certainly missed her, but it was important for her to have this time to herself. Plus, the kids were now attending school with their cousins, so it would be hard to uproot them again. One weekend in November I took the kids to see the 20th Century Fox animated feature *Anastasia*. The music was wonderful, and as it was such a lovely film, we saw it multiple times over the following weeks. It was a beautiful escape during a tough time.

Right before Christmas I brought the kids from Idaho to Palm Springs to the Betty Ford Center where we had all agreed to meet because Moira and I and Sophie were set to attend a family workshop at the clinic. The two youngest were too little to attend the workshop and would stay at the hotel with our housekeeper, Lulu. When Moira saw our kids for the first time again, she smothered them with hugs and kisses, and they gave those hugs and kisses right back to her. It was beautiful to see. Since we had been through rehab once before without a positive outcome, I remained cautious. Like her, I was going to take her newfound sobriety one day at a time. But there was a clarity in her eyes that I had not seen for a long time. She was fighting for her children. She was fighting for her family. She was fighting for us. And she would let nothing—not alcohol, not anything—hurt her precious children. The workshop lasted for four days, and it proved very helpful and informative for what we might face going forward. We then packed up and headed back to our home in Malibu. And when we got home, the kids couldn't wait for Moira to see *Anastasia*. She loved it too. As a family, we were at last on the road to real recovery, and I felt hopeful for the first time in years.

It was the end of 1997, and in the twenty-plus years since then, Moira hasn't touched a drop of alcohol. But there's more to this story.

Ella had her heart surgery shortly after Moira got sober for good; it seemed like one big thing after another was happening in our family.

I ended up winning an Emmy for my role in *George Wallace*, which was gratifying, yet much of my life was a blur around then. After *Snake Eyes* wrapped, within about a two-year period, I was featured in seven other movies—*That Championship Season, The Green Mile, It's the Rage, Bruno* (later released on DVD under the title *The Dress Code*), *Impostor, Mission to Mars,* and *Reindeer Games.* With the exception of *The Green Mile*, none of those movies did very well. *Reindeer Games* was a costarring role for me with Ben Affleck and Charlize Theron and another chance to work with my friend John Frankenheimer. *Mission to Mars* and *Impostor* were both leading roles. All these roles came at me at once—and as an actor, you feel hard-pressed never to turn down work. Sometimes I'd shoot one part for one movie, go to a different location and shoot another part for another movie, then come back to the first location and shoot some more on the first movie. I know I wasn't home enough. You need to travel as an actor, and acting was my work, but I regret being away from home so much and missing time with my kids when they were young.

Nine months after Moira got sober, she agreed to perform in J. M. Synge's *The Playboy of the Western World* at Steppenwolf. She took all three kids with her to Chicago to do the play while I went to Wilmington, North Carolina, to shoot the movie *Bruno.* Synge's play is set in an Irish tavern, with lots of drinking going on, but Moira stayed dry. During her time performing, she began to get back in touch with the Irish Catholic side of her family. She wasn't raised in a religious home, but her mother was Catholic by birth and her father was Methodist.

Moira regularly attended AA meetings, and one day before her performance at Steppenwolf she went to St. Michael's Church on the North Side of Chicago, searching for a meeting there. When she entered the church through a side door, still searching for the room where the meeting was held, she accidently walked into the room where the priest was still putting on his robes in preparation to perform a baptism. "Oh, I'm sorry,"

Moira said. "I'm looking for the AA meeting." The priest finished putting on his gown, then walked her into the main auditorium of the church, past the family that was waiting for him. He pointed Moira toward a door near the front. Moira said thank you and started walking away, and the priest called after her, "Pray for me." Moira turned back, smiled, waved politely, and said, "I will." As she was on her way toward the door of the meeting, she passed by an elderly French woman, a member of the parish. The woman said in a thick French accent, "My dear, you need to become a Catholic. You need to convert," and walked away.

That got Moira to thinking . . . here she was playing this Irish woman searching for strength in a play set in a tavern, and in her own life she was searching for strength to help with her sobriety. Nothing was said or done immediately. But Moira told me later she began to feel a quiet yearning for her own shooting star.

She finished up her play, then got on a plane with the three kids to meet me in North Carolina. Shirley MacLaine was directing *Bruno*, and the morning before Moira and the kids arrived, Shirley quickly gathered the cast and crew together and informed us that a literal hurricane was heading straight for Wilmington. Everyone was ordered to pack up and evacuate ASAP. All flights were filled out of Wilmington, so I hastily booked my family a flight out of Charlotte. Moira and the kids arrived on set and saw everyone frantically packing. I gave them all a quick hug hello and said to Moira, "Hi, honey. Welcome to Wilmington. We're leaving!"

We raced down the highway in our rental car, trying to outrun the fury of Hurricane Bonnie. Lightning and wind and rain and thunder chased us. From the passenger seat, Moira turned to me, quite out of the blue, and said, "Oh, when we get back home I'm going to become a Catholic, and our kids are going to go to Catholic school."

Well, I wasn't quite ready for that. I wasn't religious myself, and I didn't know much about Catholicism, even less about Catholic school. I'd had some buddies back at Steppenwolf who'd attended Catholic school in their youth, and they'd always said the nuns were overly strict, even scary. That's about all I knew. With only that image to go by, I wasn't terribly excited about my kids going to Catholic school. Moira's announcement felt like another part of that wild storm. My practical side took over and I thought, *For heaven's sake, we've just moved right across the street from a public school! The kids can walk there—and it's free!*

We beat the hurricane and sure enough, after we arrived home, Moira straightaway met with the local priest and nun and began a program to be confirmed into the Catholic Church. A week later she asked me to meet with the sister. I was reluctant, but Moira persuaded me it was important for me to go too. I went only to be supportive of Moira, yet I ended up talking to the sister for three hours. She was warm, friendly, and funny—no semblance of scariness—and she got me thinking a lot about life and God, purpose and meaning, about the importance of having a solid rock in your life. Moira and I started to attend Mass regularly, and our kids started going to Sunday school.

In the spring of 2000, I was in Chicago with Steppenwolf playing Randle Patrick (R.P.) McMurphy, the lead role in the Dale Wasserman play of Ken Kesey's *One Flew Over the Cuckoo's Nest*. I'd arranged to take off a weekend and have my understudy play the role while I was gone. I flew home on Friday, and on Easter Sunday, after two years of classes, my beautiful wife was confirmed into the Catholic Church. My children and I stood by her side, so proud of her. The fall after Moira was confirmed, Ella started third grade, Mac started fourth, and Sophie started sixth at our local Catholic school, with my full agreement. The Church and the school became a positive force in our lives, and our family only got stronger because of our involvement in the faith.

As the years rolled on, Moira began attending daily Mass, and the church became an important part of my life as well. I found that the church gave me strength and comfort and promoted service above self, all values I would particularly lean on in later years when I began to work more in support of our veterans. I saw how selfless service to others gave purpose to my life, and I was so grateful for that.

On Christmas Eve 2010, I told my wife and kids to get dressed up—we were headed for a special family dinner at Morton's Steakhouse, a place we all enjoyed. On our way to dinner, I suddenly pulled into the church parking lot. A Mass was already under way, and my family looked confused.

It was too late to attend Mass: What were we doing there? Without any of my family members knowing, I had been attending private sessions to be officially confirmed into the church. Our priest was expecting us, and in a small, quiet ceremony on Christmas Eve, surrounded by the family I love and cherish dearly, I was officially confirmed into the Catholic Church. It was a very special night in our lives. Moira was so touched. She had come a long way. Our family had come a long way, and I wanted to belong to the faith as Moira did. It meant so much to her, to me, to all of us.

In the years that followed, my faith grew, and I began to feel called by God to take greater action, compelled to use everything I'd been blessed with to serve in a more substantial way. I wanted to create something that could be there for the long haul and, over time, do good work for others. My journey of faith had basically started with Moira's need and our dark time. In hindsight, I know that God used that difficult season to deepen and strengthen me to be a better husband and father and to bring us joyfully together to faith.

I say without reservation that my wife is my hero. She lost her father, brother, and mother, all at an early age. She's had multiple surgeries on her spine, hips, and feet due to arthritis, and she's continued to forge ahead in spite of all that. She struggled with alcoholism terribly, yet has stayed sober for twenty-plus years now and has remained loving and positive through it all. She is an inspiration. Yes, an earthquake hit our family, shook our foundation, and tested our strength. But the shaking we experienced helped us find a solid rock for our lives, one that will never crumble or fall.

CHAPTER 10

Turning Point

As we rolled on toward a new century, my life continued like that of most Americans, full and busy with things significant and insignificant. And like others, I didn't realize we were all heading toward a sea of change.

I continued to have great moments in my career and much good fortune working with wonderful directors and actors. For instance, while filming *George Wallace* in 1997, I was struck by Angelina Jolie's tremendous natural talent, which was obvious to everyone on set. She put her whole heart and soul into her part. In one scene, George takes a bullet and is rushed to the hospital in an ambulance. Angelina played his second, much younger wife, Cornelia, who accompanies George to the hospital. Two camera shots show the action inside the ambulance. The first shot is from George's perspective, looking up into Cornelia's face. She says, "You're going to be all right, hang in there," while tears run down her face. The second shot is from Cornelia's perspective, looking down at George. For that shot, there's no dialogue, just a close-up of my face. When we originally shot the scene, we didn't have time to capture both images, so a few weeks later they called me back to shoot that one simple picture of my face.

Angelina wasn't scheduled to work that day, but she insisted on coming in and redoing all her off-camera work, working up real tears again, delivering her impassioned lines to George again. I could have gazed at the trees, and the expression on my face would have been fine. It was just me on a gurney with an oxygen mask on my face, looking up. But Angelina insisted. She wanted to be there for all our scenes, giving it her all, no matter what. I wasn't surprised over the next few years when her career took off like a rocket. Later I became friends with her father, Jon Voight, and *George Wallace* would mark the beginning of a gigantic career for Angelina.

Despite the alcoholism-induced chaos in my family during that season, I believe I did some of my best work ever as an actor in *George Wallace*. John Frankenheimer gave me the support and confidence I needed, and we made a great movie. I'll always be proud of that film, and today I miss John terribly. He died July 6, 2002, but before he passed I worked on two more movies with him. One was *Reindeer Games*, which didn't do as well, and the other was an HBO movie called *Path to War*, about the Lyndon Johnson administration during the Vietnam War. John wanted me to play Robert McNamara, the secretary of defense, a larger role that would have required a lot of research and preparation. But I just finished playing the lead role of Randle McMurphy in *One Flew Over the Cuckoo's Nest* on Broadway, an extremely demanding role, and I felt exhausted and couldn't conceive of tackling another major part just then. John conceded, and instead asked me to be in one scene only where I'd play George Wallace again. I already had the wigs and knew the character inside and out, so I came in for one day, and ultimately was proud to be part of what would become John's last film.

John had needed a major operation for tumors on his spine. He was a gruff sort of guy and matter-of-fact about his declining health. His operation took seven hours. I called him the next day, and to my surprise, he sounded optimistic and strong. He discussed a new film company he wanted to begin with me, and I was excited and looking forward to that. But his health turned, and the last time I talked with him he sounded very weak. A few days later, Moira and I were at a mall in Malibu when the call came. My dear friend had died. I thought the world of him. Right there in the mall, I broke down and wept.

Over the next few years, the success I had in *George Wallace* would keep me working regularly, and I was featured in seven movies between 1997 and 1999. The following year, just after the turn of the new millennium, I began rehearsals at Steppenwolf on one of the roles I'd longed to play for years, Randle P. McMurphy in Ken Kesey's *One Flew Over the Cuckoo's Nest*. When I was in high school, Barbara Patterson had taken us to see it onstage and I'd fallen in love with the story. In 1975, the film version starring Jack Nicholson premiered at the Chicago Film Festival, and somehow I scored a ticket. Jack showed up, along with director Milos Forman and other cast members. Jack, an acting hero to me, stuck his head over the railing and looked down at the crowd in the theater, and everybody cheered and shouted his name. I wasn't alone in loving the story. Terry Kinney had played the role of Billy Bibbit at Illinois State University, and Terry had wanted to direct me in the play for a long time. Finally, in 2000, we were going to do it.

Portraying McMurphy onstage required an adrenaline-fueled, full-throttle approach. He's a larger-than-life character, a Korean War veteran locked in a mental institution, and I gave the role everything I had. The sheer physical demands of the role proved difficult. Each night after I finished the play, I returned to my apartment and steamed my voice with a pan of boiling water and a towel over my head before I went to sleep. Next morning I headed to the gym, slouched in the steam room until my voice became limber enough, then went to do the play again. At one point I lost my voice entirely.

Steppenwolf opened the show in Chicago in spring 2000, and it did well. That summer we took the play to London for a two-week run, where it was a big hit. Then on April 8, 2001, we opened it on Broadway, where we played 145 performances at the Royale Theater, closing on July 29. We received mixed reviews, although the *New York Times* described my performance as "a white-hot perpetual motion machine," which was certainly how my body felt. Steppenwolf won the Tony Award for Best Play Revival, and I received a Tony nomination for Best Actor.

The date we closed the show became key. In that last stretch on Broadway, we were contracted for a six-month run, which would have taken us to September 16, 2001. But toward the end of our run, ticket sales began to fall off. The show required a big cast. It was expensive to produce and difficult to perform, and tiredness dogged everybody. Shortly after the Tony Awards, I sat down with the Broadway producers and discussed moving up the show's closing date. By doing this we would encourage more sales, because then everybody rushes to see a great play before it's over. Our plan worked. Ticket sales improved for those final weeks, and we were eventually able to recoup our costs.

Moira and the children stayed with me in New York at the end of the run. After the show closed, we rented a cottage on Nantucket Island for a few weeks' vacation. Members of our extended family stayed with us too, and every day we played on the beach and window-shopped around town. We rented motor scooters and explored the island's dirt roads. We fished and sailed on the open sea. Each night we feasted on ice cream. We didn't know it, but this was the calm before the storm.

———∞∞∞———

In mid-August 2001, my family and I returned to Los Angeles. The kids started school again—Sophie in eighth grade, Mac in sixth, and Ella in fifth. Moira had remained unbending in her sobriety for three and a half years, and family life was peaceful, healthy, and fun.

One morning in September, about six thirty, as Moira helped the kids get ready for school, our phone rang. I was still sleeping. Terry Kinney, who lived in New York, was on the line. Simultaneously, Moira turned on the TV.

"Hi, Terry," I said.

"Gary, are you watching TV right now?!"

"I just got up, buddy, what's going on?"

"Two planes have hit the World Trade Center. The tops of both buildings are on fire."

I rushed to the TV.

Terry's words spilled out: "We're under attack, Gary! Terrorists have crashed airplanes into those buildings. It's bad. Really bad!"

Every American alive then remembers that moment and can answer the inevitable question: *Where were you when you first heard the news?*

I stared in shock and disbelief—along with the entire country, the entire world—as smoke poured from the tops of both buildings. Horrified, we watched on live TV as people leapt to their deaths from the upper floors of the Trade Center. The report soon arrived that a third airplane had crashed into the Pentagon. About twenty minutes later, a fourth airplane crashed near Shanksville, Pennsylvania. We later heard it was United Flight 93, seemingly bound for the White House (the target was ultimately determined by the 9/11 Commission Report to be the Capitol Building). The people on board Flight 93 had discovered that terrorists were crashing planes into buildings, and the passengers had courageously yet fatefully chosen to take back the plane. We watched the South Tower collapse and crumble in a fury of dust and smoke. Then the North Tower fell. Horror enveloped us all.

The scenes that played out on live TV were surreal, shocking. Schools closed all over the nation, and any children already on campuses were soon sent home. I didn't know what to think or feel or do. That morning I was scheduled to go golfing with an old friend from high school days, and I called to cancel, but then I thought maybe my head would clear if I could just get outside and breathe some fresh air. Maybe I could make sense of what had happened.

I jumped into my car and headed to the range. The airspace over Los Angeles usually buzzes with planes and helicopters, but by then all the nation's air traffic had been grounded, and the skies were eerily quiet. My buddy hadn't yet seen the news that the towers had fallen, so I filled him in and we tried to carry on a normal conversation and play golf, but soon we stopped the round.

Like most Americans that day, I felt adrift. I didn't know what to do, where to turn. Life for every American had radically changed, but the change was only beginning to sink in. Only a few hours earlier, my biggest concerns bounced from what my next movie project might be to what we might eat for dinner. Halfway through my golf game on the morning of 9/11, it hit me that normalcy was no longer possible. I thought, *What am I doing? I can't play golf today. I gotta go home to be with my family.*

While driving home to Malibu through one of the canyons, I clicked on the radio news. Newscasters speculated that today's attacks were only the beginning of more attacks to come. The reality of the morning sank in even deeper. Our country was under attack. Vulnerable. Thousands of innocent people had been killed that day. More horror lay ahead. I couldn't tell you exactly why I did this—perhaps in solidarity, defiance, tribute— but I rolled down my window, stuck out my arm and made a fist, and held it high. Tears welled up in my eyes as I still listened to the news. For some time as I drove along, I held my arm outstretched, as high as it would reach.

At home, we glued ourselves to the TV. President George W. Bush had been speaking to a classroom of schoolchildren in Florida when he first received word of the attacks. He soon boarded a plane and then touched down at Barksdale Air Force Base in Louisiana where he briefly addressed reporters. By 8:30 p.m. Eastern time, now back in Washington, DC, he addressed the nation from the Oval Office. He was clearly emotional, heartbroken. "A great people has been moved to defend a great nation," he said. He'd just been handed the distinction of being president on the day America had suffered the worst attack on our homeland in history. Pearl Harbor, on December 7, 1941, had been horrible, but Pearl Harbor had been an attack on our military, whereas September 11, 2001, was an attack on our civilian population. This day was unprecedented.

Over the next few days, we started seeing little American flags on cars all over the city. I pulled into a gas station and bought one for our car. We soon installed a larger American flag on the outside of our house. Everywhere we went, a feeling of support for the United States abounded. Fear mixed with love. We worried about America, about what had just happened, about what might come next. Yet a larger movement had begun to brew. Patriotism was ramping up, making a huge comeback. We felt that we were all in this together. We strove to come together as individuals within the same country and support one another during this senseless tragedy. We would not let this tragedy ruin us.

But the days still felt dark. Images of 9/11 kept replaying through my mind. I saw the Towers exploding and falling. I saw men, women, and children covered in dust, running through the streets of New York City. I saw firefighters running up the steps of the Twin Towers—the same steps that people inside the building had just run down to escape death. I saw people jump from the towers, their bodies falling out of the sky. I pictured the pilots killed with box cutters. I saw smoke rising from the Pentagon, and saw the huge, gaping gash in the building after being hit by a plane. I saw one lone American flag stuck on a hay bale in a field in Shanksville, Pennsylvania, marking the site where Flight 93 crashed. I saw people frantically poring over missing person posters in New York City. I saw first responders sifting through the massive mountain of twisted steel and concrete at Ground Zero, searching for bodies and any signs of life. The images replayed and replayed in my mind. They wouldn't leave.

The attacks occurred on Tuesday. The following Friday morning, President Bush flew to New York and toured the still-smoking Ground Zero. As he stood on top of a pile of rubble with retired firefighter Bob Beckwith, the president put his arm around Beckwith in solidarity. Using a bullhorn, President Bush began his now-iconic speech by calling out to searchers: "America is on bended knee, in prayer for the people whose lives were lost here, for the workers who work here, for the families who mourn."

A searcher called from the back of the crowd, "I can't hear you!"

Instantly the president called back, "I can hear you! The rest of the world hears you! And the people—and the people who knocked these buildings down will hear all of us soon!"

A raw nerve had been touched, and the rescue workers at Ground Zero began to chant, "USA! USA! USA! USA! USA!"

President Bush called for a National Day of Prayer and Remembrance for that same Friday. In the afternoon, I took my family to our church in Malibu. Mourners packed the church. We couldn't find a place to sit, so we stood with others along a side wall. People looked stunned, and quietness settled on the church. Father Bill, our priest, began his message by saying simply, "This has been a tough week." Then he paused. I don't remember anything else specifically that Father Bill said that day—my mind churned so much—but I know he talked about service and volunteerism, about supporting each other through times of need, and about how service to others can be a great healer. At the end of his message, we all sang "God Bless America." Tears rolled down my face as I tried to choke out the words, but I couldn't get them out. My crying became too much. I gave up and just let the tears flow.

My heart broke for the families who'd lost loved ones on 9/11, and I ached for the enormous waste and destruction of lives and human potential. I was highly concerned for our nation, for the future, for my own children. That same Friday night, impromptu candlelight vigils cropped up across the country. In Malibu, a vigil formed on a street corner not far from our house. After we returned from church, Moira and I and the children headed out the door for the vigil, but before we'd reached the sidewalk, I said, "Wait," ran back to the house, and lifted our American flag from its holder. I carried the flag with us to the vigil.

On the street corner, faces looked somber, but strangely triumphant in unity too. One voice began to sing "My Country, 'Tis of Thee," and we all joined in. When that finished, someone began "The Star-Spangled Banner," and we sang with all our might. When the national anthem finished, I raised the American flag over my head. As if on some unseen cue, everybody turned toward the flag and recited the Pledge of Allegiance.

The memory of Father Bill's message mingled with the sorrow, passion, and patriotism I felt at the vigil. As we walked home that evening, I wondered what I could possibly do to support my country during this terrible time.

———— ✻ ————

In October 2001, our troops began to deploy to Afghanistan in response to the attacks of September 11. Osama bin Laden, the leader of the terrorist organization Al Qaeda, had planned the attacks and trained the perpetrators. The son of a billionaire, bin Laden had been born in Saudi Arabia, but the plot to attack America had been hatched in Afghanistan. Bin

Laden and Al Qaeda were harbored and supported there by the Taliban, who controlled the country.

Our troops soon started taking their first casualties. Each name on the nightly news I held close. Our servicemen and -women fought the terrorists on *our* behalf, and our servicemen and -women were now getting wounded and killed. I felt a terrible sadness for them and their families.

I wrestled with many issues. Anger, anguish, and despair flooded my mind. So many innocent people had been killed on 9/11. Nineteen radical Islamic terrorists had trained to kill Americans at flight schools within our own country. The terrorists had been taught how to fly our airplanes by my fellow citizens, unaware at the time that the men they trained were plotting to use the airplanes as weapons. I didn't want our country to be at war. I didn't want our servicemen and -women to have to be deployed. But I knew we had to respond.

An issue of justice remained unanswered. What happened on 9/11 revealed absolute evil, and evil must be confronted and defeated. That meant our nation's defenders were going to be called upon to do the dangerous and difficult job of combatting our enemies. When I thought about it that way, I was fully in support of that response. If we didn't respond, then who would be attacked next? If we didn't do something, what other innocent people would die?

As a country, we started to wake up to the fact that when it came to national security, we had been far too complacent. We'd failed to see the signs, to connect the dots of the threats to us.

We still had a collective memory of the First Gulf War, its two parts code-named Operation Desert Shield and Operation Desert Storm. Back in the summer of 1990, right before I'd auditioned for *A Midnight Clear*, Saddam Hussein, leader of Iraq, had pushed his armies into neighboring Kuwait and claimed it for himself. A coalition of thirty-five nations, led by the United States and Great Britain, came to Kuwait's aid. I remembered turning on the TV and seeing the entire night sky lit up by antiaircraft fire. Saddam's troops blasted away at our bombers as those planes rained fire on Saddam-controlled Baghdad. By the third week in February 1991, Saddam had been driven out of Kuwait; the First Gulf War was over, but not before we'd lost 383 Americans, with many more wounded. I never imagined then that one day I'd travel to Iraq myself.

In February 1993, just before I went to shoot *The Stand* in Utah, news came that a truck packed with thirteen hundred pounds of explosives had been parked in a garage at the North Tower of the World Trade Center in New York. Terrorists lit the fuse and the truck exploded, killing six innocent people and injuring more than one thousand. Investigators later learned that the terrorists had planned to bring down one tower and topple it into the other, ultimately bringing down both Twin Towers and killing everybody inside. Most of the bad guys were caught this time, but not all. Investigators found the information on where the truck had been rented and discovered that the idiot who'd rented the truck had actually used his real name. He was eventually linked to a group of terrorists, including one of bin Laden's partners in Al Qaeda, Khalid Sheikh Mohammed, who was not apprehended in 1993 and was later named the main architect of the September 11, 2001, attacks. Today, it astounds me to think that radical Islamic terrorists had planned and tried to bring down the Twin Towers a full eight years before they eventually succeeded. Why didn't we see it coming?!

On April 19, 1995, I was working on *Truman* in Kansas City and turned on the TV news to see the chaos unfolding in downtown Oklahoma City. Two domestic terrorists had detonated a truck packed with explosives in front of the Alfred P. Murrah Federal Building, killing 168 innocent people and injuring another 680. Another terrible day for our country, coinciding with my wife's birthday. That coincidence made the atrocities seem even more personal.

On June 25, 1996, Hezbollah terrorists bombed a housing complex called Khobar Towers in Saudi Arabia. Coalition forces had used the complex as housing in their operation to enforce a no-fly zone in Iraq. Nineteen American Air Force members were killed, with many others wounded.

On August 23, 1996—a full five years before the attacks of 9/11—bin Laden officially declared war on the United States. He was angry that American forces were still in Saudi Arabia, where we'd been stationed since the First Gulf War. The Saudis expelled bin Laden, so he'd moved his terrorist training organization to Sudan, and then to Afghanistan. In February 1998, he declared war on the United States a second time, lumping the West and Israel together with this declaration.

He was serious about his declaration. On August 7, 1998, two US embassies were simultaneously truck-bombed by bin Laden's Al Qaeda henchmen—one in Tanzania and the other in Kenya, killing 224 and injuring more than four thousand. After the truck bombings, the FBI placed bin Laden on their Ten Most Wanted list.

In October 2000, the USS *Cole* was bombed by bin Laden's Al Qaeda while on a routine refueling stop in a harbor in Yemen. At lunchtime, with many sailors aboard ship lined up for chow, two suicide bombers piloted a small speedboat close to the vessel and blew themselves up, killing seventeen sailors and injuring another thirty-nine. A United States battleship had been blown up. If that isn't an overt act of war, I don't know what is.

After 9/11, I started remembering all these events and thinking, *Why didn't we connect the dots better? Why weren't we better prepared?* I was afraid for my country, for my family. A plan began to form in my mind to do something bigger than myself, something that would support our country in its response to the reality of terrorism. I concluded that the best way I could do this was to support our nation's defenders. I didn't know yet what this would mean. But I knew I wanted the men and women who were deploying to know they were appreciated, and that a grateful nation backed them up. The thought of our returning warriors facing any sort of treatment similar to what our Vietnam vets received when they came home was very troubling to me. I couldn't stand the idea of our troops going off to fight Al Qaeda on our behalf and then being mistreated upon return. We couldn't make the same mistake twice.

On the first anniversary of 9/11, I was asked to emcee the Chicago 9/11 memorial event held in Daley Plaza, in the middle of the city. More than one hundred thousand Chicago citizens packed the area, and tears flowed. It was a very somber day. I wasn't primarily known for my work with veterans yet, but I'd been doing bits and pieces along the way. People knew I'd created the veterans' nights at Steppenwolf. I'd supported the

DAV since 1994 when *Forrest Gump* came out. I'd helped raise money to build a veterans' memorial in Lansing, Illinois, and I'd supported the American Veterans Center awards ceremony in 2000. (And over the next decade, I was always somewhere on September 11, hosting some kind of memorial event.)

But I had yet to make a full commitment.

Over the next few years, the hunt for bin Laden continued. (His eventual killing on May 2, 2011, in Pakistan by SEAL Team Six and other participating units prompted Al Qaeda to vow vengeance). But in 2003, focus was shifting toward Saddam Hussein in Iraq. US intelligence believed Saddam had significant chemical and biological weapons, perhaps even nukes, that he planned to use against us. I felt deeply conflicted about this. It looked now like a second war would be started, and I hated the idea of more war. Yet I held a deep concern for the future of America. What would my own children experience in this new post–9/11 world?

Slowly, America adjusted to the new normal. We took off our belts and shoes in the airport. We consented to random pat-downs. We couldn't go all the way to the arrivals gate anymore. We saw young people enlist and head off to war. We began to understand we were fighting a new kind of war against a cowardly enemy who blended in with the population, an enemy who often used children and civilians as shields, an army of suicide bombers, a war that wouldn't be over anytime soon.

Yet life continued for America, and work continued for me. In February 2003, I shot the movie *The Human Stain*, starring Anthony Hopkins, Nicole Kidman, and Ed Harris and directed by Robert Benton. I played Nathan Zuckerman, a writer who develops a theory about how the characters played by Anthony and Nicole are killed. In one scene, I go out to the middle of the lake to confront Ed Harris, the bad guy, who is ice fishing. We needed a frozen lake, but shooting wasn't set to begin until mid-March. So Ed and I were asked to shoot the scene in February on a frozen lake just outside of Montreal. It was freezing cold. Ed's character wore plenty of clothes, but my character had only a thin overcoat. My teeth chattered as the camera rolled. And in that period I often felt myself shaking for other reasons, ones that had nothing to do with the weather.

In early March 2003, the shoot finished, and I came home. My brother-in-law Jack Treese and I got to talking—debating, really. He was a hawk about our country and was convinced we needed to go into Iraq. Because he'd been a combat medic in Vietnam, I took his views seriously. Unmistakably, Saddam was an evil killer. His sons were evil killers. Saddam tortured and killed many, including his own countrymen, in unimaginable ways: by tearing people apart, feeding them to wild animals, lowering them into vats of acid, burning off their limbs, and raping women in front of their families. He squandered millions of dollars given to him by the United Nations' humanitarian oil-for-food program and used it instead to pay the families of Palestinian suicide bombers $15,000 to $25,000 every time they blew up Jews in Israel. Some 117 of these bombings were carried out.

On February 5, 2003, Colin Powell made a convincing presentation to the United Nations that Saddam continued to build weapons of mass destruction in spite of UN Resolution 1441 demanding that Iraq comply with its disarmament obligations set forth in previous UN resolutions. Saddam had killed some 5,000 women and children by having Iraqi jets drop poison gas on them. All told, he killed as many as 250,000 Iraqis, 50,000 to 100,000 Kurds, and many other men, women, and children. This post-9/11 world was a frightening place, and Saddam Hussein was an evil, evil man—no question about it.

Yet I was not completely on board with sending our troops into a new war zone in Iraq. "I just don't want to see any more of our men and women get killed," I said to Jack, my adrenaline rising.

We debated each other hotly for some time, and eventually I blew up and walked out of the house. For an hour I circled the block, thinking, cooling off. All kinds of political problems were bound up with the plan to go to war with Iraq. To name just one, a few years earlier we'd actually supported Iraq when they were at war with Iran. As I walked, the hawk and dove parts of me tore at each other. I wanted evil to be confronted, but I didn't want anybody to have to actually do it. We'd invaded Afghanistan nearly a year and a half before. Our men and women were getting killed and wounded, and we still hadn't found bin Laden. Yes, we had removed the Taliban, and Al Qaeda was on the run, and I was glad about that, but I was reluctant to open up another battlefront and go into Iraq because more Americans were going to get hurt and die.

I debated and debated myself, circling the block. Finally, a switch flipped. I decided the necessity of the cause outweighed the problems associated with the invasion. Evil needed to be confronted, and Saddam was evil. Period. He needed to be stopped.

A few weeks later, on March 20, 2003, our troops began the invasion of Iraq in a mission titled "Operation Iraqi Freedom." A month after the war began, I watched on TV with the rest of the world as our troops and the Iraqis wrapped one end of a chain around a tank and the other around the statue of Saddam Hussein in the town square in Baghdad—and yanked that bastard down. The local Iraqis, filled with rage, surrounded the statue and beat Saddam's image with their shoes, a sign of great contempt and disrespect in that culture. The evil dictator finally had been toppled—figuratively and literally—and he was now on the run. (Eventually he was caught hiding in a hole in the ground near Tikrit. Saddam was tried by the Iraqi judicial system and executed on December 30, 2006.)

Shortly after the liberation of Iraq began, something big began to stir inside me. My thinking turned a corner, and I made a decision to go all in, making my commitment to support our troops stronger, more permanent. And as there was clearly a divide brewing in our country over whether we should or should not be fighting a war in Iraq, I had a fear that our troops, like those who fought in Vietnam, would be caught in the middle, not feeling supported and appreciated for their service. A fuller mission began to galvanize in my mind, heart, and soul. I began to feel a new and compelling calling to serve directly. I didn't want to serve only a little bit, then go back to my golf game. I wanted to do something lasting.

Throughout my entire life, I'd always been the type of person who chose to act—not in the theater sense of the word, although I did a lot of that. I mean *take action*. Whether it was starting a band that lip-synced for a living room full of neighborhood kids, or working with my fellow high school students to fashion our own theater company, or taking a great production to New York, or moving out to Los Angeles so I could work in the movies—I'd never been the kind of guy who sat around and talked, or wondered, or thought about stuff without doing something about it, at least not for long. My response had always been to take action—and hopefully doing so would benefit other people along the way.

In those early months of 2003, I realized like never before the cost of freedom, and I knew freedom needed to be defended. I knew places existed in our world without freedom, and I knew that without freedom, none of the good and fulfilling ways we in America aspired to live our lives would be possible. This realization helped fuel me more than ever before. It made me profoundly grateful for being an American, able to live in this land of freedom, able to make something of my life. When it came to my service, I wanted to be all in, all the time, living out my calling every single day for the rest of my life.

I can most certainly say that what happened to our country on September 11 broke my heart and changed me forever. It forced me to rethink everything. What do I really believe? How do I want to raise my kids? What kind of example do I want to set for them? What can I do to give back to this great country I love? How can I use my good fortune to help? It was a turning point and marked the beginning of a new level of service. I found that the more I gave, the more I healed.

Two months after watching the statue of Saddam Hussein being pulled down, I was on a plane to Kuwait.

Nothing would ever be the same.

A Bridge Between Worlds

H i, I'm Gary Sinise, and I'd like to go on a USO tour. Please call me back." I left my number on the voice mail.

A couple of weeks went by; all I heard were crickets. I concluded the USO must receive a large volume of calls with requests similar to mine, so I called again and left a second message. (This was April 2003, and fax machines were still big, so I sent a fax too.) "Hi, I'm Gary Sinise, and I'd like to go on a USO tour to support the troops. Please get back to me."

Chirp, chirp. Those crickets were deafening.

The United Service Organizations (USO) has been around since 1941, and the driving purpose is to enable Hollywood celebrities and volunteer entertainers to go to wherever troops are—both domestically and overseas—and help boost morale. USO representatives say hello, shake hands, scribble autographs, and put on live shows. Most of all, USO reps bring messages of affirmation and encouragement from back home.

Many famous entertainers have been part of USO tours over the years. In World War II and on into the Korean and Vietnam conflicts, USO reps included Abbott and Costello, Fred Astaire, Lucille Ball and Desi Arnaz, Humphrey Bogart, Cab Calloway, Bing Crosby, Marlene Dietrich, Duke Ellington, Judy Garland, Betty Grable, Connie Stevens, Raquel Welch, Cary Grant, Rita Hayworth, Laurel and Hardy, Ann-Margret, Glenn Miller, Marilyn Monroe, Martha Raye, Ginger Rogers, Mickey Rooney,

Frank Sinatra, Fats Waller, John Wayne, many others, and, of course, Bob Hope.

In more recent years, USO entertainers have included Trace Adkins, Drew Carey, Jay Leno, Steve Martin, Marie Osmond, Sinbad, Bruce Willis, Robin Williams, Jessica Simpson, Carrie Underwood, Toby Keith, Kellie Pickler, Wayne Newton, and many more.

When I called in 2003, this was before *CSI: NY*. So I concluded the USO didn't know who I was. Although I'd done a lot of movies by then, I was still mostly known for one role. I called again in May and left a third message—this time more strategic. "Hi, this is Gary Sinise calling again. I'd like to go on a USO tour. I want to do as much as I can to support the troops. Please call me back. Oh, by the way, I'm the guy who played Lieutenant Dan in *Forrest Gump*." Simultaneously, I asked my publicist, Staci Wolfe, to help me double-team them, and she reached out to them as well.

A representative from the USO returned my call the very next day. A big USO tour was coming up the following month, she explained. Would I like to be a part of it?

I grinned. "Absolutely. Lieutenant Dan would be happy to go."

Called "Project Salute," the upcoming tour marked the first large-scale USO visit to the Persian Gulf region since the start of Operation Iraqi Freedom. More than 180 entertainers would come along. Signed up already were Wayne Newton, Kid Rock, Alyssa Milano, Leeann Tweeden, Brittany Murphy, Lee Ann Womack, Neal McCoy, Paul Rodriguez, John Stamos and Rebecca Romijn-Stamos, the hip-hop band Nappy Roots, the Dallas Cowboys Cheerleaders, football players, basketball players, and many more. Even Robert De Niro was set to show up midway through the tour.

I was really looking forward to this trip, wanting to do my part to support and thank our troops for defending us, and to let them know we were thinking about them. I'd never been to a war zone before and didn't know what to expect, or what exactly I would see or do once we got to Iraq. But I was ready to go. On June 16, 2003, I flew from L.A. to Washington, DC, where tour members gathered for the first time. A few performers looked as excited as I felt, but mostly we all just shook hands and climbed aboard the plane, a donated 747 from Northwest Airlines, and headed overseas. I was an actor who wanted to do something positive for the troops. I had no other plans.

Our plane touched down in Kuwait City late afternoon on June 17, and after going through customs we checked into our hotel to get some rest. The next morning the USO officials split us up into three groups. My group made a stop to visit folks at Camp Doha Army Base just outside the city, before heading to Camp Arifjan, the main military installation for all US branches of our military. After visiting with a group of troops there, we boarded several large, tandem-rotor Chinook helicopters, and the pilots flew us to Camp Udairi. The ramp of the helicopter was open in the back, and from the air I saw a huge sprawling tent city in the middle of the Kuwaiti desert. Someone said we were about fifteen miles from the Iraq border, and the camp could accommodate some fourteen thousand troops. Already the temperature soared. It might have been 110 degrees Fahrenheit outside, maybe more, although it was hard to tell. The air felt sticky, sandy, and as we touched down I squinted at the clouds of dust that rose off two man-made ridges of sand surrounding the camp. A string of barbed wire topped the ridges, and guard posts dotted the perimeter.

We all scrambled out of the helicopters. Generators hummed nearby, and a few helicopter rotors were still winding down, making it hard to hear. I smelled a whiff of plastic portable toilets, as a tan-colored US armored vehicle with a machine gun turret on top barreled down the road close to us. Saddam's statue had been pulled down in Baghdad a few months before, and Saddam was on the run. I felt safe, but my eyes darted to and fro, keeping a sharp lookout for I don't know what. *We're in a war zone,* I reminded myself.

A USO representative motioned for us to follow him, and he led us to a big tent near the center of the camp. The tent had an entrance on each side. Generators worked overtime to pump in air-conditioning. We headed for one door, and at a door on the other side, a line of at least a thousand troops waited in the heat to get in. As we headed in, they started to applaud. The atmosphere inside crackled. Maybe another thousand uniformed troops already inside the tent broke into applause when we came into the tent. I took a deep breath. *What have we done? They deserve the applause, not us.* But wow! It was amazing. Even with a little air-conditioning, it was hot as hell in there. But nobody seemed to care. We lined up, and the troops lined up and quickly started to file past us.

We smiled and shook hands and posed for pictures, and everything happened quite quickly. The very first soldier I met said, "Hey, Lieutenant Dan, you got legs!" And then each one down the line just kept calling me Lieutenant Dan over and over. I realized they didn't know my real name, so I went with it. I tried to look each person in the eye, tried to ask each soldier where he or she was from, tried to ask how things were going, but nothing I did felt very deep, because we had to keep the line moving; there were so many people to see.

Two hours later we needed to leave. The same USO representative herded us back toward the helicopters. As the helicopters began to take off, I looked off into the distance in the direction of Iraq and envisioned hundreds of our tanks rolling across the border a few months before. I looked out again across this vast tent city in the middle of nowhere. Soon, it would be renamed Camp Buehring in honor of Lieutenant Colonel Charles H. Buehring, who would be killed in the coming months. As the sun began to set and the base disappeared in the distance, I reflected on what had just happened. We'd seen nearly two thousand troops in two hours. I wondered, *Did we actually do any good?* The helicopters ferried us back to Camp Arifjan. It was night now, and after we landed and shook the cotton out of our ears, we headed back to the hotel for a night's sleep. Tomorrow we would be getting up early to head up to Baghdad. As tired as I was, it was hard to sleep that night.

The next morning I grabbed a quick bite to eat, gathered with the rest of my group, and shuffled off to Arifjan where a big C-130 military transport plane waited for us. The heat beat down from the sun. Inside the C-130, two long lines of foldable seats faced each other from either side of the airplane. I found my seat and strapped myself in. Toward the back of the plane, I noticed pallets of equipment and supplies. We were all part of the cargo.

The man to my right wore a button on his shirt bearing a photo of two young men, one a New York City police officer, the other, a firefighter with the FDNY. We struck up a quiet conversation, and I learned he wasn't an entertainer. The two young men were his sons, and both sons had died on 9/11. He was there because he wanted the troops overseas to know that America supported them. The man was maybe in his midsixties and spoke with a low rasp. Scars ran across his neck, and later I found out he'd survived throat cancer. The man carried a chunk of rock. Concrete maybe. He showed it to me, then passed it my direction so I could feel it too. I ran my hands over its rough surface. It felt like any old piece of rubble. Puzzled, I asked him what it was all about, why he was carrying all this extra weight.

He swallowed once, twice, then his eyes grew wet. He whispered, more hoarsely than before, "It's a piece of the World Trade Center."

A few hours later we landed at Saddam International Airport on the outskirts of Baghdad, Iraq. In early April 2003, this was the site of one of the fiercest battles of the war as the Iraqis fought hard to keep control of runways. It would soon be renamed Baghdad International Airport (BIAP). The temperature must have climbed to 120 by the time we arrived. The air felt thick—like the Mojave Desert on the hottest summer's day. Security looked tight, and we were informed the airport was mostly safe (although a few months later a civilian airplane was struck by a Russian-made SA-14 missile shortly after takeoff). I longed for a bottle of water.

When we clattered down the cargo plane's ramp, I could only shake my head in disbelief. In front of us, waiting in two long rows of uniforms, stood American soldiers. Thousands strong. Lining our route all the way from the cargo plane to the hangar like a happy gauntlet. We simply walked forward and shook hands on the way to our destination. Soldier after soldier. Marine after marine. Sailor after sailor. Airman after airman. Smile after smile. I felt choked up inside. Happy to be there. Honored. Grateful. So incredibly grateful. We were here for them. But they had our backs. They weren't going to let anything bad happen to us. They were there for us.

Inside the hangar, another five thousand troops waited for us. Kid Rock led the charge along with a few members of his band. Country singer Chely Wright walked with Rebecca and John, followed by model and sportscaster Leeann Tweeden and Nappy Roots. I came last, and we all made our way onto the stage.

My shirt was soaked. It must have been 130 degrees inside the metal hangar. Oven-hot. Noisy. Echoes bounced off the metal walls. The troops looked ready for a show, but I glanced at Kid Rock and he kinda shrugged. No one in our group had heard anything about a show, so we weren't exactly prepared. Luckily, a soldier-led rock band had entertained the troops just before we arrived, and their equipment still sat on the stage. Kid Rock grabbed an electric guitar, John Stamos sat in on the drums, Kid's bassist hopped in, and country singer Chely Wright jumped on a microphone to sing some backup. They all fired up the opening chords to "Sweet Home Alabama," and the crowd went nuts. It was a crazy good time, sweat flying off the stage as the energy built. When the song finished, a few football players joined us onstage and were introduced, and the crowd cheered. Leeann Tweeden, dressed in a sexy red, white, and blue top, was a knockout doing interviews with the troops throughout the hangar with her camera crew from *The Best Damn Sports Show Period.* Nappy Roots launched into an impromptu hip-hop tune, and when they were done with rockin' the hangar, someone introduced me as "Lieutenant Dan," and the crowd went nuts again. I got up and said a few words. Everybody in the crowd was smiling. Clapping. The energy ramping up. From the front of the stage, I took a good look at the crowd. The expressions on the troops' faces fascinated me. There they were, all piled into that hangar where it felt like a sauna. Sweat beaded on every forehead. But in spite of the heat, everyone was having a rocking good time. It was surreal to be there.

When I stepped off the stage, I collected my thoughts. I'd heard some stories already. I knew some of the troops in that hangar had already experienced some bad stuff. They'd lost buddies, seen arms and legs lost to artillery and rockets. The man who'd sat next to me on the plane took the stage, along with two other 9/11 family members. He held up the piece of the World Trade Center, took the microphone, and spoke of what had happened that terrible day. The noise hushed. Soldiers nodded, and some bowed their heads. We'd heard that many of those same troops had volunteered right after 9/11. When the man was finished speaking, he passed the chunk of the Trade Center to a soldier at the front of the crowd. The soldier held it carefully, almost reverently, nodded, then passed it to the soldier next to him. One by one, each soldier touched the piece of concrete as it made its way around the hangar. That chunk of rubble seemed symbolic, even sacred. It represented a moment of great change in America. A change that each and every one of these service members were a part of. A cause so much greater than any one person.

Kid Rock and the gang headed back onstage and blasted away for a few more tunes. I stood backstage while the show rumbled along, and an officer came up and asked me to come with him to meet some soldiers who were getting ready to leave the base. He wondered if I would simply say goodbye to them. I nodded and said sure, then went alone with the officer outside of the hangar and over to a squad of soldiers standing on the tarmac. Fully armed. Fully suited for battle.

"Where you guys headed?" I asked.

One just grinned.

The officer spoke for him: "Into combat."

I simply shook hands and tried to say a few encouraging things. The squad members climbed aboard the truck and rode away, and it hit me anew what these soldiers' jobs were all about. In my mind I said a silent prayer: *Let them all be safe. Let them all return home again to the people who love them.*

I headed back into the hangar. Once the concert finished, I was able to sort through the crowd and locate Captain Justin Morseth, a young rifle platoon leader with the Third Infantry Division. His father-in-law sat on the board of directors for Steppenwolf, and Justin's wife had given me a letter to give to him if I could find him. And I did. We were indeed able to arrange to meet backstage, and there among the loud noise of five thousand sweaty troops enjoying the entertainment, Justin smiled at the letter when I hugged him and handed it to him. He opened it right there and read it on the spot. Mail was finding its way to the troops, but there was something special about having a letter hand delivered from home, he said. The kind word from home absolutely made his day. And Leeann's camera crew caught the whole thing on video.

We boarded the C-130 again, strapped ourselves in, and flew back to Kuwait. It was a good day, but I was beat. In the evening, we landed, grabbed some quick chow, and returned to our rooms in the hotel around nine o'clock. For a few minutes I simply wandered around my room, culture-shocked to stand again in the civilian world. I felt jet-lagged, dusty, exhausted, and I knew I stank. For a while I sat on the bed, replaying the day in my mind, trying to take it all in. Then I peeled off my clothes, turned on cold water, and stood under the shower until I almost felt normal again. I dried off, threw on boxers and a T-shirt, lay down on the bed, and closed my eyes.

I must have dozed off, but when the phone rang I opened my eyes. My watch read just after 11:00 p.m. An official from the USO was on the line: "Hey, Gary. General Tommy Franks is heading back up to Baghdad first thing tomorrow morning. He wants to take a small group with him. This part of the trip is optional. You in?"

"Count on me," I said. "I'm ready to go right now."

I didn't know exactly where we'd be going or what we'd be doing, or even if I could sleep the rest of that night. But I knew General Franks, a four-star general, was as tough as they come—and whatever he was doing, I wanted to go his direction. Not only had Franks led the 2001 invasion of Afghanistan that had ousted the Taliban regime, he'd also led the 2003 invasion of Iraq that had ousted Saddam Hussein. The general had just retired a few weeks earlier, on May 22, 2003, but he would still be active in his position until July.

Early the next morning, we met on the tarmac at the airbase. It was a smaller group this time that included John Stamos and Rebecca Romijn-Stamos, Alyssa Milano, and Robert De Niro, who shot footage with a small video camera. General Franks greeted us with a smile and a hand-shake, and we snapped a few pictures for posterity. I'd met lots of celebrities before, but I couldn't quite believe a man of this magnitude was standing right before my eyes. We flew up to Baghdad again, but this time no double-sided wall of troops greeted us. This time, instead of staying at the airport, we donned flak jackets and helmets and climbed into a convoy of trucks that sped us into the heart of the city. Images of Saddam lined the street. Paintings of his face still hung everywhere. We saw huge concrete pillars with big iron busts of Saddam's head on top. One was toppled, lying facedown in the dirt. You couldn't go anywhere in Baghdad without being reminded who the dictator had been. Three helicopter gunships hovered above us the whole way, providing security for the convoy. We were in the heart of the battlefield now. This was urban warfare, and anything could happen.

When we finally pulled up at our destination, I did a double take. There stood the front gate of Saddam's Al-Faw presidential palace, a grandiose concrete structure with columns and arches, domes, and courtyards, now occupied by US and coalition forces.

The palace was cold and unwelcoming from the outside, although surrounded by calm artificial lakes. Inside, the main structure was huge with enormous chandeliers hanging everywhere and intricate, massive mosaic tiles on the ceiling and walls. Someone said the main structure was some 450,000 square feet, with sixty-two rooms and twenty-nine bathrooms. In its day, Saddam had kept a zoo on the grounds, as well as horse stables, a cinema, date groves, and more. But Saddam himself had rarely stayed here. He kept several different presidential palaces scattered throughout Iraq and preferred a different palace downtown.

We visited US troops inside the compound, shook hands, and signed autographs. General Franks greeted them right along with us. I could see the service members held just as much admiration for General Franks as I did. It wasn't every day he was able to shake hands with the troops, and they recognized it as a high honor. We must have each shaken two to three thousand hands and taken as many pictures. We also got to look around the palace and see a few things, and I took a picture of a giant mural on a wall. The painting depicted a massive missile that I was told was pointing in the direction of Israel. Saddam's taste in fine art. I got to sit in a giant throne given to Saddam by Yasser Arafat. So surreal to be there. It was a long day, and the ride back to Kuwait on the C-130 was quieter than when we'd traveled to Baghdad. Tomorrow we would leave Iraq. But our trip was not over; there was more to come.

From Camp Arifjan, the next day we boarded a C-130 and General Franks led us up to Camp As Sayliyah, Qatar, where Central Command for the whole region had been located. General Franks and I sat together on the plane, and we talked the whole time. At the camp, we visited more troops, and Kid Rock put on a big show that evening. They introduced me again as "Lieutenant Dan," and again the crowd went nuts. I took the microphone and said a few words. When I stepped down, it was dawning on me more and more that the name "Lieutenant Dan" encouraged people far more than the name Gary Sinise, and I felt fine about that. This was about being here for the troops, and if meeting "Lieutenant Dan" would make their day, then that was all right by me. Country singer Neal McCoy took the stage, and he brought up General Franks to sing the old Roger Miller song "King of the Road." I gathered General Franks didn't sing onstage very often, but he belted out the tune heartily, while the crowd clapped and cheered.

(After the trip was over, General Franks and I stayed in touch for a while. The following year he came to Chicago and surprised me with an award for supporting the troops.)

Just like that, the trip was over. Six days total. Just a small taste of life in Iraq. I didn't know it then, but within six months I would be back again, with several trips to come in the years ahead.

On the flight home, I reflected on what I'd seen and experienced. I'd shaken countless hands, posed for thousands of pictures, and talked with so many service members. I'd seen a lot of smiles and felt a lot of spirits lifted. I stood behind the troops a thousand percent. If they were going to be there, fighting this war for us, helping to liberate that country, then I was going to do all I could to support them. The simple act of show-ing up seemed to carry much weight. I wanted our troops to know they were appreciated, and if going to where the troops were and shaking some hands could help, then that's exactly what I wanted to keep doing.

When I returned home on June 21, 2003, I called the USO immediately and asked where I could go next.

Two weeks later, I was on another USO trip, this time to Italy, visiting US troops stationed there.

Late August, early September 2003, I found myself in Germany with the USO, visiting troops at various bases around the country and also at Landstuhl Regional Medical Center, the main overseas hospital where soldiers wounded in Iraq or Afghanistan received medical care before being flown back to the States.

When I came home from Germany, a week later I visited troops at Fort Stewart and Hunter Army Airfield in Georgia, home of the Third Infantry Division, who'd done much of the work to take Saddam International Airport. My brother-in-law Jack had met my wife's sister, Amy, while serving at Fort Stewart, so I asked Jack to come with me on that trip.

Two days later, on September 11, 2003, two years after the terrorist attacks on our country, I walked into Walter Reed Army Medical Center and National Naval Medical Center at Bethesda for the first time, meeting wounded troops in both hospitals in one day. At Walter Reed, I met a soldier wheeling himself down the hallway whom I'd seen two weeks earlier at Landstuhl. Back in Germany he was fresh off the line, unable to get out of bed. Now in Washington, DC, he was able to get around in a wheelchair. It felt good to see progress.

A few weeks after that, in October, I visited troops at the Naval Base Coronado in San Diego. The USO set up a trip for me where I drove myself down and said hello to the troops at the base and boarded the aircraft carrier USS *John Stennis* and took pictures and signed autographs aboard ship. My wife and kids joined me on this trip, and they loved meeting the troops and seeing me at work supporting them.

Then in early November 2003, I flew with the USO overseas again with Wayne Newton, Chris Isaak, Neal McCoy, and a couple of Dallas Cowboys Cheerleaders, this time visiting troops at Al Dhafra Air Base in the United Arab Emirates, returning for a second time to Camp Doha, and visiting more troops in Kuwait and at Camp Anaconda / Balad Air Base in Iraq.

All told, I'd taken six trips in six months.

On each trip, I felt a new surge of adrenaline. I wanted to help the troops so badly. My goal was to spread out as far as I could, as fast as I could.

I don't think anyone back then could have possibly known what lay ahead for our military in the war against terror. How long the wars would last. How brutal they would become.

As years went on and the wars continued in Afghanistan and Iraq, the fighting became harder for coalition forces. Before I'd left for my first USO trip, the president had already given his now-infamous speech under a banner that read "Mission Accomplished" on the aircraft carrier USS *Abraham Lincoln.* That happened on May 1, 2003, but clearly the mission was far from over. President Bush had never himself uttered the words "mission accomplished," and he'd clearly stated during that speech that "our mission continues," and "we have difficult work to do in Iraq," but the damage had been done by that banner. Controversy swelled back home in America, and more of our troops were getting hurt overseas. I would continue to make trips to the war zones in Iraq and Afghanistan to meet our fighting men and women in a variety of places and under many different circumstances. On one of my trips, I visited a small combat unit stationed at a forward operating base in Habbaniyah, Iraq. The day I arrived, there was sadness and tension and anger in the unit. The day before, a sniper had killed one of their buddies, and they were all eager to find the terrorist and bring justice to him. This was simply one day in Iraq for just one of our units living in a combat zone. They would live with this death, and surely many others, for the rest of their lives. Each time I heard this kind of news my heart broke. I felt for these warriors, and I so desperately didn't want any controversy surrounding this current conflict to spill over and hurt our troops or their families. I didn't want to see these wars turn into another Vietnam, where our defenders were forgotten. They would have a difficult enough time returning home with the scars and wounds of war. I wanted our servicemen and -women to know people still backed them up, and I wanted to do everything in my power to help them stay strong.

News reports from the war in Iraq were seldom good, and I still feared for America, for my family, and for what the future held. In 2003, Sophie turned fifteen, Mac turned thirteen, and Ella turned eleven. I was spending a lot of time away from my family, but Moira and our kids told me how much they supported what I was doing. With Vietnam vets in her family, Moira knew how important it was. I think my wife and children knew that by letting me go, they also helped in the effort. They wanted us as a family, as Americans, to do whatever we could.

And then there were the hospitals.

I did not have good feelings about hospitals.

Back when I was nineteen years old, smoking finally caught up to my mom's mom, Grandma Millie. I loved Grandma Millie; she was fun and loved that I acted in plays. She was diagnosed with emphysema and lung cancer and went into the hospital, where she quickly lost a lot of weight. With the exception of being born in one, and having my tonsils removed when I was five, I'd never spent any time in a hospital before, and I wanted to visit her. But I was scared. I'd seen death only once before, and I hated it.

When I was about nine years old, my grandpa Les had contracted Buerger's disease, where blockages occurred in the blood vessels of his feet and hands. Grandpa Les had lived with his mother then, a staunch Christian Science follower who didn't believe in doctors. One of Grandpa's toes literally fell off, and with a rubber band his mother tried to put it back on and hold it there so it would heal. He died slowly, wasting away bit by bit, a horrible death for anyone to endure.

I wasn't terribly close to Grandpa Les, but I still cared about him greatly. Grandma Millie and Grandpa Les had divorced when I was young. After their first divorce they remarried each other, then divorced again, a tug-of-war relationship where feelings for each other rose and fell.

After the second divorce, we never saw Grandpa much, and his funeral was the first funeral I ever faced. I took a soldering gun and burned some lettering into a piece of wood. The message read, "I love you, Grandpa, love Gary," and I showed it to Grandma Millie. When I arrived at the wake, the lid of the casket lay open. My grandmother had placed my message inside the lid. Grandpa Les was dressed in a suit, and with the embalming and makeup he looked okay. They buried him with the message from me inside his coffin.

Years later, when Grandma Millie went into the hospital, I still had these memories of how Grandpa Les had died, and my gut roiled at the thought of visiting her. But I screwed up my courage and went anyway. She'd tried to fix herself up for us, because she knew we were visiting that day, but one glance told me she was not doing well. Her arms were as thin as sticks, her fingers bony and gaunt. She'd withered away to maybe forty pounds, almost to nothing. She smiled, and we talked a bit, and when I hugged her to say goodbye, I couldn't believe how light she felt in my arms. I loved her and hated to see her looking like that. Sadness filled me, and when I walked out of her hospital room, I felt heavy and unnerved. I never saw her again.

From that day onward, hospitals represented death to me. My belief was one-sided, I knew, faulty in its entirety, because hospitals can be places of healing and hope. But those beliefs weren't part of me yet. If you showed me a hospital as a young man, I instantly started to sweat.

In 2003, on the USO trip I took to Germany, the ride from the hotel to Landstuhl seemed to last forever. I fidgeted in my bus seat, my hands clammy, my heart racing. What would I do when I saw the troops in the hospital? Seeing a skinny grandma was one thing. But what if a patient was missing arms and legs? What if I was taken to the burn unit? I wanted to be on this tour, but I didn't know if I had what it took. I'd met wounded vets earlier at the DAV convention in 1994, but those vets had been living with their injuries for a long time. The vets I was set to meet this day would be fresh off the battlefield, their injuries raw, many still fighting for their lives.

Our bus stopped in front of Landstuhl, and I climbed down the steps. Right then, another bus pulled up, and we just stood and stared. A plane had just landed from Iraq. A dozen or more US Army and Navy medical personnel swarmed in and went to work. One by one, the service members were carried off the bus on stretchers. A battery of medical machinery came along with them, a bustle of hoses and tubes and IVs, and I could see each wounded service member's face. Eyes closed. Mouths grim. Soon the bus was empty. I took a deep breath, looked at my USO escorts, and said, "Okay. Let's go."

Through the doors in Landstuhl, we walked to a big, open room full of wounded service members. Maybe thirty guys total were standing or sitting in chairs around the room. A few burns or cuts, a few sprains and splints, but nothing too bad. These were soldiers whose wounds weren't life-threatening. These guys would be patched up and sent back to the battlefield.

All was quiet at first. Somber. I could smell the antiseptic. Feel the harshness of the fluorescent lights. A lot of these soldiers had thousand-yard stares. I wore a USO baseball cap and just stood there at first, not knowing how to get started. The silence felt uneasy, awkward. But I knew I needed to dive in. I needed to go to someone and introduce myself and say hello.

Just then, one of the wounded soldiers looked up. He looked straight into my face, broke out in a big grin, and exclaimed, "Lieutenant Dan!"

A dam broke. The other guys all looked at me and roused themselves. The ones who could walk crowded around me, and the whole mood in the room changed. Soldier after soldier introduced himself. They asked me questions about *Forrest Gump*, and I told them some funny stories. A USO rep had a Polaroid camera and started taking pictures of me with the guys, so I signed the backs of the Polaroids and handed them out.

Maybe half an hour passed. Not long. But when I left that room, I couldn't help but notice how the mood in the room felt different. Now there was laughter. Joy. And I knew a change had occurred in me too. This first room full of banged-up service members had forced me to get outside of myself. They'd helped me focus on who I was truly there for—them, not me. It was a reminder that this trip was about lifting them up and not about my own fears. So, on the walk to the next ward, I told myself to stop thinking about how I felt and focus instead on how the troops felt. My job was to help relieve their pain, to help give them something else to think about, to help them heal, to spread a bit of cheer.

Other rooms proved more difficult. That day in Landstuhl I visited some severely wounded service members. One soldier was in a coma, not aware of my presence. Another soldier was so filled with painkillers he couldn't lift his head off the pillow. I spoke with a man whose face had been burned. Another was missing an arm. Some of the wounded weren't even soldiers, although they were casualties of war too.

The United Nations Headquarters in Baghdad had been blown up a few days earlier. The UN special representative to Iraq had been killed. A civilian had been meeting with the representative at the time of the bombing. He lay in a bed in a coma, missing both legs, and his adult-aged daughter sat with him, waiting for him to wake up. When I first walked into the room, she looked so sad, so filled with grief and exhaustion. But after I said hello and introduced myself, she managed a smile, and I sat with her while she shared his story with me. She worried because he didn't know yet his legs were gone. A real-life Lieutenant Dan. Not on the front lines, but definitely a casualty of war.

Later, when I boarded the bus, I knew there was much healing still to be done. Not only for the civilian with the missing legs, but for all the service members. And for our country. My heart was still broken about 9/11, as it was for many of us, and I knew again that the wars weren't over yet, that much more pain lay ahead. More troops would be wounded. More flag-draped coffins would be sent home.

The gears of the bus downshifted as we crested a hill. Far in the distance lay the lights of the city we were returning to for the evening. I felt strangely grateful again. Grateful I could do something. Grateful for every wounded person inside that hospital—for the sacrifices they made and the bravery they displayed. Grateful for every family member who sat beside each bedside, waiting, hoping. Grateful for the doctors and nurses and hospital staff who'd devoted their lives to help the healing.

That night I lay awake a long time. As I reflected on the day's events, I knew something big was shifting inside of me. A transformation was now under way. I was no longer primarily an actor, even though I would appear in roles for many years to come. I was becoming an advocate, and my job was to carry a nation's gratitude to the troops. I wanted to let them know the country they loved hadn't forgotten about them. We hadn't forgotten the sacrifices of America's defenders and their families. And we wouldn't forget—not ever, at least not if I could help it.

I didn't fully know the totality of what my new role would hold. I knew I would never stop saying "thank you"—a good start—but maybe that wasn't enough. A new generation of wounded veterans was growing, crying out for help, and maybe I could do a bit more. How? I didn't know just yet. But I would start with the single steps that were in front of me. I would remember standing in our church on the National Day of Prayer just after 9/11, recall the feeling I had and the words of our priest that had great healing power. Perhaps God was calling me to do a little more.

CHAPTER 12

Honor. Gratitude. Rock and Roll.

"Jenny, I don't know if Momma was right or if . . . if it's Lieutenant Dan. I don't know if we each have a destiny, or if we're all just floating around accidental-like on a breeze, but I . . . I think maybe it's both. Maybe both is happening at the same time." Standing over the grave of his wife, as a gentle wind blows, Forrest Gump speaks these words to his departed wife, Jenny, after she's been laid to rest under their special tree.

I often wonder about these things. God's plan for us. Destiny. Or if life is a series of random accidents as one small seed is planted, and years from now the "history we don't know" is changed.

I think about how a ragtag kid, struggling in school, happened to be standing in a high school hallway at the exact right moment the drama teacher came walking by, changing the course of his life, and how that would lead to his getting together with some buddies and starting Steppenwolf Theatre. Or how one supporting film role for that kid became such an important story for wounded veterans everywhere. Certain events in our lives, certain turns we happen to make, or not make (if I'd gone right instead of left, if I'd gotten out of bed a little later that day), can lead to larger and more purposeful things that we never imagined—things that can inspire and reach many people for good.

In 1997, I played the role of Stanley Kowalski in *A Streetcar Named Desire* at Steppenwolf. Terry Kinney directed the play, and he hired a Chicago composer named Kimo Williams to create some original music for the production. A professional musician and professor at Columbia College, Kimo had fought in Vietnam, and we became friends. Kimo had heard I played a little music myself, so more than once he invited me over to his house for a casual jam session. The intensity of *Streetcar*, however, was exhausting, so during the show's run I never took him up on the offer. But after we closed the show and I was set to head back to L.A., an evening became free. Kimo called up a couple of other musicians he knew, we ordered some pizza and beers, and we banged around on guitars, drums, keys, and bass. It was just a simple, fun evening with some like-minded guys. I didn't know it then, but I think a tiny seed of something may have been planted in the back of my mind that would grow into something great in the coming years.

My next movie was *Snake Eyes* with Nicolas Cage, filmed in Montreal. Some of the local guys on crew had a band, and one guy kept a small rehearsal studio, so we all got together one evening and jammed. A driver on set owned a club with a dance floor. He heard about our jam session and invited us to play at his venue. I had hardly picked up my bass since my early twenties because I'd been so focused on Steppenwolf and my career, but playing at a club sounded fun. We needed another guitarist for the club session, so I called Kimo and offered to spring for a hotel and fly him up to Montreal if he'd play with us at the club. He said sure. We went into the rehearsal studio, learned some tunes, invited all the cast and crew from *Snake Eyes*, and threw a party. All of us musicians twanged onstage while everybody else bopped around on the dance floor. It was a relaxed and fun and crazy good time. I even spotted Charlie Sheen—in town making a movie at the same time—on the dance floor in a black fedora, arms in the air, rocking out with our cast and crew. From then on, whenever I was in Chicago, I'd call up Kimo if I had a free evening, and he'd get the guys together. We'd play a little music and eat pizza and hang out. That's how we started.

After 9/11, my life's focus radically changed, as it did for so many people. The transformation didn't happen all at once, but my mind-set definitely shifted. I still cared about my acting career, but in an earnest and new way I cared about so much more than acting. Wherever I went, I looked for new ways I could support the troops. I had no formal backing or team of people alongside me. As I went from acting job to acting job, I simply did whatever I could that related to this new thing I'd come to care about.

In 2003, about two weeks before my first trip to Iraq with the USO, I called up Kimo and said I'd like to put together a music event to honor the troops. I figured we could find a venue in Chicago and host a show, inviting any troops nearby to come and hang out. We'd play some fun cover tunes that would make them smile and try to honor them with a free night out. That was my big idea.

Kimo was associated with the National Veterans Art Museum in Chicago, a really cool place with a big area devoted to artwork done by Vietnam veterans. Kimo liked my idea, so he arranged for us to hold the event in the museum's large upstairs room. We contacted the USO, because we figured they'd know some military personnel we could invite. We ordered pizza and beer. A bunch of troops came over, we put on a show, and everything seemed to go well.

All the band members except me were professional musicians. Even so, our band sounded a little ragged at that hastily-put-together first show. We all sort of knew some songs, but we hadn't gelled yet as any kind of band. What we lacked in cohesion, we made up for in enthusiasm and volume. For that first show, I played bass. Kimo played guitar. A singer with a tremendous voice named Gina Gonzalez played acoustic guitar and sang with us. My longtime keyboard player, Ben Lewis, played that first show, and his brother Matt played trumpet and belted out some tunes. A fantastic Chicago-area guitarist, Ernie Denov, was there as well, and along with Ben has been with the band ever since. That informal event on June 10, 2003, is now considered the first USO concert my band ever played. We were just Gary and his buddies, *playing for the troops.* That last phrase began to take a greater hold of my soul. Without knowing it, we joined what we loved doing with a new motivation—and when joy connects to mission, a life's purpose begins to take shape.

Two weeks later, I went on the USO trip to Iraq. I watched how Kid Rock's band really entertained the troops and brought smiles to their faces, and I saw by their expressions how the troops felt when someone with a big name showed up just for them. I saw how slumped shoulders turned into lifted spirits. How maybe a soldier would walk into the venue with a thousand-yard stare, but by the end of a show he had a new light-ness in his step. The songs of America had reminded him of home, and in a small way, perhaps even reminded him of the freedom he was fighting for. Seeing this transformation was so moving to me. On the 747 on our way back to the States, even though I was tired from the trip, I was full of energy, pumped up and inspired by what I had just experienced. I was standing with some of the USO folks and said, "Gosh, I'd like to take a band on tour. I play music too. You think I could put on a show?" They nodded politely and changed the subject. I'm sure they were thinking, *Oh great. Another actor with a band.*

But I didn't ignore the vision starting to take shape within me. After I returned from that first trip to Iraq, I immediately asked the USO where I could go next. They set up another handshake tour to visit troops in Italy two weeks later. They said I could take a few people with me, so in addition to asking my brother-in-law Jack Treese, I called up Kimo. Both guys said yes, and it was great to have these two Vietnam veterans coming on the trip with me.

On July 4, 2003, the USO held a big outdoor celebration at Carney Park, a recreation center for US troops near Naples, Italy. I shook hands there. We watched Mustang Sally, the all-girl band from Nashville, enter-tain the troops. They put on a great show, and once again I felt the desire to do something like that too. Two days later we visited the troops at the Air Force National Security Agency at La Maddalena, Sardinia, and toured the USS *Emory S. Land*, a US Navy submarine tender. From there we met with troops at Aviano Air Force Base, where I had the great privi-lege of experiencing a ride in an F-16, before heading down to Sicily to see troops at the Naval Air Station Sigonella.

I saw how important these handshake tours were for the troops, but I couldn't get the idea of a band out of my mind. Still, I needed to think through a strategy. Plenty of professional bands were already entertaining the troops—and doing a great job. What could I do that they couldn't do—particularly when I wasn't even a professional musician? I began to wonder what sort of message the troops would receive if a new band was put together solely for their encouragement. Maybe this band could be started from the ground up with that mission in mind. Maybe this new band wouldn't exist for any other reason than entertaining the troops.

Maybe this new band, in a way, would always belong *to them*.

I called up the USO and mumbled through my vision. I still had no fleshed-out plan. Again, they humored me for a second but quickly changed the subject, wanting me to continue with the handshake tours. They mainly wanted more well-known bands with bigger names to do the entertaining. The USO's mission is to deliver celebrities to the troops, and while I was slowly rising in my profile as an actor, I understood their point of view regarding musical acts. Still, I felt my idea had merit. I kept talking it up, kept nudging them about it, kept going on USO tours, and eventually they softened. Maybe I just wore them down, but I think they saw how devoted I was to the overall USO mission, so finally they said okay.

Wow. It was actually happening—meaning we needed some songs to play. I called Kimo. "Guess what?" I said. "Next February, we're going on a tour with the USO. And—oh—we gotta figure out something to play."

Kimo chuckled. "Great, Gary. I'll call the guys. We'll figure it out. Let's get some songs together and rehearse."

Even I was shaking my head that the USO had agreed to take a chance on us. USO organizers had never heard us in concert, and it's not like we had a CD we could hand over so they could hear our sound. In addition, I wasn't a songwriter or a professional musician, and I didn't have any established music tours that anybody could point to. I didn't even really have a band at the time. So I have to salute the USO officials, because the decision showed tremendous flexibility and vision on their part.

But they trusted we would deliver a great show. And I think they agreed to send me on tour because I was Lieutenant Dan. I'm sure they crossed their fingers and hoped I could play.

A short while later, they told me where we were going. First up were two back-to-back shows at the Naval Support Facility Diego Garcia, a small base on a remote island in the Indian Ocean. I'd never heard of it before, but a smaller show was okay by me. Probably the USO representatives figured that if we stunk, nobody would hear about it from the tiny island of Diego Garcia. From there, our schedule called for a stop at a naval base in Singapore where we'd do another show, then on to South Korea for three shows: the US Army Garrison Humphreys, Kunsan Air Force Base, and Camp Casey.

I was excited and also a little nervous. I felt a personal responsibility to put on a professional-caliber show for the troops. Our troops were worth it. I didn't worry about getting booed off the stage; I just didn't want to let the troops down with a bad show. Fortunately, our tour was still a couple months away.

Around the same time that the officials from USO World Headquarters in DC agreed to set up a tour, and just before my second handshake tour to Iraq, we asked the Chicago chapter of the USO to set up a concert, preferably at a smaller venue. We needed experience playing for the military under our belts. The USO representatives agreed and set up a show for some two hundred recruits on November 6, 2003, at Naval Station Great Lakes. It's the navy's only "boot camp." We played okay, but I knew we needed more practice. Still, our first show on a military base felt great, and I got to deliver a message that I would continue to deliver over and over in the coming years: Thank you, and I am grateful for you.

A few weeks later in November 2003, I headed back to Iraq for a second time with the USO. This tour had already been set up prior to my band's creation, so I flew overseas alone. Chris Isaak was set to give a concert at Camp Anaconda near Balad. He found out I played bass and asked me to jump in with his band onstage. Johnny Cash's "I Walk the Line" proved a big hit with the crowd. The show had maybe five thousand troops in attendance, and between songs I took the mic and said a few words of encouragement. Somehow, the show felt different, although at first, I couldn't put my finger on why. What was it exactly? Bigger crowds? A bigger name onstage? Then it hit me. I was playing for the first time in a war zone.

Camp Anaconda, also known as Balad Air Base, was a big base. Under Saddam Hussein, it was the most important airfield used by the Iraqi Air Force. The base was captured by the US as part of the invasion in April 2003 and was pretty beat up when I was there in November. Parts of some runways still could not be used because of bomb damage. We visited the base hospital and saw many of the wounded who were being stabilized to be sent home. I was staying in a building that had taken a beating during the battle for the base, and it was very rugged, with no lights or plumbing, a tiny army cot to sleep on, and porta potties down the road. I learned to always keep a large empty plastic water bottle by the bedside.

One night, I awoke to the sound of what I thought were noisy pipes. The sound kept going, and I realized it wasn't pipes. I got up and walked out into the darkened hall where, for security detail, a few soldiers were standing by. I asked what I'd heard.

"Mortars," one said. "They're shelling us on the other side of the base." My heart sank a bit. But since the soldiers didn't seem too worried, I went back to the little cot in my room and tried to get some sleep, one eye open for the rest of the night.

Back home, in early February 2004, right before we were to head overseas with the band, Steppenwolf's board held a fund-raiser golf tournament in Palm Springs. They needed entertainment, so I gathered Kimo and the band and we played, basically cramming our rehearsing in as tight as we could. We learned enough music to play for ninety minutes solid. If a show called for two hours, we were sunk. But hey—the golfers thought we were pretty good.

A week after the fund-raiser, which was our second official practice, Kimo and I and the crew headed overseas as a band for our very first time. Almost until the moment we left, the band still didn't have a name. But during those first handshake tours in the summer of 2003, it had occurred to me that if I were ever able to bring a band on tour, it needed to be called the Lt. Dan Band. Nobody knew who Gary Sinise was, and the troops always identified strongly with the *Forrest Gump* character. The Lt. Dan Band seemed natural and proved a straightforward choice. So that's the band that flew off on that first tour.

Diego Garcia is a million miles from nowhere and takes nearly twenty-four hours to get there. First London, then Hong Kong, then Singapore, then onto a US Navy jet for another five-hour flight to a little atoll in the middle of the Indian Ocean where our US military base sits. It's so far away that getting entertainment to the island is a rare thing. So even though the "Gary Sinise" of Gary Sinise and the Lt. Dan Band was a mystery, Lieutenant Dan was not. The character was well-known already, and word seemed to have spread among the troops that the real Lieutenant Dan was here to play for them. So, while it wasn't a huge crowd to start, this was our first overseas crowd, and it seemed pretty good to us. And we had another show there the next night, so we assumed word would spread that, although not quite Earth, Wind & Fire, we'd still be a fun show.

We were introduced, and a few people whistled and wahooed. Still backstage, my heart pounded, and I looked around at my band members. We were all jet-lagged, and the energy of playing was going to be all over the map. Yet we all made a silent pledge: we would go big with everything we had. One by one, we filed onto the stage, me wearing fatigue pants and a tank top because of the heat. I glanced at the people milling about in front of us, and we blasted away into our opening song. I closed my eyes, and the nighttime temperature seemed to soar. A minute later when I opened my eyes, I looked out again, and the crowd seemed to be getting a little bigger, and they really seemed to be having a good time. Midway through the show, we launched into "Purple Haze." Kimo was channeling Jimi Hendrix while Ernie Denov played his electric guitar behind his head, giving it his all. For the next song, Gina Gonzalez channeled Janis Joplin, singing the hell out of "Piece of My Heart." By the time our show finished, my tank top was drenched in sweat, the crowd had swelled a bit more—and everybody had been partying hard, dancing like nobody was watching. I started breathing easier, and for the first time it felt like we were taking off. When we got to Singapore, the secretary of the navy introduced us, and the crowds grew a bit bigger. Then we went to Korea and did three shows there. At every venue, importantly, the troops seemed to have a good time, especially at Kunsan Air Base where they packed into the officers' club and I would meet Colonel Robin Rand, who would rise to the rank of four-star general and become a dear friend in the coming years.

Our time in Korea proved particularly eye-opening, even startling. Americans are so blessed to live in a free society, yet many people are not so fortunate. The band toured the demilitarized zone (DMZ) between North and South Korea near Camp Bonifas, a United Nations Command military post. When I traveled there, between the two countries lay a foot-wide strip of concrete, about four inches off the ground. That was the borderline. The North Korean guards and the South Korean guards could come right up to their respective edges of the border and look across. I stood right next to that border, and there was probably no place on earth where you could feel more vividly the difference between freedom and slavery than there, staring into the eyes of a North Korean soldier just a few feet away. Several blue-colored buildings overlapped the line, with doors at either end of the buildings. The North Koreans could enter from their side, and the South Koreans could enter from their side. In the middle of each building is a common area with a table that straddles the border. Over the years, meetings and negotiations between the two countries have been held at that table.

Our band has traveled to South Korea three times—in 2004, 2009, and 2015—and each trip we visited the DMZ. More than once we saw North Korean guards studying us with binoculars and taking our pictures—official photos taken by guards wanting to know who was getting so close to the border. During several trips we toured the insides of the blue buildings. You could actually walk around freely inside these buildings—technically on either side of the border. On one trip, a North Korean guard came right up to the window where I stood inside the building. He snapped my picture, then stared at me for some time. I snapped a picture of him in return, then simply tried to hold his gaze and smile a bit, in the interest of maintaining goodwill. The man didn't smile back. In his eyes I saw a deep and distant sadness, a haunting, almost blank despair.

On each of our trips to the DMZ, I felt terribly sad for the people of North Korea and for their inevitably difficult experiences living in a totalitarian society. For more than six decades, they have known only slavery. The soldiers of North Korea, their families, and their fellow North Koreans, all forced to worship and serve their supreme leader, while all those years ago the people in the south had the American military on their side and have been far more fortunate. The South Koreans have a tremendously skilled army too, and they work well with our forces in defense of their country, while the North Korean regime has defended only themselves, ruling through terror for decades. The existence of multiple labor camps has been verified in modern-day North Korea, and reports indicate an equivalence to Nazi concentration camps. In the twenty-first century, these things still exist. Reports say life outside the prison camps hasn't been much better. Since military action was halted in 1953, the United States military, along with the army of the Republic of Korea, has provided a defense and security, and the people of South Korea have lived free because of it. One military force on the Korean peninsula has oppressed, prohibited freedom, and struck fear into the hearts of the people. Another military has provided freedom to its citizens. Two nations: one has flourished, the other has starved in darkness.

Freedom is truly a precious thing.

Our visits to the DMZ also held a few absurd moments. Officials on each side of the line had held an unspoken contest as to who could put up the biggest flagpole. The North Koreans would build a little bit on theirs, then the South Koreans would build a little bit on theirs. This went on for years until finally the South Koreans gave up. So now, on the North Korean side, one little hamlet of buildings exists with a huge skyscraper of a flagpole in the middle. The height of this structure is so glaringly out of proportion with the buildings around it, you look at it and go, "Yep. That's a flagpole, all right."

By the time of our second visit, *CSI: NY* had grown pretty big and was a hit even in South Korea. On the South Korean side at the DMZ sits a gift shop. We were inside browsing when a bus filled with Asian tourists pulled into the parking lot. Everybody climbed out, and although I pulled my baseball cap down a little lower, I was spotted. It turned into mayhem at the DMZ, everybody wanting my picture and autograph. The star of a hit American TV show was mobbed by Asian *CSI: NY* fans at the DMZ gift shop. Surreal, but that's the power of television.

Our tours went smoothly. On that first band tour in 2004, we'd set the tone and format: we played our same set at each show, and I would talk to the troops a bit. My message was one of pure gratitude. I spoke my thanks that they were there, doing what they were doing. I told stories about my own family members who'd served with the military and mentioned how thankful I felt for them. I talked about getting involved with the DAV in 1994 and described how profoundly grateful I was for the people who sacrificed so much for the sake of freedom. I shared about 9/11, and expressed thankfulness for all the first responders on that fateful day. I told how events of that terrible day had motivated me to get out and support the men and women who were deployed. The message I was able to deliver was equally as important to me as performing the music. I loved playing, and I loved seeing the troops having a good time. Yet these concerts also enabled me to directly communicate a strong word of thanks, a central part of our shows from the beginning.

Soon after we came home from that first tour, I landed the role with *CSI: NY,* so my schedule quickly became a lot busier. But I wanted to keep doing the tours. I figured that during the nine and a half months each year when we filmed, the band could head out on weekends in between shoots. And in summer when the show was on hiatus, we could head overseas. The USO must have liked what we did overseas, because they soon said yes to setting up a domestic tour for us. Within three months, we were on the road. Three bases. Three states. Fort Polk in Louisiana, Goodfellow Air Force Base in Texas, and Kirtland Air Force Base in New Mexico. We were off and running.

For the first several years of playing for the troops, each summer we toured overseas when I was finished shooting my show for the season. As we ramped up more and more, we played thirty, forty, sometimes fifty shows in a year. During the television season when I was working on the show, we toured bases around the States on weekends. At the end of the workweek, I'd finish shooting, and I'd jump on a plane to meet the band somewhere. We would play two to three shows over the weekend, bussing from base to base, then jump on a plane to head home and go back to *CSI: NY*. The more I did, the more I wanted to do. In the early and middle years of the war, when the insurgency was at its height, our servicemen and -women were experiencing difficult times, and I found myself constantly wanting to do more, help more, and reach out wherever I could.

Compared to today, the Lt. Dan Band then sounded pretty raw. Yet from the start we came in with lots of energy and heart, and our mission has always been clear: we're here for the troops. Period. This band isn't about gaining recognition or becoming an international rock show or making any money. The mission has always been about encouraging our defenders. The people who fight to protect our freedom need to know they're supported by the country they love. It's all about honor, gratitude, and rock and roll.

Along the way, some band members have left, and new ones have come in. Kimo left the band in 2012 to focus on his own veterans' charity work. Gina left shortly afterward, preferring to stay home more to focus on her own music. Today, twelve regular members plus myself make up the band, along with a great crew. We're still a cover band. We play songs people *like*, everything from classics by Journey, Bruce Springsteen, and Stevie Wonder to contemporary songs by Bruno Mars, The Band Perry, Sara Bareilles, the Dave Matthews Band, Beyoncé, the Zac Brown Band, and others. We dip into pop, rock, blues, Motown, soul, country, even tunes from the 1940s big band era, which World War II vets love. We're deliberately a show for all ages, and it's common to look out and see kids dancing along with their dads and moms and having a great time. Our goal is always to have fun and rock the house, and in the middle of each show I throw in a couple of familiar lines from *Forrest Gump* like, "Life is like a box of chocolates," which crowds the world over recognize and cheer for. We play a certain few songs at nearly every show. "Another Star" by

Stevie Wonder is a crowd favorite since it talks about falling in love, and the beauty of days that go well—and just for fun, in the tradition of great 1970s bands, we put a huge drum solo in the middle. Everybody loves a drum solo. And we always end with Lee Greenwood's "God Bless the USA," a powerful and emotional closer.

Our level of musicianship rose quickly in the early days. The level was never bad, yet with the number of concerts we played, combined with our common purpose, we gelled quickly. Quality players and singers were crucial from the start, because I wanted the troops to have a first-class show. If anyone's wondering, yes, I do pay my musicians and stage crew. They're all professionals, and this is what they do for a living—and they work hard for me. But I don't personally receive any money for the work I do with the Lt. Dan Band.

One thing I love to do at every show is feature different members of the band up front and let them showcase their talents. I'm technically the band's "front man," but other than the Beatles and the Police, there aren't many bands with bassists as front men. I don't sing, so during each concert I'll come to the front of the stage and thump along on my bass for a while, then I'll head back upstage and let other members of the group perform down front.

Today, in the seventeen years since we've been around, the Lt. Dan Band has played more than four hundred shows for troops. This band is another part of my mission of service to honor our defenders, and we've played all over America and all over the world in service to that mission. The show has been crafted and fine-tuned over the years, but the basic message remains the same. We are a band created solely for the troops' enjoyment. We are here today to say the hugest thanks we can, and to reflect the overall appreciation of a grateful nation.

CHAPTER 13

Perfect Timing

Back in 2002 and 2003, I wasn't sure where my movie career was headed. I'd had a solid string of hits in the 1990s followed by some up and down movies around the turn of the millennium. I appeared in several movies during those first couple of years of the 2000s—*Impostor, A Gentleman's Game, The Big Bounce,* and a few others—but none of them did any business. *The Big Bounce* was a small part, but it was shot in Hawaii, so I took it. It starred Owen Wilson and Morgan Freeman, my only time acting with either of them. My scene with Morgan? I fall down the stairs. He walks up, puts his hand on my neck, checks my pulse, and says, "He's dead."

So the career had slowed down a little at this point.

But one movie made during that season shone a bit more brightly: *The Human Stain* with Anthony Hopkins, Nicole Kidman, Ed Harris, and myself in the cast. Based on the novel by Philip Roth, the film premiered at the Venice Film Festival in August 2003, so along with the film's director, Robert Benton, and some of the producers, we all traveled to Venice for that. Although it received mixed reviews when it opened in October that year, it felt good to be part of another movie with great actors. In a moment of on-screen silliness, I had a wonderful Fred Astaire and Ginger Rogers–type dance scene with Anthony. My character, Nathan Zuckerman, is a bit reserved and inhibited, and Anthony's character tries to snap him out of it.

When the song "Cheek to Cheek" comes on the radio, he yanks Nathan out of the chair and spins him around until Nathan is laughing. Not many people have danced with Hannibal Lecter and lived to tell about it.

In 2003, I starred with Joely Richardson in a warmhearted Hallmark movie for CBS called *Fallen Angel*, a lovely little Christmas movie about an L.A. attorney who returns to his deceased father's home in Maine where he's reunited with his past. It was a love story, and I really hadn't done that type of thing before. It also turned out that my work in the movie and track record of solid performances caught the attention of the CBS executives.

The movie aired just before Christmas 2003 and did well, with some eighteen million viewers tuning in. The network execs were happy with the ratings, and in early 2004, just as I was heading out on my first overseas USO tour with the band, I got a phone call. One of my agents told me that CBS was offering me the lead role in a big new TV series. CBS planned to do a third spin-off of *CSI: Crime Scene Investigation*, the award-winning forensics crime drama. The original *CSI* had been set in Las Vegas and was a massive hit. The network had already spun it off in another series, *CSI: Miami* with David Caruso, and it had also done well. The new spin-off they offered to me was tentatively titled *CSI: New York*.

Lead roles don't come along every day—and I felt grateful for this initial offer. Network execs expected, reasonably, that *CSI: NY* would become a big hit—they were going to give strong support. That sounded really good to me. But strangely enough, my first reaction to the offer was mixed. I wasn't sure if I wanted to go into a weekly TV series. I'd always been an actor who moved from role to role and stayed flexible, and I couldn't envision myself settling in and playing the same role week after week.

My agents set up a meeting for me to meet Les Moonves, the president of CBS, to discuss the role. The meeting went well. Then I sat down with Anthony Zuiker, the creator of the *CSI* franchise, for another conversation. We met at the Sagebrush Cantina in the San Fernando Valley for nearly four hours, and Anthony described how he envisioned the spin-off. The lead detective was named Rick Carlucci in the pilot script, and Anthony wanted Rick to be a fast-talking, hard-hitting, no-nonsense New York crime scene investigator who got things done. We tossed around a lot of ideas and hashed it out in a productive meeting, but still I didn't say yes right away.

I set off for Diego Garcia, Singapore, and South Korea, and all during the tour, in every free moment, I considered the role, trying to figure out if I should accept. The show would receive a lot of attention and support from CBS. They held a great stake in making a successful third show in the franchise, and my agents and manager felt it was a good move for me. And I did love many of Anthony's ideas. My family also encouraged me to do it. Even though the show would be set in New York, it would be filmed mostly in Hollywood, and as I had traveled so much over the years, Moira really liked the idea of my working closer to home. So did I. It felt like something big, something life-changing, was about to happen, although I couldn't exactly see the future. But how would I feel about playing the same role week after week? That was still something I was trying to wrap my head around. As a character actor, changing things up from role to role is what I had always tried to do in my career. It's a major element in what I love about acting. Inhabiting different people, different personalities. But I started thinking more about my family and my financial situation and the whole idea of steady work, something actors rarely get to experience, unless on a successful series. I went back and forth with this. Then I considered that by taking this offer, if the show did well, I'd not only have a steady job, but having that steady job could help me in my ongoing mission to support the troops. It would be hard to go overseas regularly, but I could still travel to military bases around the States on weekends. I could go forward with my new mission without needing to worry about scrambling for a paycheck all the time. And, come on, it was a leading role on a major network, a quality show in a very popular franchise, and I liked the creative potential offered by the part! What was I thinking? Finally, it all started to make sense.

When we came back from the tour, I said yes to *CSI: NY.* Just before we shot the pilot, I met with Anthony and told him I liked the character, but I didn't feel like a "Rick Carlucci." Could we change his name? I also wanted to give him a military background before he became a detective, to reflect my support of the troops. Anthony liked my suggestions, and we made the main character a veteran of the Marine Corps who served with the First Battalion Eighth Marines, surviving the 1983 Beirut barracks bombing attack and deploying in Operation Desert Storm. (In the third season, we did an episode called "Charge of This Post" where my character talks about his past with the Beirut bombings.) One of his most memorable lines is when he says he wants to serve his country more than anything else in the world.

Anthony asked me for ideas for a new name, and I gave him a list of suggestions for both the first and last name. The name I liked most was Mac, for obvious reasons. For the last name, I suggested the surname of Lieutenant Dan. Anthony wrestled around with the suggestions, along with some others, before coming to me and saying, "Let's do it." Right away, I felt gung ho for my character's new name: Mac Taylor.

In the spring of 2004, we shot the pilot episode in New York as an episode of *CSI: Miami*, near the end of their season. David Caruso's character in Miami must go to New York to follow up with a case, and while there, he meets Mac and the *CSI: NY* team. Even before the pilot aired, CBS execs decided to proceed, and we started shooting our first regular season in July.

CSI: NY officially premiered September 22, 2004, and the first episode, titled "Blink," did well from the start with more than nineteen million viewers tuning in. Anthony added the idea that Mac Taylor had lost his wife at the World Trade Center on 9/11. I had become friends with several 9/11 family members by now, so the idea of honoring family members and first responders this way—by having Mac be a character who shares their loss—appealed to me. In the first episode, a crime victim is in the hospital in a coma, her eyes wide open. Toward the end of the episode, Mac Taylor sits with her while nobody else is in the room and shares a story about how, after the 9/11 attacks, he went back to the apartment he shared with his wife. In the closet was a balloon, inflated by his wife, and Mac realized the breath of his now-deceased spouse was still inside that balloon. It's a beautiful scene.

After that moment in the episode, Mac goes to Ground Zero. We were filming in the summer of 2004, and television crews had not yet been allowed to shoot at Ground Zero. Anthony secured permission, but we needed to go there at 2:00 a.m. when nobody else was around. At the time, Ground Zero was just a big, empty fenced-in pit; nothing had been rebuilt. We took a small crew, and we shot Mac simply standing there, near the pit. There's no sound, and I rest my head on the fence and close my eyes in thought. You see Mac's wedding ring on his finger. The camera pulls back and tilts up in a wide shot of the night sky where the Twin Towers used to be. It's a very powerful moment.

That first season we worked hard and put in lots of long hours. When a show is just beginning, everybody is finding their feet. Between the first and second season, CBS execs took a closer look at the show and decided to reshape its look. The mood of the show was a little dark at first. The offices were set in what looked like a warehouse, and the entire season I wore a dark suit and tie. At the end of the first season, CBS execs decided to rebuild the entire set. Our new offices were now set on the thirty-fifth floor of a high-rise where the sun blasted through the windows and lit up the rooms. In the first episode of the second season, you see us moving boxes into the new offices, and I throw out a line, something like, "I'm just about done moving." That was all the explanation given. Yet behind the scenes, the move had been major. CBS invested a lot of money in the new set, and the new look really improved the show.

Right around that time I started getting more serious about golf. A number of my buddies played a lot, and I wanted to join them. I'd dabbled for years but had never been much good, always too busy to practice. But now I decided that if I ever found a spare moment, I'd head out to the range and hit a bucket of balls or try to sneak in nine holes between responsibilities. I even took lessons and worked with a pro for a while. Somehow the CBS execs found out.

Each year, CBS televises a big charity pro-am golf tournament sponsored by AT&T. It's all for a good cause, and the idea is that two professional golfers team up with two amateurs, the foursomes play together, and it's broadcast on national TV. I still didn't know much about golf, but somehow in 2005 I got asked to play in the tournament. Actually, the term is "strongly encouraged" to play. *CSI: NY* was still young, and network execs recognized the opportunity for publicity when announcer could introduce me and plug my new series.

I headed to the tournament in Pebble Beach, between Monterey and Carmel, California, my knees shaking. You play for three days, then if you make the cut, you advance and play a fourth day. Each of the first two days is at a different course. The third and fourth days are at Pebble Beach. Samuel L. Jackson and I were in a foursome together, and each of us was paired with a pro. To call Samuel an "amateur" is misleading. The man is an absolute golf ace. (He's actually talked publicly about the clause written into his contracts stipulating he gets to play golf at least twice a week while making movies.) The other celebrities in the tournament were all aces too—Andy Garcia, Ray Romano, Kenny G, Michael Bolton, George Lopez, Tom Dreesen, Bill Murray. I, on the other hand, am a golf knucklehead.

On hole number one, Samuel and I stepped up to the tee box. Samuel teed off first and hit his ball 280 yards right down the middle. A crowd had gathered to watch, but it wasn't very large yet, and the people all applauded nicely. (As the tournament progresses, the crowd grows substantially bigger.) Then my turn came up. "Ladies and gentlemen, now on the tee, from the new hit series *CSI: NY*, Gary Sinise!" Yikes. Already my stomach ached. As I prepared to take my swing, I was sweating, and inside I was shaking, but I put on a good face, acting through my fear. I let loose with a nervous swing and sliced the ball down the fairway. *At least I hit it*, I thought. The crowd tried to be polite, clapping in that small-crowd golf kind of way.

Few of my next shots went well. A slight rain fell, and I hit a ball into the woods, another into a water hole, another into a sand trap. Between the ninth and tenth holes, we passed the parking lot and I seriously considered jumping into my car and never looking back. But then I reminded myself that for an actor, the show must go on, so I powered up to the tenth tee and tried again. My golf pro caddied for me, so he gave me a few pointers along the way, and sometimes I hit a few good shots in a row. But nothing kept the feelings of panic under control.

The good news was that Clint Eastwood hosted the tournament, and he subsequently became a friend as well as a big supporter of my foundation. The bad news is the second day went no better than the first. I hit the ball all over the place. By the third day, Saturday, we played at Pebble Beach, and the crowds had swelled. About midway through the course, as Samuel and I walked to the tee, the pro I was with knew the course and the tournament, and just before we turned the corner, he said, "Okay, get ready." We turned the corner, and a massive crowd greeted us with applause. Literally thousands of people lined this hole, all the way from the tee to the green. My knees quaked. Again, Samuel's shot flew straight down the fairway. I wound up with another big swing and launched. It didn't look pretty, but again, at least I hit the ball and it stayed on the fairway. Still nervous but somewhat relieved, I glanced around for a tree I could throw up behind.

On the tee at the eighteenth hole, in the distance, I could see that the grandstand surrounding the green was packed with people. And the fairway was lined with spectators all down the right side from tee to green. The Pacific Ocean was to our left. *At least it's a beautiful day,* I thought. *Here goes. My last drive. I'm going to nail this shot and walk to the green like a champion.* I stepped up to the tee. The crowd grew quiet. I set up. Took my swing. Hit the ball, and . . . uh-oh . . . it soared over the crowd to the right. A polite little applause followed. I cracked some sort of joke and folks laughed. I wasn't about to chase my ball into the crowd, so I said, "Guys, I'll just walk it in from here and enjoy this beautiful day. You guys finish strong." Samuel and the pros all kind of nodded and chuckled. They finished up, and I walked it in. I never pretended to be much of a golfer. It was a truly humbling few days. I was glad I did it, but I was also glad it was over.

I think the ratings for *CSI: NY* actually went down after that.

On my first USO trip to Iraq in 2003, I sat on the C-130 transport plane next to a man wearing a button with the picture of his two sons. His name was John Vigiano. His younger son, Joe Vigiano, was a highly decorated New York City police officer, and his older son, John Vigiano Jr., served with the FDNY in Brooklyn at Ladder 132, Engine 280, a station that lost six firefighters that terrible September day.

John Vigiano Sr. and I became good friends over the years and remained so until his death in 2018. He served in the Marine Corps and is a legendary New York City firefighter himself. Both of his boys were family men and absolute heroes on the job. John Jr. was known as one of the best firefighters in his department, and Joe had taken three bullets in his career and received multiple awards for valor. John Sr. talked to his sons on the phone each day before work. His last line to each of them was always, "I love you." He lost both of his sons in the Twin Towers' collapse on 9/11. They laid down their lives trying to rescue others. John Jr. was thirty-six; Joe was thirty-four.

After we returned from Iraq, John Sr. introduced me to many of New York's bravest at the FDNY who inspired me with their selflessness and willingness to help others. John also proved a great inspiration to me in my Catholic journey. He was a man of deep faith who loved God. After losing both his boys and searching for their bodies among the rubble for days and days, John easily could have despaired or turned bitter. But he saw many people who came from all over America to help search for other people's loved ones. He met many fellow Americans who passed out food and water to the rescue workers and who gave wherever they could. In light of the outpouring of support, John said to me, more than once, "I believe more good came out of September 11th than evil." I will never forget that.

John invited me to Ladder 132, the very station where his son John had worked, to meet the guys, have a classic chicken parm dinner (lots of bread, lots of pasta, lots of fun), and take a tour of the firehouse. The guys told me that if a bell rang and they needed to go out on a call, I should be ready too. So they dressed me up in full firefighter gear, and sure enough, a call came. We all jumped on the truck and headed out, sirens blaring. Somebody had fallen down an elevator shaft, and the guys set out to rescue him.

Once we got to the site, one of the firefighters handed me some sort of tool and told me to look busy. Other engines from other houses were coming, and they didn't want to explain me. Sure enough, other firefighters arrived, and they all sort of glanced at me and grinned. Turned out, the guys from Ladder 132 had handed me some sort of tool that no respectable firefighter would ever use in that specific rescue operation—so to their trained eyes I stuck out like a sore thumb. Like changing a flat tire with an egg beater. This was firefighter humor at its best, and everybody enjoyed a good laugh about it afterward, including me. The firefighters became an extremely important part of my life. These were the guys who were there during the first battle in the new war of the twenty-first century. They had lost friends and loved ones and seen horrific things that terrible day. I wanted to support them however I could, and many became great friends of mine. We've undertaken a number of initiatives together over the years. In 2016, to say thanks for championing their work, the FDNY commissioner Daniel Nigro made me an honorary battalion chief. My pals were all there for me, including John Vigiano, who drove into the city from his home in Long Island for this special day. I was and remain humbled to receive that recognition from the FDNY.

In spring 2007, one of the firefighters I'd met on that first day, Mike Hyland, took me out to Coney Island, to nearby MCU Park, where the minor league Brooklyn Cyclones play baseball. Work had begun on a memorial for the firefighters of Brooklyn killed on 9/11. Mike introduced me to Brooklyn-born resident Sol Moglen, who had dreamed up the idea to put beautiful panels with laser-engraved images of the first responders on the outside wall of the ballpark. About a third of the first responders killed on 9/11 had come from Brooklyn, and standing there, looking at the faces of the first responders who lost their lives, was very powerful. Sol explained how they wanted to expand the memorial to commemorate all 416 active duty first responders killed in the line of duty that day—including firefighters, Port Authority officers, NYC police officers, New York Department of State officers, New York Fire Patrol officers, responders from private emergency medical services, a canine rescue dog, and Father Mychal Judge, a fire department chaplain who was the first to lose his life at the Trade Center on September 11.

A total of 417 faces on the wall.

Right there, I offered to help them raise money to complete the memorial.

On August 11, 2007, I donated my band, and we put on a concert at Brooklyn College that raised the funds to enable the expansion of the memorial, today named the Brooklyn Wall of Remembrance. The first responders memorialized on that wall gave everything. On May 18, 2008, the memorial was finished, and I was honored to help dedicate the wall at a huge ceremony. Rain poured, yet everybody stood solemnly in tribute. It was an amazing day, underscoring what great people serve at the FDNY and what fine work they do. I'll always feel honored and blessed to have been able to help them establish that memorial to honor their fallen brothers and sisters.

In 2011, for the premiere of *CSI: NY* season 8, I wanted to do an episode that featured the Brooklyn Wall of Remembrance and pitched it to our executive producer and show runner, Pam Veasey, who loved the idea. Pam assigned John Dove and Zachary Reiter to write the script. Both New Yorkers, John was actually a former New York City detective who was at Ground Zero on that terrible day. This script was very personal to them, as it was to me, and they did a fantastic job. We filmed the episode titled "Indelible" where Mac Taylor makes a speech at the wall. Art imitating life slightly, as Gary Sinise had made a speech at the wall on the day of the dedication. I suggested to our producers that we have a number of real-life first responders and their families standing with me in the scene, and they enthusiastically agreed. So I invited these special friends who had lost loved ones on 9/11 to be in the scene with me, with John Vigiano by my side. The premier date fell two weeks after the tenth anniversary of 9/11, and viewers tell us still today how much they love that episode. To me, it's one of the best shows we did on *CSI: NY*, and one of the most special scenes I've ever done.

<hr />

Initially, we'd received a six-year deal for *CSI: NY*. That's standard. It's not a guarantee your show will last for six years, but if ratings show promise, then you're locked in for that time. About three or four years in, CBS started talking about adding another season. So my agents did a little renegotiating, and we added a seventh season to the contract. It went year by year from then on.

During all those years of TV work, I found the work honed my short-term memory. I could put lines into my head for a scene, deliver the lines, then almost erase my mind like a chalkboard so I could put new lines in for the next scene, then do it all over again the next day. The series as a whole is driven by plot, so we all needed to stay close to the scripts. You can't really improvise forensic science, and the writers were very specific in how they wanted things delivered.

In the beginning, the show revolved mostly around the work of solving murders—the science, the clues—but as the series went on, we delved into the personal storylines for each character. Melina Kanakaredes starred with me for the first six years. We were in a lot of scenes together and had great chemistry, I thought. Sela Ward replaced Melina for the last three years, and she was terrific too. We had a wonderful team of writers and producers, an amazing crew, a fantastic cast—Eddie Cahill, Hill Harper, Anna Belknap, Robert Joy, A. J. Buckley, and Carmine Giovinazzo—and I felt blessed to be part of the show, deeply appreciative of how well it was received, and forever privileged to work with such an excellent group of people.

I had two linked setbacks on the show. Season 1, episode 21 featured a chase scene, shot on March 17, 2005, my fiftieth birthday. Carmine and I were working at night in an old subway tunnel in San Pedro, California. The two of us run after a suspect down a set of stairs into the subway. I warmed up and stretched out, and we did one take, then we headed back up the stairs and came running down for another take. Up and down we went. Take after take. On take seven, we were running hard down the stairs, and I still felt good, then *whack*—like a baseball bat walloped me in the back of my calf. I spun around to see if someone had kicked me, but nobody was there, and I collapsed on the floor in agony. Pain shot through my leg, and my whole body started shaking. I tried to get up, but I couldn't put any pressure on my leg.

I was taken to a car and then to the hospital. I had a gastrocnemius tear in my calf muscle. It was very painful. The doctor gave me crutches, a wrap, ice, and morphine, and the driver took me home to the San Fernando Valley. It was a Thursday night, about eight o'clock, and nobody was home. Moira had taken the kids to a school event. I sat on the couch and put my leg up. I felt blurry, buzzing on the morphine. The house was empty, I felt miserable, and I couldn't help but mutter, "So this is fifty. Happy birthday, bud."

About an hour later, my family came home. Everybody fussed over my leg and wished me a happy birthday. Cake and ice cream and cards appeared as if by magic, and a lot of love and care were shown.

Back at work, though, we still needed to finish shooting the episode. So we eventually completed the chase scene by having me sit on a stool and shooting close-ups that showed only my face popping into the frame. I'd be huffing and puffing as if I'd been running. The rest of the episode I'm either sitting at a desk or leaning against a wall. The final two episodes of the season were rewritten slightly so I could take it easier. But as I recovered, I gave those final two shows everything I had.

Years later, in season 7, I was running after a bad guy again. I caught him and slammed him into the side of a truck. *Whack*—the same baseball bat hit my leg again, only this time my other one. I went down, my body went into shock, and it turned out I had another gastrocnemius tear. I now had a matching set. All nine seasons had physical stuff, and our stunt coordinator always took special care to determine which stunts I should or shouldn't do, depending on their difficulty. I was fifty-seven, almost fifty-eight when the show finished its run, and though I always tried to keep in shape, the body has its limits. I found most of them.

The end of season 4 and the start of season 5 featured a big two-part show, the first part a real cliff-hanger where a kidnapped Mac Taylor is knocked out and thrown into a car; then the car is dumped into the Hudson River. In the second part, Mac wakes up as the car goes down and escapes just in time. We shot the first part of that scene in a big tank in the San Fernando Valley. The plan was to shoot me inside the car as it slid underneath the water. I'd give the signal to be let out by banging on the car door. A diver with air tanks was stationed just outside my door, and his job was to listen for my signal, then yank the door open for me so

I could swim out. Another diver with air tanks would be in the back seat of the car in case anything went wrong. His job was to quickly reach over and give me air in case of any delay.

We did the first take, and everything went smoothly. The director called for a second take. The camera rolled, the car started submerging, and as I slid underneath the water inside the car, I banged on the door, but this time, nothing happened. I banged again. The door still didn't open. Completely submerged, I could feel the air bursting inside my lungs. I couldn't see a thing. I fumbled around, trying to reach back to the diver in the back seat so he could hand me air, but I couldn't find him. I panicked, my lungs throbbing. I lay back against the opposite door, banged hard with my legs, and kicked the door open myself. I was nearly inhaling water by then, but at last I swam out, reached the top, and sucked in a huge lungful of fresh air. Angry and frightened, I swore and shouted. Everybody looked alarmed, trying to figure out what had gone wrong. Turned out the diver outside the door hadn't felt my first two bangs. The diver in the back seat had tried to find me, but everything was happening so quickly, I was already out and up before we connected.

Everybody was highly apologetic. We had worked out the safety precautions beforehand, and the first take had gone smoothly. But it was a fresh reminder to me on those risky shoots of the need to work out every contingency plan beforehand. As for me, takes were over for that scene. We flew to New York and shot the rest of the scene, with me walking out of the actual Hudson River, the car submerging in the background. That moment—and my calf issues—aside, everything went relatively smoothly on set, and I loved coming to work at *CSI: NY*.

Apart from being artistic director at Steppenwolf, my role as Mac Taylor was the only job I've held for a long period. The network stayed solidly behind the show, and I was grateful for this good run. The production team appreciated what I wanted to do for our military and veterans, so they agreed to flexible shooting. As one example, in the 2012 season I had the opportunity to go to Kuwait and give a concert in January. One concert then home. *CSI* gave me a couple of days off from shooting, so I finished work one night, got on a plane the next morning, and flew to

Kuwait City, returning to Camp Arifjan for a concert there the following night. The day I arrived I got in a nap, headed to the airstrip at Arifjan, boarded a Blackhawk, and flew out to Camp Buehring to visit troops. I was there for about three or four hours then jumped on the helo again for the ride back. Next day I visited with more troops, did our sound check, played the concert at night, and then headed to the airport for a late-night flight home. There and back in seventy-two hours. It was a great visit with the troops, although as soon as I returned home I was back on set with a ton of scenes to catch up on. No rest for me that week.

From 2004 until 2013—nine seasons and 197 original episodes in all—I portrayed Detective Mac Taylor on *CSI: NY*. The show ranked as high as number seventeen on Nielsen and evened out to about ten million viewers per episode, considered quite good. Today, it's been shown in more than two hundred markets all over the world and continues to run in syndication. Eventually comic books, novels, a video game, and even a slot machine in Vegas came out, all based on the show.

Although at first I didn't see what a blessing it would be, the series became one of the greatest gifts ever handed to me. Nine seasons on television is a tremendous success, and it gave me resources I never could have imagined. It allowed me the financial and logistical freedom to take good care of my family and continue my mission of supporting the troops. It gave me a greater public platform to spread that message of support. Without the financial blessings that resulted from the series, I never could have done the service work I'm doing today at the level I'm engaged in. The timing of the series was perfect, coming at the exact right moment, and has helped me with the mission I feel I was called to all those years ago. I will always be proud to have portrayed US Marine Corps veteran and 9/11 family member Detective Mac Taylor on *CSI: NY*.

CHAPTER 14

Helping Children

We suited up in helmets and bulletproof vests and drove out in a convoy of Humvees to visit one of the Iraqi elementary schools that US troops had been working to improve. It was November 2003, my second tour of Iraq with the USO. The school itself wasn't considered dangerous, but the roads out to the school and back were always suspect, particularly when traveling with US military. Troops had built walls and restrooms at the school, repainted sections of the building, and installed windows and ceiling fans, and they wanted to show us what they'd been working on.

Keep in mind that our troops had only been in Iraq for eight months or so. The statue of Saddam had fallen in Baghdad in April, and the insurgency had now started to pick up. During the next few years, from about 2004 to 2007, the insurgency would grow, and Iraq would become a highly dangerous place indeed.

On this trip in 2003, Wayne Newton, Chris Isaak, country singer Neal McCoy, and I all traveled in the convoy together. Soldiers operated as our security detail. When we arrived at the school, the headmaster came out to greet us along with Iraqi teachers, interpreters, a few Iraqi parents, and a welcoming cadre of children. They greeted us warmly and beamed with pride about their new school. Boys and girls played together outside. Inside, they were taught separately, in about eight classrooms total.

We all said our hellos. School representatives led us on a tour of the school building. Boys filled the first classroom we stepped into, and I was shocked and surprised when the boys all shouted, "Lieutenant Dan!" Everybody burst out laughing, including me, and it turned out that one of the soldiers had coached them how to say that before I arrived. When the laughing subsided, I turned to Wayne Newton and said, "Well, I think I'm going to be living with 'Lieutenant Dan' for a while."

Wayne chuckled and replied, "Yeah. Lieutenant Dan is your 'Danke Schoen.'" I chuckled back. The German-titled love song was inextricably linked with Wayne, even though he had recorded and performed many other hits. In 1963, when he was just twenty-one, Wayne had recorded a version of the song that shot up the charts. And in 1986, his recording rode a new wave of popularity after Matthew Broderick lip-synced it in the hit comedy *Ferris Bueller's Day Off.* This was my second tour with Wayne in six months. He had always been a big supporter of the troops, first singing with the USO as a child. Over the years, Wayne did many other USO tours and performed with Bob Hope during Vietnam.

It wasn't all fun and games at the school. The children themselves seemed happy, grateful for an education, and proud of their school. Conditions at this school had definitely improved since Saddam ran the country. I couldn't help but notice how many children sat at each desk. The desks looked longer than typical American school desks, perhaps built to seat two comfortably. Yet three to four children huddled at each. Each little group would share one pencil stub, passing it back and forth among themselves, working on just a few sheets of paper. These desks and pencils were the only school equipment I saw. The walls at this school were bare—and not because they'd recently been painted. I asked a few careful questions, and it turned out that the sparseness of school supplies was typical of area schools. Few pencils, sheets of paper, or books were available. Certainly nothing close to the mass of erasers, glue, rulers, binders, geometry sets, art supplies, maps, posters, lettering charts, sports equipment, and backpacks we saw at home. When I asked why the Iraqi children didn't have more supplies, the surprising answer came back: "Because we can't get them here."

The kids themselves seemed smart and kind. I tried to put myself in their shoes. What would it be like to go to school in a war-stricken country? What would it be like to go to a school consisting solely of students, teachers, and a small building with only eight classrooms? No gym. No library. No sports field. We continued from classroom to classroom, where all the kids greeted us enthusiastically, and cheered readily for the US soldiers. It was obvious just how much the troops cared about the children, and just how safe the children felt around the troops.

At one point I pulled out a picture of my own children, squatted down next to a group of Iraqi schoolgirls, and showed them my family. The interpreter explained who the kids were in the picture. The girls beamed and giggled, and talked with each other, very excited. Through the interpreter, they asked more questions about my own kids.

The headmaster of the school wanted to show me something. Through the interpreter, he explained how he'd made a plaque and put it up in his office, a tiny room. The plaque was written in Arabic and English. He was very proud. The plaque read:

BY THE GRACE OF GOD, AND THE COOPERATION BETWEEN THE FREE IRAQI PEOPLE AND THE COALITION FORCES, AL-MAJD PRIMARY SCHOOL HAS BEEN REBUILT. THIS SCHOOL IS DEDICATED ON 20 SEPT. 2003 FOR THE EDUCATION AND A NEW GENERATION OF FREE IRAQI PEOPLE. MAY THIS WORK STAND, UNDER GOD'S WATCHFUL EYES, AS A TESTAMENT TO THE HARD WORK AND DEDICATION TO FREEDOM OF IRAQ AND THE COALITION FORCES. CONTRACTOR: AL-ANWAR CONTRACTING CO. COALITION FORCES: 205 MI BRIGADE

I never forgot that. At this moment, prior to the insurgency, it showed they had a lot of hope for the future.

At one point in one of the classrooms, Wayne beckoned me over to form an impromptu quartet with Chris and Neal, and we sang "You Are My Sunshine" for the kids. When we finished, they clapped heartily. We spent several hours at the school, just talking with the children and troops and school officials, giving high fives and playing simple games with the kids, taking many photographs that I still have, and trying to ingrain in the minds and hearts of Iraqi children and their parents that they weren't forgotten by the world. They were respected and valued. They *mattered*. And our troops were there to help them.

As we headed back to the base in our convoy, an idea started to per-colate in the back of my mind, but I didn't say anything at first. It wasn't a big idea initially, just simply reflecting the phrase that was digging deep roots into my heart:

I can do more.

After I returned home to the States, my idea started to take shape. I knew it wouldn't be feasible for me to fly to Iraq each month to help with USO handshake tours. I needed to do something from home to let the troops and Iraqi citizens know they weren't forgotten.

I called the principal for my children's school and asked if I could come in and talk to the kids about what I'd seen in Iraq. I explained that I could show a video and photographs. Then perhaps we could ask all the kids if they'd like to put together a care package of school supplies for the Iraqi children. Once the supplies were gathered, I could send the care package over to the military base in Iraq where I had contacts, and the troops I'd just met could return to the school and pass out the supplies.

The principal liked the idea. We held an assembly, and I talked to the kids about the trip and explained my plan, and all the kids seemed excited about creating care packages. The principal sent notes home with the kids, and they went to work collecting school supplies, teddy bears, soccer balls—anything the Iraqi kids might enjoy. We also had the kids write letters of encouragement and goodwill to the Iraqi kids. I didn't know how many supplies we'd gather, but I figured anything would help and at least it would be a gesture.

Supplies trickled in. Over the next few weeks, more and more supplies arrived. By January 2004, we'd filled twenty-five big boxes. I mailed them to the base in Iraq. The troops drove out to the school again and handed out the supplies to the kids I'd met on my trip. The soldiers wrote back to me, sending photos and videos and describing the wonderful day and the happy smiles on the faces of children, teachers, and Iraqi parents.

I started thinking, *Why not keep this flow of goodwill going?* Not only from my own children's school, but from other schools too. My plan was still very grassroots. Schools could get addresses of military bases themselves, or I'd help supply addresses; then the schools could simply duplicate the model. I went on radio and TV a couple times and explained how others could do what we'd done. The model stood to be win-win all around. Iraqi children and their parents would be helped. The troops would be supported and encouraged and would know that the American people were not forgetting about them. People at home could pitch in and help in a positive way. We didn't hear a lot of good stories in the news about the war, but I knew those good stories were out there. I not only wanted to tell those stories, I also wanted to help create them.

A soldier I knew had been in touch with *New York Times* bestselling author Laura Hillenbrand, who a few years earlier had written the inspiring book *Seabiscuit*, about an underdog racehorse who persevered and ultimately became a champion. Another soldier had asked Laura if there was any way to send Arabic translations of *Seabiscuit* to him. He'd been reading the book, and while helping at an Iraqi school, a child had seen it and asked him about it. The soldier had told the child the story of the famous racehorse. Other kids had gathered around and listened, spellbound.

Laura had been trying to get her book translated and shipped overseas so she could donate copies to the children, and here I was trying to ship school supplies over, so it made sense that we meet. Like me, Laura wanted to support our troops and do more to help the children, yet due to a decades-long debilitating and incurable case of chronic fatigue syndrome that hits her with severe nausea and vertigo, Laura is rarely able to leave her house. Thankfully, in recent years she's gotten a bit better, but still she's limited to mostly staying close to home. I grew to admire this wonderfully brave and gifted person who would go on to write another bestselling book, *Unbroken*, about the life of World War II hero Louis Zamperini. We became fast friends and talked over our ideas.

She wanted to help the troops. I wanted to help the troops. Together we decided to start a school supply program, initially naming it Operation Iraqi Children (OIC), emphasizing the grassroots approach. We came up with a motto—"helping soldiers help children"—and created a logo of a helmet filled with school supplies. We created a website where people could go and follow guidelines about how to gather supplies and ship them over to the troops to give to the kids. I went on TV a couple more times to promote what we were doing, and Laura called her contacts. The idea began to spread, and people started to reach out to us.

What started as a simple suggestion, an encouragement to our fellow citizens to send school supplies to Iraq, quickly needed to take a new direction. We were giving people the guidelines, but we had no way of knowing if supplies were actually getting through, or what kind of supplies were being sent. I received a call from Mike Meyer, a Vietnam veteran working for the VFW. Mike had seen me talking about the program on TV and introduced Laura and me to Mary Eisenhower, granddaughter of President Dwight Eisenhower. Mary ran a humanitarian organization based in Kansas City called People to People International (PTPI), which had been started by her grandfather. She offered to partner with us and essentially fold our program into her organization. Now we were able to take supplies into our own warehouse and package and ship them ourselves. I continued to promote the program on radio and television, sending people to our website, and we began to receive supplies from people all over the country. We were also able to raise funds, allowing us to purchase additional supplies ourselves.

Mary and Mike connected us to representatives of FedEx, who offered to support our initiative by donating the shipping to Kuwait. FedEx CEO Fred Smith approved it. Getting supplies from Kuwait into Iraq was tricky. It involved more steps and higher clearance levels, so at one point I went to the Pentagon to ask for help, but with the war in full swing, it was difficult to get a consistent commitment. We worked to find as many ways as possible to get the supplies where we wanted them to go. We eventually had a good system in place.

In April 2004, we held a press conference at the airport in Kansas City saying we were ramping up efforts yet again. We developed a volunteer base, and I did benefit concerts for OIC with the Lt. Dan Band. Supplies poured in. I started talking about the program more and more on radio and TV. Even more supplies poured in. We quickly learned to create two-pound school "kits" with big plastic Ziploc bags so each child would receive roughly the same amount of supplies. Our volunteers assembled the kits, complete with pencils, erasers, and other basic school supplies. A buddy of mine from high school, Mike Fisher, owned a container supply company in Chicago and offered to donate Ziploc bags. Over the years, Mike would donate thousands of these bags to OIC.

On April 20, 2004, we shipped six hundred school kits, along with two hundred stuffed animals, for distribution to schools in Balad and Baghdad. On June 8, 2004, we shipped another two hundred kits and three hundred stuffed animals for distribution at Iman Primary School in Ishan Hamzah, Iraq. Two weeks later we shipped another six hundred kits to Hillah, Iraq. We were off and running. In 2004 alone, we made nineteen shipments—and we were only getting started.

Blankets, jackets, shoes, socks, soccer balls, art supplies, soap, and backpacks—we added all these items the next year. Items donated, or purchased through funds raised from the American people, were distributed to the children by our troops. We received a massive donation of Crocs shoes and shipped those. Year after year we kept going. It proved a very successful program.

The success was largely due to the simplicity of our overall goal. OIC was a mission of encouragement, hope, and love. The program expanded over the years to include shipments to other countries, and the name of the program was eventually changed to Operation *International* Children. (That way we could still call it OIC.) Yet our mission always stayed the same—*helping soldiers help children*. Eventually we were able to help children in Afghanistan, the Philippines, Haiti, Djibouti, and the United States, where supplies were flown to kids adversely affected by Hurricane Katrina. I pictured our program as something in the spirit of our GIs walking through a bombed-out town in Germany after World War II.

They'd hand out chocolate and candy to the kids, and while those actions certainly didn't solve all the world's ills, the GIs' actions had let the citizens know that the soldiers were there to help, not hurt.

Over the next few years, we received sack loads of letters from school-kids who thanked us for the supplies, along with many other letters from soldiers, telling us the program allowed them to extend the hands of friendship to people in these communities.

We were able to establish strong relationships with soldiers on the ground, including Lieutenant Colonel Donald Fallin, who for a period of time took a lead role in distributing our supplies. Another lieutenant colonel named Drew Ryan wrote to tell us about how his troops had visited the Iraqi town of Albu Hassan where villagers had suffered tremendously under Saddam Hussein. When Saddam had wanted to build a new air-field for himself, he simply confiscated farms without ever giving the Iraqi citizens any compensation or jobs. When Saddam was ousted, Lieutenant Colonel Ryan arrived. Many structures in Albu Hassan were dilapidated. The elementary school was a simple mud-walled building with a palm thatched roof that birds often nested in. No running water. No heating for cold winter mornings. No air-conditioning for the hot months—not even fans—and temperatures in the area reached 130 degrees. Lieutenant Colonel Ryan and his troops rebuilt the primary school and built a completely new secondary school with ceiling fans in each room, windows with glass and screens, lights, and a new roof. Through OIC, the troops delivered pens, pencils, notebooks, maps, and soccer balls—and held medical clinics for the students and community members at the school.

One of my favorite letters came from an Iraqi teen, who wrote to us in broken English.

> My name is Hadeel and I am 18 years old girl from Iraq, Baghdad. i am very greatful to your help to iraqi children . . . its nice to know there still good people in this world . . . infact you made alot of kids happy because you gave them the hope of new life and the encouragement and the feeling they are important. Id like to thank Gary sinise . . . he is realy charitable and noble man . . . i wish i could see him to thank him in the

place of all iraqi children . . . thank you Gary we love so much. infact thank you all and let God bless you!

Troops told us the deliveries from OIC helped in unexpected ways. For instance, an American soldier gave a stuffed animal to a little Iraqi girl, about five years old. The next day, a convoy of American soldiers drove down the road, about five vehicles in the convoy running at about forty-five miles per hour, and they saw this same little girl in the street, still holding her stuffed animal. She wore a worried look on her face, so they pulled over to make sure everything was okay. She shifted the stuffed animal in her arms and pointed to a little mound of dirt just up the road in the direction the convoy headed. The troops checked it out. An IED was hidden in the dirt. This little girl, after receiving a stuffed animal from a US soldier, very probably saved the soldiers in that convoy from being seriously injured or killed.

I got to help in a few unique situations. A convoy of US troops was headed down the road and Iraqi kids ran out to greet them when suddenly all hell broke loose. An insurgent's rocket hit the convoy and blew up. One of the boys, about thirteen, was tragically caught in the cross fire and severely wounded in one arm. The US troops gave him emergency medical attention on the spot, then rushed him to a base hospital. He lived, but his arm couldn't be saved. Later, a soldier who'd met the boy connected him with a doctor in San Francisco who'd offered to arrange for the boy to get a prosthetic arm. Out of the blue, I received an email from this soldier, asking me if there was some way we could help get the boy to San Francisco.

This request really caused me to choke up. Immediately, I arranged to pay for plane tickets for the boy and his father to come to the States. I just didn't want to wait for any red tape or anything. But getting the boy and his father out of Iraq proved trickier. I called a friend at the state department, Susan Phalen, who'd spent time in Iraq. She arranged for the boy and his father to drive from Iraq to Jordan first, where she personally met them and accompanied them from Jordan to San Francisco. The boy received his new prosthetic, and he and his father flew home. It was a tough story in many ways, but for me, it felt important to have this personal touch and engage with real people, not just numbers or theories.

Somebody I met thanked me for my work in support of the troops. He told me he had a friend serving at a military hospital in eastern Afghanistan, Major Catherine Crespo, a nurse. I reached out to her, asking if she needed any school supplies for the local children. She worked at the 349th Combat Support Hospital at Forward Operating Base Salerno and said she didn't need any school supplies, but described how the medical staff saw many injuries from IEDs. These weapons can cause real devastation to the human body and leave behind dirty wounds that must be left open to heal. One tool of modern medicine that helps phenomenally with open wounds is a device called a wound VAC. The hospital used them so much they burned through the machines quickly, and it was slow going to get replacements from the Department of Defense. She asked if we could help.

I had no idea what a wound VAC looked like or how much it cost. I called a buddy, a surgeon, who put me in touch with the manufacturer, a company called KCI. The devices cost $25,000 each, certainly more than pencils and shoes. But the company CEO's father was a marine, so when the CEO learned what we were doing, he promptly donated three wound VACs, sent them to our OIC warehouse, and we quickly shipped them to Afghanistan. Catherine wrote, "These wound VACs most assuredly saved hundreds of lives, maybe more. They continued to be used by the medical units that followed us after we left."

Our focus, however, stayed mainly on school supplies and shoes. Throughout the years, we heard many positive stories from troops who were able to help children and parents. Troops would go into a village in the cold winter and see kids running around barefoot. They'd describe seeing children put on a new pair of shoes for the first time. The kids' faces lit up with joy. Or the troops would just carry items along out on patrol and see a group of kids or mothers and donate shoes right on the spot. Troops described conversations with parents of Iraqi children who said what a big difference a simple gift of new school supplies made.

Seldom was I able to distribute supplies myself, but once in a while I was offered the rare and wonderful experience of being part of a distribution team. In 2009, on my second trip to Afghanistan, my band came along, as well as my industry pals Kristy Swanson, Kevin Farley (Chris Farley's brother), Leeann Tweeden, and Mykelti Williamson. It had been three years since my first trip to Afghanistan with the USO. Then, I'd taken along my brother-in-law Jack, and after a stop in the United Arab Emirates we arrived in Afghanistan where we roughed it a bit, sleeping in makeshift barracks, plywood rooms with rickety cots and wooden bunks. A C-130 had taken us to Bagram Air Base, where I visited with hundreds of troops before setting off for several small forward operating bases (FOBs) via Blackhawk helicopters. There I shook more hands and took just as many pictures, it seemed. Now, after three years, I was back, only this time with both school supplies and my band. This was a morale-boosting concert trip for the troops, and we were set to play three shows: one at Bagram Air Base, one at Camp Leatherneck for the marines (our stage was two flatbed trucks backed up into each other), and one at Kandahar Air Base, where I'd serve turkey, gravy, and all the fixings to our troops on Thanksgiving Day.

We flew on American Airlines to Frankfurt, where we spent the night, then boarded a C-17 for the flight to Afghanistan. The plane was filled with pallets of ammunition and supplies, and we found room wherever we could fit. Upon landing at Bagram Air Base, I was met by Major General Mike Scaparrotti, and while the rest of the people on the trip stowed their stuff and rested up, Mike flew with me by Blackhawk helicopter to a small Afghan school near Forward Operating Base Garcia, near the Pakistan border.

OIC staffers had preshipped five hundred backpacks filled with school supplies to the small FOB. A soldier at the FOB had emailed me earlier, asking me if it might be possible to get them some school supplies. We already had the trip and the Thanksgiving dinner planned, so I thought it would be great to surprise the soldier by going out to the FOB in person to help hand out the supplies to the children. To say that this soldier was shocked to see me is an understatement.

We landed in the Blackhawk right at the Afghan school. Soldiers were already there with several trucks filled with supplies. Security was tight.

A couple of hundred children were already lined up, and the atmosphere was charged with excitement. An interpreter explained what OIC was all about and who I was, then we went to work. It took about two hours to hand out all the backpacks. The children were amazing. Although some did not have shoes on their feet, and clearly all were very poor, they were wide-eyed and grateful and some of the most beautiful kids I'd ever seen. I took photos with them, gave high fives, and tried to take it all in. We didn't have long at the school, so when the backpacks were all gone, we jumped back on the Blackhawk and flew back to FOB Garcia where I visited with some one hundred fifty troops stationed there. The entire area near the Pakistan border was considered dangerous, laced with Taliban insurgents.

Years went by, and our program ran strong. Eventually, as our troops started being pulled out of Iraq, our program began to wind down. We stopped shipping to Iraq in 2011, and continued to ship to Afghanistan until 2013, when we officially closed OIC. Altogether, the program lasted for nine years, and during that time, OIC delivered 340,967 school supply kits, thousands of shoes and backpacks, more than fifty pallets of sports equipment, more than half a million toys, and eight thousand Arabic-language copies of *Seabiscuit*. OIC remains one of my favorite programs of all those I've been involved in.

※

The children of Iraq and Afghanistan weren't the only kids affected by the global wars against terrorism. In the early days of the war, I sat in my office thinking about all the casualty reports we kept hearing in the news. A heavy sadness washed over me. By then, I'd already done six or seven USO tours and met a lot of troops, and some of those men and women I'd shaken hands with had now died. My heart ached for their families, specifically for the children of US service personnel who'd lost their moms or dads in the conflicts. (As I write this in 2018, nearly seven thousand Americans have been killed in the wars against terrorism, with many thousands more wounded.)

I went online and searched for organizations specifically geared toward helping children, and found Intrepid Fallen Heroes Fund. I'd met some folks on my first USO tour who worked with Intrepid, so I reached out to them and ended up on their board for a few years to help raise awareness for their initiatives. They're connected with the Fisher House Foundation, which provides a network of conveniently located homes where the spouses and children of wounded service members can stay for free while their loved one is recuperating in the hospital. I also got involved with the Tragedy Assistance Program for Survivors (TAPS), which focuses on grief management for loved ones of fallen heroes.

Still, I wanted to do more. I received a call from Roy White, who'd been involved with an event held a few weeks earlier, right before Christmas 2006, called the Snowball Express. Roy wanted to know if I'd help the next year. Their idea was simple. They brought the children of our fallen heroes to Disneyland just before Christmas to allow them to meet each other, to see that they were not alone in their grief, and to bring some joy and new happy memories to this special group of children who were experiencing so much sadness, especially at Christmas.

Roy came to my office, along with early event coordinators Greg Young and Bill "Monsoon" Mimiaga, and they showed me a video of the Snowball Express event. I loved it! The kids looked like they were simply having fun, exactly what I wanted to be a part of. This was something that focused specifically on the kids. I made a financial commitment on the spot and donated my band to play for the kids at the 2007 Snowball Express. While we can never do enough for these children and their families, I wanted to do at least something.

There's no playbook on performing shows for grieving children, and my band and I learned things along the way. The following year, 2007, we held the first Lt. Dan Band concert for the kids at a theater called the Grove in Anaheim. We played the song "Hero" by Mariah Carey, a slower, moving ballad. In advance, we'd thought about this choice in the set list, and I wanted the kids to be strong, to know they are heroes to us. But because it's an emotional song and I wasn't sure how they were going to take it, I put Miami Sound Machine's "Conga" in the set list as our next tune, a fun, fast-moving song, so we could shift the mood, just in case. We often perform "Hero" during our concerts for the troops, and I dedicate it to the families of our fallen and families of our wounded. It is always moving and well received as I remind them that when they are going through these difficult times, they should know there is strength and hope and a hero inside them that will help them find the way. And they are heroes to me. But sure enough, when we played it for the children, we quickly saw that the song meant something different, something heartbreaking—a reminder of the hero they had lost—and the mood quickly became somber. Kids started to cry—not what we wanted at all. We wanted the music to bring them joy and fun and help lift their spirits. We wanted them leaving feeling better than when they walked in. So when the song ended, I stopped the show, bent down, and simply hugged the children in the front row, one after another, as tears ran down their faces. Then we started up again with "Conga," and that changed the mood and helped spark joy in the kids again. From then on, whenever we played for Snowball, I decided to only do songs that were going to make the kids happy.

One family I saw backstage at Snowball that first year was the wife and children of Air Force Major Troy Gilbert, an F-16 pilot. I'd met the Gilberts in early 2006 at Luke Air Force Base in Arizona when I attended a ceremony for my friend Robin Rand, who was being pinned as a brigadier general. Later that year both Robin and Troy deployed to Iraq with the 332nd Air Expeditionary Wing under Robin's command. On November 27, Troy was killed while flying a combat mission in Anbar Province, Iraq, in support of Operation Iraqi Freedom. He went down with his jet while protecting twenty soldiers on the ground below who were battling insurgents. I saw Troy's wife, Ginger, and their children that day at Snowball before we played the concert. Surprisingly, nearly ten years later, I would receive a phone call from Robin, now a four-star general, inviting me to attend a funeral for Troy at Arlington National Cemetery. Troy's body had been missing for a decade. Al Qaeda insurgents had removed him from the crash site. By the time our forces got there, only a piece of his skull was found in his helmet. The skull was buried at Arlington. In 2013, an additional limited amount of remains were recovered, prompting another burial at Arlington. Finally, in 2016, the rest of his remains were recovered by US Special Forces and returned home. On December 19, 2016, Troy was laid to rest. He is the only US service member to have been buried at Arlington three times. At the end of the final ceremony, we all looked to the heavens as the missing man formation of F-16s flew through the sky. One aircraft abruptly broke away from the pack, in memory of the fallen pilot. It was a powerful and emotional moment. Troy's wife is a wonderfully strong woman, and I know the Snowball event in 2007 helped her and her children through a very difficult time.

Backstage at my first Snowball event, I also met Jim Palmersheim, an American Airlines pilot and Operation Desert Shield/Storm veteran who at that time was volunteering in support of the new Military and Veterans Initiatives (MVI) program at American. The airline has done a lot of caring for veterans. AA lost two planes on 9/11, and their representatives were now doing all they could to support our nation's defenders. American Airlines had supported the first Snowball Express event in 2006 and were supporting it again the following year. An instant friendship sprang up with Jim.

A year later, in 2008, I volunteered my band to do another concert to support an organization called Coalition to Salute America's Heroes at their event in Orlando, Florida. They serve and support our wounded service members, and I'd begun helping them back in 2004. At this 2008 event, American Airlines was lending travel support. Jim Palmersheim was there and had now become managing director for Military and Veterans Initiatives at American. After the event, he and I sat down for a drink and I told him all about Operation Iraqi Children. Our minds started cooking up an idea, and he arranged for an American Airlines plane to ferry school supplies to Iraq—twenty-two tons of school supplies on that one flight alone. It was a big donation and a big trip. Over the years, AA has done great things for our veterans and for the families of our troops.

From that first event in 2007, I've supported Snowball Express every year since. In 2008, I couldn't bring in my band due to scheduling difficulties, but I still wanted to support the kids. So, on the Snowball Express weekend, after my shoot at *CSI: NY* finished at 6:00 p.m., I jumped into my car and headed down to Anaheim, where I took pictures with kids and signed autographs, then presented the organization with a donation of $10,000 from Moira and me.

In 2009, the event moved to Dallas, the main hub for American Airlines. A huge group of volunteers and local sponsors got on board, and the cities of Dallas and Fort Worth made available many great things for the kids to do. From 2015 to 2017, my concert for the kids was held in Fort Worth at the Naval Air Station Joint Reserve Base. The entire Snowball Express four-day event includes magic shows, parades, skits, bowling, and face painting. Scholarships are given out to older teens. The most moving part of the event comes when the children march down the street surrounded by cheering residents of Dallas–Fort Worth, each child, upward of fifteen hundred of them, holding a balloon. The children have written messages on the balloons to their fallen parent. The balloons are released into the sky. The messages of love soar into the heavens. Dallas rolled out the red carpet for these children for nine good years, and each year the Dallas volunteers did absolutely everything possible to make sure the children had a great time.

I love this event for the kids so much that in 2018, we brought Snowball Express under the Gary Sinise Foundation umbrella of programs, and moved the event to Walt Disney World Resort in Florida. Dallas is terrific, but to change things up and give the event new life, it was time to move to "the happiest place on earth." Some one thousand kids and 668 parents and guardians came in 2018, and everybody had a great time.

New children come to Snowball Express each year, and it's sobering to realize they are not new because they haven't heard of the program before, but because each year our troops continue to give their lives. When children turn eighteen, they graduate from Snowball to make room for additional children. Each year we see returning children too. It's moving for me to stand onstage and see these children grow up, year after year, always with the loss of their parent in mind. It never really goes away. Some of the older teens adopt a mentoring attitude, and they take the younger children under their wings and help them through their difficult experiences.

I could not be prouder to be a part of creating opportunities for joy, friendship, and communal healing by connecting families struggling with loss to one another. Together, they share a common bond and can feel part of a bigger family. The children meet and interact with others who understand what they have been through, and help each other through this unique and terrible experience. It cannot be overstated what an event like this can mean to a child who has lost a parent in military service. Struggling with their grief can be overwhelming, and uniting together with hundreds of other children experiencing a similar tragic loss can be the magic that carries them throughout the year.

One of the children's favorite songs that we do year after year is "Life Is a Highway" by Tom Cochrane, covered by Rascal Flatts and featured in the movie *Cars*. The song's got a great up-tempo feeling, and it always sets the crowd dancing. During that song, I always welcome the kids to come up onto the stage with us so they can bop around with the band. Word gets out beforehand, and kids pile up in front of the stage waiting for the moment they know I'll invite them up. There's so much joy on their faces during these moments. It's such a blessing to interact with the kids this way.

At the same time, I'm always reminded of the solemnity embedded in these moments, of the incredible cost represented in the faces of the children who come to this event. I feel for these families so deeply. I hurt. How profoundly grateful we all must become—as individuals, as a nation—when we realize anew the magnitude of the sacrifice given for us. Freedom is never *free*. Someone has to pay.

Last year, one girl wore a T-shirt to the event with these words printed on the back: "In honor/memory of . . ." and underneath the words was a blank box where kids could write in the name of their fallen hero.

In black marker, the girl had written simply, "My Daddy."

CHAPTER 15

Flurry of Action

The first time I met Moira's father, things didn't go so well. Steppenwolf had just gotten under way, and we were working out of the rented church basement. I sported a mass of scruffy hair and typically wore torn blue jeans and a raggedy T-shirt. Staying true to the 1970s struggling-artist motif, I looked pretty wild. And yes, I'll confess, my internal self mostly focused on me, my dreams, and my big ideas.

Moira's family lived in Pontiac, Illinois, about one hundred miles south of Chicago. At one time, her dad had worked in book publishing in New York, but they'd moved to this smaller town in the Midwest where he'd entered the real estate business. He golfed at the country club, wore suits to work, and belonged to the Union League Club, a respectable men's organization with branches in cities around the country.

They heard we were dating, so Moira's folks drove from Pontiac to Chicago to have dinner with us. Although we'd met before, this was the first big meet-the-parents event. They wanted to see if this kid was worthy enough to be dating their daughter.

I am *sure* they had their doubts.

Moira's dad made dinner plans for us at the Chicago branch of the Union League Club. Moira and I were at different places that day, so she told me when and where to meet. After working at the theater all day, I was running late. So I jumped into the car and raced downtown, still sporting my raggedy jeans and T-shirt. I had no idea what the Union League Club was. When I showed up, the maître d' stopped me at the front door and sniffed, "Young man. You cannot enter this establishment looking like *that*."

"I . . . I came all the way from the suburbs." My voice climbed to a plea. "I have to meet my girlfriend's parents. I'm late!"

"I'm afraid that's impossible. You need a suit jacket. You can't come in here."

"I don't have one. Please. They're Mr. and Mrs. Harris. Ask them. They'll tell you."

The maître d' sighed heavily. "Wait here." He disappeared and apparently rummaged through the coatroom, because he came back with a suitcoat and ordered me to put it on. It fit tight through my shoulders and was short on my arms, but I wasn't complaining, even when he crossed his arms and added, "You still can't go in the front way. We'll take you around the back."

We walked around the building into the alley, past garbage cans and cardboard boxes. He escorted me onto the freight elevator. When the door opened at the assigned floor, he made sure the coast was clear and ushered me to the correct dinner table.

Moira breathed a sigh of relief that I'd finally made it. Her dad took one look, a bit dismayed and bewildered. Her mom bit her lip in concern. I apologized for being late and fumbled my way through the next two hours of dinner. The tone didn't change much. When it came to my dating their daughter, let's just say they weren't overjoyed.

But there's more to that story. Hang on. We'll get to it soon.

In my office today, in our Center for Education and Outreach, we keep something we call the "Call to Action" list, which has the various organizations and causes I've supported since 9/11. What cheers me most is that it reflects the number of strong organizations that have come together to stand behind our nation's defenders and first responders. We truly are a country that gives back. And I never want America to lose this drive.

The groups on that Call to Action list focus on issues as varied as the personalities of the people we help. Some initiatives directly help active-duty service members. Others support the wounded. Some shine a light on veterans' families. Others entertain the troops and boost their morale. Still others honor veterans from wars past. Beginning in 2003, my aim became to do as much as I could, as fast as I could, with as many organizations as possible, to benefit as many people as possible. I want our nation's defenders and first responders never to be forgotten. What follows are just a few stories from those years.

In 2005, I got a call from my buddy, actor, producer, and director Joe Mantegna. He's appeared in everything from *Three Amigos* to *The Godfather Part III*, and we have a lot of mutual friends. And both of us grew up in Chicago. Each year since 2002, Joe has been a part of the National Memorial Day Concert in Washington, DC. He knew I was working with the USO, so in 2005 he asked me to be a part of the concert too. They were doing a segment on the history of the USO and wanted me to bring my band to be part of the segment. I said yes immediately.

If you've never seen it before, the ninety-minute concert is all about honoring our nation's defenders, their families at home, and those who have made the ultimate sacrifice. The concert is free and held annually on the West Lawn of the United States Capitol Building the night before Memorial Day. Music is performed, documentary footage is shown, and dramatic readings are presented. It's all broadcast live on PBS, and it's one of the network's highest-rated programs. The idea is to unite the country in remembrance and gratitude for all who have served and who have sacrificed their lives. Whether by participating or watching, we as a country can say thanks—and that we do not forget.

The logistics for the Lt. Dan Band's participation proved tricky. We were just finishing an overseas USO tour, so we flew straight from London to Washington, DC, and promptly prepared to play at the National Memorial Day Concert. We'd only been together as a band for about a year and a half, and now we were rehearsing onstage backed up by the National Symphony Orchestra. When it came our turn to perform, we played "Ain't No Mountain High Enough" and "God Bless the USA" along with the symphony—and the force of music in tribute to the troops pulsing from the stage felt incredible. An audience of between two and three hundred thousand people sat on the lawn, and another ten million watched on TV. As the size and purpose of the crowd washed over me, the reason for the event became unmistakable. We were here to say thank you. Period. When we finished our songs, I set down my bass, went to the microphone, and said a few words of thanks and encouragement for our nation's defenders. And for the next ninety minutes I narrated different segments of the show.

The following year Joe asked me to cohost the show with him. I've been doing it every year since, plus joining in the parade held the day after. (I missed one year only, 2017, when my granddaughter was born.) Cohosting this show with my dear buddy Joe, while acknowledging the sacrifices of our military families, is one of the highlights of my year.

In 2007, I was introduced to the Congressional Medal of Honor Society, a prestigious and uniquely exclusive group of American heroes. The Medal of Honor is the highest award given to any individual serving in the Armed Services of the United States—and you receive it only for valor in action against an enemy force. Over the years, I've become close friends with a number of recipients. The stories of these recipients are amazing, and we need to write dozens more books to tell them all. But something happened that absolutely humbled me. Medal recipients knew about the initiatives I backed to support our troops, so they decided to give me an award. That sure turned the tables, and for a while I wondered if I could even accept such a thing. I concluded that any award for me would only help shine a brighter light on the many causes I was involved in to help our veterans. I accepted and came to a special Medal of Honor Society event in Seattle to receive their Bob Hope Award for Excellence in Entertainment. It's given to performers who positively portray military personnel in film or theater. In my case, I received it for two reasons: my performance as Lieutenant Dan and my support of our nation's defenders.

A year earlier, at a concert the band played called Rockin' for the Troops put on by Operation Support Our Troops America, I'd met a Medal of Honor recipient, Vietnam veteran Sammy L. Davis. In his battle days, with a broken back and not knowing how to swim, Sammy had used an air mattress to traverse a river while under enemy attack. His actions helped rescue three wounded American soldiers. A scene in *Forrest Gump* shows President Lyndon Johnson placing a Medal of Honor around Forrest's neck. Filmmakers used original footage of Sammy and spliced Tom Hanks's head onto Sammy's body. We shared a chuckle about that, and over the years Sammy became a wonderful friend and today is an ambassador for my foundation.

One open door led to another. Backstage at a USO concert at Luke Air Force Base in Arizona, I met Dave McIntyre, a USO board member and the CEO of TriWest Healthcare Alliance, which provides healthcare for our nation's military. He offered to help my mission however possible, and eventually helped pay for my band to play at various USO shows around the world. The USO only offers a small per diem for performers on tours. While I work for free, my band members all make their living by performing, and the USO per diem isn't enough to pay their fee. So prior to Dave's offer, I funded my band out of my own pocket or by raising funds here and there from various pals of mine. To keep my band engaged, I wanted to find as many opportunities to play as possible. Sometimes if I had a show at a military base on a Friday, I would look for a local venue to play at on a Saturday and offer to bring my band there. But the clubs do not pay enough, and I found myself having to supplement the expenses of the band, simply to give the band members an additional gig that weekend. I was feeling the strain. Dave's generous support allowed us to play at even more USO shows.

Dave also sat on the board of the Medal of Honor Foundation and was one of their main sponsors. After the event in Seattle in 2007, Dave told me that the society was considering doing an event the following year in Los Angeles. Would I be interested in supporting it? I was immediately on board and took Dave to see the Reagan Library in Simi Valley, a fantastic, high-roofed, multiwindowed venue that allows people to sit indoors underneath the Air Force One airplane that served seven US presidents from 1973 to 2001. Dave had never been to the library before, and as it's one of my favorite spots in the area, I knew it would be the perfect venue for the Medal of Honor event. Dave agreed, and thanks to his encouragement, I was one of three cohosts of the Congressional Medal of Honor Celebration of Freedom from 2008 to 2012. The event was a magnificent black-tie affair, and each year I was able to recommend performers from my industry to receive the Bob Hope Award for Excellence in Entertainment. I've made many great friends within the society over the years. I serve on advisory groups for the Medal of Honor Society and the Medal of Honor Museum Foundation and continue to do events with them each year. I feel so privileged to be part of the work of these incredible heroes.

⸜⸝

Beginning in 2003 with trips to Landstuhl, Walter Reed, and Bethesda, visiting our wounded in military hospitals around the country became more and more frequent for me. In subsequent years, in a stream of hospital visits, I met many incredible people. Elaine Rogers, president and CEO of USO of Metropolitan Washington–Baltimore, the USO responsible for multiple USO facilities in the DC area, is a dear friend and dedicated troop supporter who has served the USO for more than forty years. Elaine and her team have accompanied me on several of my hospital visits over the years, and we have done many great events together, including our annual Salute to the Troops event where we bring dozens of our wounded from the hospitals to Las Vegas for a big morale boost.

I'll never forget my first trip to the DC hospitals. After a bomb exploded in Iraq in July 2003, Marine Staff Sergeant Mark Graunke Jr. lost an eye, hand, fingers, thumb, and right leg. I met Mark on my first visit to the National Naval Medical Center in Bethesda, Maryland, on September 11, 2003, where he was recovering. He was the first wounded service member I visited on the first of many trips over the years to the DC military hospitals. He wanted to talk about Lieutenant Dan, and we shared a few stories and I sat with him for quite a while before I went on to the next room. I saw many soldiers and marines who'd been wounded in Iraq and Afghanistan—as well as in places we don't normally associate with today's wars. Two marines I saw were being treated on ventilation machines for malaria after serving in Africa. They were both very sick, unconscious, with tubes down their throats. Their families stayed with them in the hospital, and I sat with the families for some time. It is sobering to realize our service members can become wounded, ill, or injured in so many ways and places.

That afternoon I was at Walter Reed for the first time. I visited with so many wounded heroes that day, including the first of many triple amputees I would meet in the coming years. Just twenty-one years old, US Army Specialist Hilario Bermanis was serving with the 82nd Airborne Division in Baghdad. On June 10, just ten days before I would be in Baghdad myself, Specialist Bermanis and a fellow soldier came under attack while guarding a weapons turn-in point. A rocket-propelled grenade killed his friend and took both Bermanis's legs and his left hand. As Bermanis lay in his bed, his father stood by his side and told me what had happened and how Hilario was from one of the tiny islands in the Federated States of Micronesia. Three years earlier, wanting to be an American soldier, he had gone to Guam to sign up for the US Army. The week after my visit, in a ceremony at Walter Reed on September 17, 2003, Bermanis was awarded US citizenship. I will always remember that first visit, meeting Specialist Bermanis and so many others, seeing this young man in a hospital bed missing three out of four limbs. It made a lasting impression on me.

In the spring of 2004, I was back at Walter Reed on a Thursday evening and learned that every Friday a local Vietnam veteran named Hal Koster hosted free dinners for wounded veterans at a nearby steakhouse. Hal sponsored those dinners himself—the bills ran into the thousands of dollars—and his motivation was simply to get our wounded vets out of the hospital for an evening to relax and enjoy a good dinner. The vets I met that Thursday invited me to attend the next day along with them in the big private room Hal provided. Not every wounded vet was able to leave the hospital, but those who could really looked forward to the evening out. I stayed an extra day. I tried to pay for my own dinner, but Hal refused. After I got home, I sent some money to Hal to help pay for one of the Friday-night dinners. From then on, whenever I visited Bethesda, I'd try to attend a dinner if I could. Hal's actions are another wonderful example of gratitude from one of our citizens. Hal eventually named his program the Aleethia Foundation, and it's still running to this day.

———— ∞∞∞ ————

For several years, my schedule prevented me from visiting the Brooke Army Medical Center in San Antonio, our nation's primary burn center for wounded troops. But in 2009 I made a commitment to get there and flew myself from California without the aid or invitation of any supporting agencies.

The hospital's chaplain agreed to escort me around to the various rooms. Burn injuries are very tough. I introduced myself to each service member I met and tried to spread a bit of cheer. Troops were burned on their faces, hands, arms, legs, and torsos. Some were missing an arm or leg, or pieces of their scalp. I ordered myself not to show any reaction other than support and gratitude. One young soldier looked badly burned on her face and arm, and I met her as she walked down the hallway, tugging her IV behind her. We talked for some time, and I tried to offer a bit of encouragement. Today's wounded troops are not only our nation's sons, but our nation's daughters too.

The chaplain wanted me to visit one family in particular. They were caring for their severely wounded service member, a marine master sergeant named Eden Pearl, who'd been part of the Marine Corps Forces Special Operations Command (MARSOC). I'd met a lot of severely wounded vets by then, but the severity and extent of Eden's wounds set him in a category by himself. His family, especially his wife, Alicia, remain some of the strongest, most courageous people I've ever met.

Eden was muscular, tattooed, and once sported a bushy red beard. They called him "The Viking." Other marines knew him as an exemplary combat leader. He'd served in Kosovo from 1999 to 2001, helping to prevent ethnic cleansing. In 2003, he was one of the first marines on the ground in Iraq. He redeployed to Iraq in 2004 and 2005, then deployed to Afghanistan in 2009.

In August 2009, Eden and his unit were involved in a massive gun battle against terrorists in the area surrounding a small Afghan village. The battle raged so intensely that the marines made the difficult decision to leave the village so they could return at a more strategic time. As they left, the Humvee that Eden rode in struck a hidden roadside IED, exploded, and burst into flames. An interpreter and the driver, Army Corporal Nick Roush, were killed immediately. The remaining four troops inside the vehicle received severe burns, but none as terrible as Eden. Here's the remarkable thing. Eden was finally pulled from the vehicle and placed under a burn blanket. Still coherent, the first thing he did was ask if his troops were okay.

The family asked me if I'd go into the intensive care unit for a while to sit with Eden. I nodded, and a nurse fitted me with a gown, gloves, and booties, and placed a nylon hat over my hair. The family stayed outside while the nurse led me in. All was quiet in the ICU. My footsteps made no sound as I approached the marine in the bed.

I stood for a moment, taking in what I saw. Eden was burned on more than 90 percent of his body and was covered by bandages. Burn gel covered any exposed areas of skin. His eyes were slightly open, with burn gel covering his face. He'd suffered a traumatic brain injury and was missing both legs and one arm. I'd seen many, many badly wounded service members by then, but Eden was the most severely wounded I'd ever met. He did not move.

The nurse whispered to me that they weren't exactly sure what Eden could hear or comprehend, but they were fairly sure some messages were getting through. I drew closer to Eden and told him he wasn't alone, that his family was there with him, that they loved and cared for him deeply, and that as a country we were immensely grateful to him for his service.

After I finished speaking, Eden's eyelids flickered. Once. Twice. The only movement he'd made since I walked into the room.

Over the next year, I would reach out to the hospital chaplain to receive updates about Eden, but the chaplain eventually moved to another assignment and I lost touch. Then, in 2012, I did an event in Chicago for the Marine Corps–Law Enforcement Foundation. A Chicago police officer started talking with me about a severely wounded marine he knew, and before he named the man I said, "Wait. I know who you're talking about. Eden Pearl. Please, tell me what you know about him. Where is he?" The police officer put me in touch with Eden's battle buddy, Marine Phil Noblin, a Florida resident. I called Phil, and he explained how Eden had moved around the country from convalescent home to convalescent home, his family always with him. Phil put me in touch with Eden's wife, and we talked and caught up. I told her about the home-building initiatives for wounded veterans that we had going by then. We talked through a few specifics of the program, then I said simply, "It would be my honor if you would let us do that for you and Eden."

Phil Noblin had raised some money to help, so I asked Phil to use those funds to purchase the land in San Antonio, not far from the Brooke Army Medical Center burn unit, and my foundation built Eden and his family a specially adapted smart-technology home. To see part of the immense burden lifted off his wife and family was gratifying. Over the next few years, in that new place of respite, his wife and family helped Eden live a quiet life, as they wanted.

Eden received all the help he could and never stopped fighting. His sacrifices were enormous, and I respect Eden and his family tremendously. In 2015, at age forty, after a long, six-year fight for healing, Eden Pearl passed away.

He will never be forgotten.

As the years went on, I found myself in a chain of initiatives. I would meet one person, who'd link me up with someone else and a different group, and from there I'd do an event, which would put me in touch with someone else at a different organization that served a different need. Wherever I looked for ways to help, a need or a contact appeared, which led to doing more and more.

As noted earlier, in 2009 I worked with Jim Palmersheim and American Airlines to send twenty-two tons of school supplies to Iraq. I couldn't go on that trip due to my shooting schedule with *CSI: NY*, but Jim went along, and I asked our Operation International Children partner Mary Eisenhower, a few celebrity pals, and some of our volunteers to go in my place. On the way back, they stopped in Germany to visit wounded troops at Landstuhl.

There, they met a young soldier named Brendan Marrocco, just twenty-two years old, the first United States service member ever to survive after losing all four limbs in an IED explosion. The blast had happened during the early hours of Easter Sunday, while Brendan was returning from a night mission in the deserts of Iraq. He was in bad shape. In addition to losing both arms and both legs, Brendan's nose, left eye socket, and facial bones were broken. He'd lost eight teeth from the blast and had taken shrapnel in his left eye and face. His face and neck had been burned, his left carotid artery severed, and his left eardrum pierced. Usually a soldier this severely wounded would die. But army medics had been making remarkable strides in treating battlefield wounds.

Jim called me from Germany and said Brendan soon would be moved to Walter Reed, and since I had a trip already scheduled to go there in about a week, I needed to visit him. During that visit, I saw Brendan and met his mother, Michelle. Under a lot of medications, Brendan didn't talk much, but he was clearly very downcast and in a lot of distress, just beginning to adjust to his new reality. It was hard to see this young man in such tough shape.

In the car on my way back to the hotel, I called up Bryan Anderson, a triple amputee soldier I met at Walter Reed in 2005 who'd become a good friend. Bryan was now out of the hospital, retired from the army. I told him about Brendan and asked Bryan if he would visit. I knew Brendan could directly relate to Bryan in ways I couldn't. Bryan has a highly resilient personality, and he'd been living with his injures for four years by then. His attitude was remarkable. He'd been blown all to hell, but he simply wouldn't let things get him down. He'd even been featured on the cover of *Esquire*. He'd also done some acting, and I'd been able to bring him on *CSI: NY*. In 2011, he published his story of courage, determination, and hope in his autobiography, *No Turning Back*. Bryan agreed to a visit and soon flew to DC to spend some time with Brendan, where he was able to help him see that there would be life beyond the injury. Putting these two together helped Brendan at a crucial time.

Yet I knew I could do more.

The following year, *CSI: NY* was shooting in New York City. Normally we shot in L.A., but from time to time we went to New York to shoot extra scenes or stock footage. While there, I got together with my fire-fighter pals, the guys I'd helped raise money to build the Brooklyn Wall of Remembrance. Sal Cassano, the commissioner of the FDNY at the time, came by the set and explained how two nonprofit organizations, Building Homes for Heroes and the Stephen Siller Tunnel to Towers Foundation, wanted to raise money to build Brendan Marrocco a specially adapted smart-technology home in Staten Island. Would I help?

Having met Brendan at Walter Reed the year before, I loved this idea and wanted to support them in any way I could. I'd met enough wounded veterans by then to know how difficult the adjustments can be. Even basic tasks can prove troublesome. Plus, severely wounded vets often need additional live-in help. I knew Brendan's brother, Mike, had quit his banking job in Manhattan and set up shop at Walter Reed to help Brendan recover. But how would they manage after Brendan was released?

As we were planning a fund-raising concert for Brendan to be held in Staten Island in August 2010, I received another call. On March 26, 2010, while leading a squad of marines on a security patrol in Afghanistan, Corporal Todd Nicely, twenty-six, had stepped on an IED buried at the foot of a bridge. His fellow marines quickly wrapped tourniquets around his wounds and administered morphine. A rescue helicopter arrived within six minutes. He became the second US service member to survive injuries as a quadruple amputee. I met Todd in the hospital, then simply said to the Tunnel to Towers guys, "He needs a house too. Let's do another concert."

Even before we played Brendan's concert, we received a third call. On May 24, 2010, Sergeant John Peck had finished sweeping a compound with a metal detector checking for bombs when he stepped on an IED. He became America's third surviving quadruple amputee.

We decided to raise funds to help build homes for all three quadruple amputees. Back before my foundation was created, it was no simple matter to raise about half a million bucks for each home project. It still isn't a simple matter today. But I wanted to do everything I could to help. We did concerts for Brendan and Todd within a year or so of their injuries. They both attended their tribute concerts, and each concert was a great cele-bration of their service to our country and raised a portion of the money to get their building projects started.

For John, he decided he didn't want to live in his home state, so his concert wasn't able to materialize as quickly. A father had approached me about raising money to help the troops. His son, Specialist A. J. Castro, had been killed while fighting in Afghanistan, and the father, Hector Castro, wanted to do something to honor his fallen son. So I proposed doing an event to raise some money, donated my band, and with the support of my foundation, we put together the A. J. Castro Tribute concert held at the Canyon Club in Agoura Hills, California. The concert raised $75,000, and with Hector's blessing, we put the proceeds toward John's house, along with a plaque eventually placed in the new home in honor of A.J. In 2012, my band performed at our seventh annual Rockin' for the Troops concert in Wheaton, Illinois, in support of Operation Support Our Troops–America. John was originally from Illinois, so I asked the OSOTA organization if they would donate a portion of the funds raised at that concert to go toward John's home. OSOTA generously agreed and donated $125,000. Finally, we raised an additional $100,000 for John from my pal Clint Eastwood, who quietly wanted to support my foundation's efforts on behalf of our wounded.

In time, we built homes for all three quadruple amputees, and this new initiative steamrolled from there. The good news was that thanks to new, sophisticated lifesaving techniques on the battlefield, more sol-diers started surviving these horrific injuries. The bad news was that after Brendan, Todd, and John, more soldiers were wounded similarly.

Staff Sergeant Travis Mills was our fourth quadruple amputee. A highly capable and resilient squad leader, he later joked that his injury in Afghanistan was only "a bad case of the Mondays." Like so many of the wounded service members I've met, Travis is one of my heroes, and we remain close friends to this day.

Navy Petty Officer Taylor Morris, a member of an Explosive Ordnance Disposal Team, became our nation's fifth surviving quadruple amputee from the wars in Iraq and Afghanistan. Immediately after the blast that took his four limbs, Taylor lay on the Afghanistan soil, fully conscious, bleeding to death. But before medics attended him, Taylor ordered them to wait and make sure the ground surrounding him was clear of IEDs. He didn't want any other service members getting wounded. Where do they find such men as Taylor Morris?!

We were able to raise funds to build smart homes for Travis and Taylor. But there would be more severely wounded service members to come. After the early concerts for Brendan and Todd, in 2012 and 2013 I would participate in another seventeen concerts to raise funds to build homes for our wounded through a program we called Building for America's Bravest. There was so much going on during this period, but even more needed to be done.

From 2004 to 2013, the entire time I worked for *CSI: NY*, I jumped at every chance to help as many organizations as possible that honored our troops and first responders. I played concerts with my band, visited our troops, and raised funds wherever and whenever I could. It was a busy period, and these initiatives became the seedbeds that grew my own foundation, which I'll tell you about soon. For now, let's get back to the story about my disastrous dinner with Moira's parents.

More than thirty-five years passed since my days as a young, scruffy-haired Steppenwolf cofounder. Over time, I developed a full-blown film career, was nominated for an Oscar, and received many other prestigious awards for acting and humanitarian work. I'd immersed the latter half of my life in charitable and philanthropic efforts, charging full steam ahead wherever I could to help the military. One effort I plunged into was raising money to build a memorial at the Pentagon, honoring the 188 people killed at that location on 9/11. I did two concerts for that initiative, and just as we were ready to launch the building effort, an event was planned for the same Union League Club in Chicago where I'd met Moira's parents. Pentagon officials sent Brigadier General Vince Brooks to be part of the event, and I was set to talk about the memorial fund-raiser.

This time I arrived at the Union League Club in a suit and tie. This time the maître d' opened the front door for me and said, "Mr. Sinise, come right in." This time, nobody brought me up the freight elevator.

I sat near the front of the crowd at the dinner, and moments before I took the stage, I lifted my glass ever so slightly in private tribute to Moira's father. The opening lines of my speech recalled the first time I'd visited the Union League Club, and I could only chuckle at the trajectory of my life from then to now. I held no hard feelings—not to the club, not to the man who became my father-in-law. Back then, so many years ago, he was only concerned for the daughter he loved, like any good father would be. He wanted to see his daughter cherished. He simply wanted any potential son-in-law to make something worthwhile of his life.

A healing power exists within service work. My heart had been broken after that terrible day of September 11, 2001. Fear had crept in as to what the future would hold for our country and for my family. I needed to do something to help assuage that fear, to help heal that broken heart, to stand behind our country with everything I had, and to honor those who had been lost by taking action to remember them.

Inspiration and mentoring are so important in our life's journey. We can all point to men and women throughout our lives whom we have learned from, and who, by their example, have inspired us to become better people. I can truly say that over the years, the veterans, active-duty service members, first responders, and family members, and the many great Americans I have met along the way who've taken up the charge to support them, have done that for me. I have been motivated and inspired by so many who have devoted their lives to service and volunteerism, and I have tried to do a little more by taking action.

And I have found that the more I served, the more I knew that this calling was just, and true, and right and that this healing power was giving me new strength to continue to carry on. Eventually, everything came together, pushing me to create an initiative of my own—one that would eclipse everything else I'd ever done.

CHAPTER 16

The Gary Sinise Foundation

For a moment I thought it was a joke. Early one morning in October 2008, I was puffing away on my treadmill at home when my cell phone rang. A voice said that the president wanted me to come to the White House in December to receive the Presidential Citizens Medal, the second-highest civilian award in the United States and one that recognizes people for exemplary acts of service for the country.

I'd been to the White House and met President Bush a few times before. In 2004, I introduced six Medal of Honor recipients at a July 4 celebration at Ford's Theater, which the president attended. And I'd spoken at the presidential inauguration in 2005. That experience was wild. Ryan Seacrest emceed with many other entertainers performing. My job was to introduce Neil Armstrong, Buzz Aldrin, and some of the other Apollo astronauts in a special salute to America's space program. The day was freezing cold, and as soon as I walked out, I glanced over and saw President and Laura Bush sitting to my right. I then looked straight ahead at the teleprompter and everything went blurry. Thanks to the subzero temperatures, my contact lenses had started to frost over. I panicked. *Holy cow—this is live TV. There's a massive crowd out there, and I can't see the prompter.* Luckily, I knew the astronauts I was supposed to present, so I cleared my throat, ad-libbed a few lines, and jumped to the introductions.

In 2006, after we'd started Operation Iraqi Children, the president had invited me to a meeting at the White House along with leaders from other nonprofit organizations that support our troops. Officials from the Department of Defense were working on an initiative called "America Supports You." Basically, they had created a big database and website that listed many organizations that supported the troops—and they wanted the troops to know about it. Later, the Lt. Dan Band played twice at the Pentagon for the America Supports You initiative. At one of the shows, Donald Rumsfeld danced in the front row.

And on Veterans Day 2006, President Bush delivered remarks at the annual wreath-laying ceremony at the Tomb of the Unknown Soldier. I emceed the event, introducing many of the distinguished veterans present and speaking about the dedication and service of veterans and active-duty military personnel.

I was honored to have been asked to do all these things. But this was something completely different. I was being asked to come to our nation's capital again, this time to receive the Presidential Citizens Medal. I never expected this kind of honor. The rewards of my mission are the smiling faces of service members and their families. They're the ones in the spotlight. Yet here I was, on the phone with a White House representative who was saying I could bring family members to the ceremony. I stammered my thanks and hung up. On December 10, 2008, I brought Moira, our children, and my parents, along with several other family members, to the White House. There were thirteen of us in all. We stood outside the Oval Office. The door opened, and President Bush said heartily, "Come on in, Gary." The citation was read. We took some pictures and chatted with the president. The entire ceremony lasted maybe ten minutes. Not long. But it was the honor of a lifetime.

⸙

The busy pace started to catch up with me toward the end of that long "call to action" season. From 2003 to 2010, I kept volunteering more and more, helping many different organizations and charities anywhere I could. I performed regularly with the Lt. Dan Band at concerts overseas and around the country while I was working full-time on *CSI: NY*. My family had never complained that I stayed away too much. They understood the sacrifices military families must make, and they saw one of their roles in this mission as giving up some time with me. Moira especially saw it this way. With Vietnam vets in her family, she knew and understood the importance of what I was trying to do for our service members, and she was behind it 100 percent. But I'd been away a lot, and as much as she kept supporting me, I knew it was tough on her. Still, while the pace was beginning to wear on me and my family, I could also see the support effort was doing some good for these military and first-responder families, so I kept at it.

In 2009, I had an incredibly busy year. So many different volunteer projects and events, including an announcement on September 11 at the Beacon Theater in New York City that 9/11 was now a federally designated National Day of Service and Remembrance. In 2002 David Paine and Jay Winuk, whose brother Glen had been killed at the World Trade Center, had founded a group called "One Day's Pay" to encourage our fellow citizens to devote that single day's pay to service and volunteerism. Their idea was that this tragic day could not only be a day of remembrance of the terrible loss and of honoring those who perished that day, but also of memorializing the incredible spirit of the American people coming together during that time to help one another. I wanted to support them and joined the group's advisory board in 2004 to help promote this idea.

In 2007, they changed the name of the organization to "My Good Deed" and a few years later—eight years after the attack on our country—I was thrilled to help David and Jay make the announcement at the sold-out event that this day had become an official day of service. The effort continues today on the anniversary of the attacks, under the name "9/11 Day." By reaching out to help others, we honor all those who lost their lives that day. In so many ways, this concept resonated with me, as I felt called to service and volunteerism myself, and I wanted to continue to encourage our fellow citizens to take action. And so, in 2009 I picked up the pace. I did two overseas tours: one in the summer to Korea and

Okinawa and another while shooting *CSI: NY*, when I managed to get time off at Thanksgiving to go to Afghanistan and Germany for three shows and several handshake events. That year alone saw eighteen USO concerts, at home and abroad, plus an additional fourteen military support and charity concerts, as well as many other events, hospital visits, and fund-raisers.

In May the band played a concert at Fort Hood, Texas. The following November, a terrorist attack at the base killed thirteen people and injured thirty-two. Just awful. One of our own soldiers had been radicalized and had opened fire on his fellow service members. I wanted to do something to help, so I called the commanding general and offered to bring my band for a healing and support concert in the following month. This turned into a large USO event with several entertainers performing, including Dana Carvey and the Zac Brown Band. The concert took place a little over a month after the shooting, and people on base were clearly in need of support and encouragement. I was grateful to have a part in helping them heal through that difficult time. Sadly, in the fall of 2013, I would make a similar offer, this time reaching out to Navy Yard in Washington, DC, to provide a healing concert after the terrible shooting there that took the lives of twelve people and injured eight more.

Another busy year was planned for 2010: thirty-five concerts and additional events in support of our troops. They were still out there fighting, and I kept doing so much because so much needed to be done. But I was tired. I wondered how long I could keep up this pace. Would I be able to continue like this, or would I burn out?

Yet I envisioned a future doing still more, and I wanted to figure out a way to ramp up, not pull back, my work since I could see the positive effects these efforts were having. The question was how. I began to consider consolidating my mission under one umbrella, continuing the work while focusing my priorities in the most effective way possible. Having teamed up with many organizations and efforts in the military support space, I had learned a great deal about many different areas of need. I could strategically harness the incredible power of the many volunteers who worked alongside me over the years and could help serve them and our military, veteran, and first responder communities more effectively too. I could still point donors in a good direction and encourage the generosity of the American people to support quality projects I was involved in, but I could do it more consistently under this one umbrella. And since I would be building a bigger team, delegating more responsibilities to other people, I thought perhaps I could do even more while spending a bit more time with my family, something I had been longing to do for some time.

Thinking all of that through, the solution became clear: my own foundation. I had been on the ground floor of other nonprofits in the past, such as Steppenwolf and Operation International Children, and I knew I needed great people around me to get things started. At the time, I had a little office at CBS Studio Center in Studio City, on the lot where we shot *CSI: NY*. Organizers and volunteers came to the office to help me with various initiatives. That's where I met Judith Otter. She'd moved from the East Coast to the West Coast to marry Ben Robin, my longtime hair and makeup pal. Judy was educated at Juilliard and had spent several years as a professional ballerina. Following her dance career, she held several senior-level positions at leading financial institutions as well as board positions at a few philanthropic organizations. In 2009, I was very busy. I hadn't really gotten to know Judy well yet, but as she had recently relocated and had not quite settled into a job, I asked Ben to ask her if she would like to volunteer in my office. She agreed and began coming in to answer phones, helping to organize events I was putting together, whatever needed to be done. As time went on we got to know each other better, and it quickly became clear that she was a leader and someone I could rely on. So I offered her a small salary, and she began coming in to the office every day. Judy is a tremendously hard worker, a skilled manager with a lot of business experience, and has a very strong work ethic. In early 2010, I told her I was going to start a foundation and asked if she'd like to help. She accepted and I hired her, initially as my administrative director, and we went to work starting discussions with a nonprofit attorney about how to set it up. After a while Judy would begin running the foundation as executive director, and over the years became a fierce guardian, supporting me in my mission and helping me build the foundation from the ground up.

A blessing of experiencing success on television in *CSI: NY* was that I now had the financial resources to invest in hiring personnel, renting a new office, and purchasing the furniture, computers, and office equipment necessary to get us started and to support the foundation in the years to come. Judy began the hunt for the new office and located a space right across the street from CBS Studios. We then needed to begin solidifying our identity. A buddy of mine, Kiran RajBhandary, worked in branding and marketing, and I hired him to create a logo and a website. Over the next few months we went back and forth before final decisions were made on the look we were all happy with. I had been involved in so many different types of initiatives at this point. And even though I was consolidating efforts, I still wanted to keep the mission statement broad, reflecting the support work I'd done over the years, and so we could always adapt to the changing needs of our veterans. We came up with this statement:

At the Gary Sinise Foundation, we serve our nation by honoring our defenders, veterans, first responders, their families, and those in need. We do this by creating and supporting unique programs designed to entertain, educate, inspire, strengthen, and build communities.

That gave us a pretty wide berth to operate in. I'd been involved in entertaining the troops, visiting the wounded in military hospitals, and honoring our heroes by supporting the building of various memorials that would remind and educate present and future generations about the sacrifices of our military and the cost of preserving our freedom. I'd helped build homes for our wounded and their families, supported our first responders, and participated in resiliency and morale-boosting events for families and children of our fallen. All that felt important to me. I'd seen much need for support in all those areas. So the mission statement had to be broad. On June 30, 2011, at an event at the National Press Club in Washington, DC, we announced the launch of the Gary Sinise Foundation. We were up and running.

Today, including the work of the Lt. Dan Band and the annual Snowball Express, the Gary Sinise Foundation has ten programs, each focused on a specific area of need. Each program emerged from a personal connection or an incident in my life.

We have our own home building program for severely wounded veterans called R.I.S.E., which stands for Restoring Independence and Supporting Empowerment—exactly what giving someone a specially adapted smart home is all about. When veterans are severely wounded, they lose much of their independence and empowerment. In a regular home that's not built for a person with an injury, it can be difficult to get around.

For example, we built a home for US Army Ranger Sergeant First Class Michael Schlitz, who served as a rifleman and platoon sergeant in southern Iraq. On February 27, 2007, Mike and his crew were conducting road-clearing missions near Baghdad when their vehicle struck a hidden IED and burst into flame. His gunner, Sergeant Richard Soukenka, and medic, Sergeant Jonathan Cadavero, were killed instantly. His driver, Corporal Lorne Henry Jr., passed away shortly after the blast. Mike rode in the passenger seat. Engulfed in flames, he was thrown from the vehicle. He lost both hands and the sight in his left eye, and sustained burns over 85 percent of his body.

Early in Mike's recovery, he started going to a program at UCLA called Operation Mend, consisting of a team of surgeons who provide free surgeries to our severely wounded veterans. When I first met Mike, he was so severely burned, he didn't have a nose and he talked through a hole in his throat. We struck up a friendship. Over the years he's had multiple reconstructive surgeries to repair the damage to his eyelids, mouth, nose, and other parts of his body where his skin was burned. Having lost both arms, he now uses two prosthetic hooks.

Mike's living situation posed innumerable challenges for him. Because of the fragility of his skin, Mike preferred colder temperatures and often needed to turn on the air conditioner full blast. His mom, Robbie, is his full-time caregiver, and she wore heavy coats to keep warm in the house. Direct sunlight is hard on Mike's eyes, so he preferred to keep all the shades drawn. We built them a home with one section for Mike and another for his mom, where the temperature and light in each section of the house can be individually governed. Mike has a special shower and a gym that he can navigate by himself. We helped restore Mike's independence and helped empower them both. Mike is an amazing individual who's dedicating his life to honoring his fallen brothers through serving his fellow veterans. An ambassador for my foundation, he helps us with our veterans' outreach as our military and veterans resource manager.

With our smart home program, we work with each wounded service member to provide exactly what they need. Mike doesn't have children, but Master Sergeant John Masson is married and has three kids. On October 16, 2010, while conducting village-stability operations in Kandahar Province, Afghanistan, John, a medic with the 20th Special Forces Group, stepped on a hidden IED and lost both legs and his left arm. Due to the severity of his amputations, he can't wear prosthetics and is confined to a wheelchair. The hallways in his house were too narrow for a wheelchair. Additionally, he couldn't reach anything in the closets, and the bathroom was too small for him to navigate alone. So we built a house for John and his family that allows him to be independent, and in turn allows his wife and children to worry less about caring for him.

Because each home is unique, budgets fluctuate from house to house. For instance, we built a home for Captain Luis Avila and his family in the Chevy Chase area of Maryland close to Walter Reed. Land in Chevy Chase isn't cheap, but Luis needs to go to the military hospital regularly for ongoing, long-term treatments. We knew that a home near the hospital would help Luis and his family immensely.

Luis served five combat tours in Afghanistan and Iraq. On December 27, 2011, Luis's vehicle ran over an IED. Luis lost his left leg, then suffered two strokes and two heart attacks, resulting in traumatic brain injury. Ultimately, he was left almost completely paralyzed. Today Luis continues to heal while maintaining an incredibly positive attitude and a sense of humor. His wife, Claudia, is his full-time caregiver and never leaves his side. She is one of the fierce fighters for the needs of our wounded service members and reminds us of the importance of also supporting our caregivers.

Each smart home is given to the veteran free of charge. The mortgage for the house and land is completely underwritten. The veteran can select what part of the country he or she wants to live in. When needed, we also provide adapted vehicles and mobility devices such as wheelchairs, Trackchairs, and Segway personal transporters. Our director of operations oversees all aspects of the foundation's home-building process. We average ten to twelve houses per year, sometimes more. From the beginning of my support of home building, on that first home for Brendan Marrocco prior to the creation of my foundation, to our most recent homes created through the Gary Sinise Foundation, I have been blessed to have supported the building or refurbishing of more than seventy smart homes to fit the needs of wounded veterans. Thankfully, we're not the only organization in America that does this. Several of these homes were built in partnership with other organizations. But about fifty of them were built solely by my foundation and our great team.

Supporting our nation's wounded veterans is close to my heart. Though it is in no way comparable, I remember the challenges of being in a wheelchair on the set of *Forrest Gump*. I found it difficult enough to have my legs bent underneath me, but of course, I could always stand up and walk again. Being able to provide these supportive services for our many real-life Lieutenant Dans is an incredible honor.

We have another program called Serving Heroes. I've always held great compassion and empathy for someone who serves his country by going off to war, who perhaps is wounded or sees his brothers and sisters in arms lose their lives or become wounded, then comes home and is mistreated or ignored. Sometimes the simplest gestures can remind our veterans and active-duty service members how much we appreciate them.

Before the foundation was created, Moira and I drove to LAX one day to pick up Ella, who was flying home from university. We arrived an hour early, so we walked over to the USO building to see if we could say thanks to any veterans or active-duty service members there. I signed some autographs and took a few pictures; then I got to talking with the USO representatives on duty. I asked if they had any upcoming days where a lot of troops would be coming through the USO, and they did, so I simply volunteered to buy lunch for them as a way of saying thanks.

When the day of higher traffic arrived, we bought a bunch of barbecued ribs with all the fixings for the troops, and USO reps and volunteers passed out the food. I continued to do this each month until it eventually became the foundation's Serving Heroes program. We've expanded to serve free lunches not only in USOs but in VA hospitals and different travel hubs wherever high numbers of troops pass through. We do this both domestically and overseas, and we've now served more than one hundred thousand meals to the troops. Buying lunch is simply one more way of telling the troops, "We appreciate you," and "We haven't forgotten about you." The idea came from those times when I've seen a service member in a restaurant and secretly picked up the check, leaving a little note of thanks behind. Anyone can do it, and I hope more people do. But I love those rare moments when I am able to pop in and serve up some baked beans for the troops in person. It's a great feeling.

The foundation is now the sole sponsor of Steppenwolf's Veterans' Night through our Arts and Entertainment Outreach program. For every play Steppenwolf has performed since the early 1980s, the final dress rehearsal is set aside as Veterans' Night and includes free dinner and a free show for anyone who has ever served our country. Since the creation of the Gary Sinise Foundation, we have supported more than sixty-four hundred veterans attending these special nights. It's been a wonderful way to help our entertainment community extend a supportive hand to our defenders and it's gratifying that all these years later, through the support of the American people who donate to the foundation, I can still be a part of this work.

From the beginning, I wanted the foundation to support our first responders. The seeds for our First Responder Outreach program were planted after 9/11 when I was introduced to members of the FDNY and became involved with the Fire Family Transport Foundation in New York and the Brooklyn Wall of Remembrance. Like our nation's defenders, our police and firefighters work hard to protect our cities. It's dangerous work, and we want to do everything we can to make sure they're not forgotten.

Through our First Responder Outreach program, we reach out and support police, firefighters, and EMTs in any areas of specific need. For instance, Green Beret Edward Cantrell and his wife, Louise, had two young daughters, Isabella and Natalia. During Edward and Louise's eight years of marriage, Edward completed six combat tours and received four Bronze Star Medals and a Purple Heart. After he returned home for good, they lived in a house built in the 1920s, and in the early-morning hours of March 6, 2012, their house caught fire. Edward wanted to get Louise out quickly, so he helped Louise jump from the second story of the house, and they made it out safely. Edward wrapped himself in a blanket and ran back into the blazing home to rescue their daughters while Louise ran to a nearby nursing home and dialed 911. Tragically, Edward and the girls never emerged. Firefighters found all three inside the home, killed from smoke inhalation. Edward was thirty-seven, Isabella six, and Natalia four.

When I heard about this story, my heart broke. I wanted to do something to support Louise, as well as encourage the firefighters who'd responded that night. The tragedy hit them all. So I asked our ambassador John Masson, who lives near Fort Bragg and is a former Green Beret, to reach out to the firefighters at the Cotton and Hope Mills fire departments in North Carolina, to see if there was anything they could use. Firefighters from the two small towns had responded to the blaze, and one station needed a new river rescue boat, while the other needed a new equipment trailer.

The foundation decided to purchase both the boat and the trailer and dedicate them in honor of Edward, Isabella, and Natalia. Louise's little girls had loved dancing, and in their memory Louise had already started a foundation called Dancing Angels to fund scholarships to help young dancers fulfill their dreams. When the equipment was ready, I flew out to North Carolina and we held a ceremony in their honor, surprising Louise with the dedication of the equipment. Moira and I also made a donation to the Dancing Angels Foundation. Louise is an amazing woman full of resilience and courage.

Over the years, the Gary Sinise Foundation has provided grants for equipment and support for families of first responders who have been wounded or killed in service. Among other things, we've provided additional transport vehicles to departments around the country. This began with a donation of an SUV Moira and I made to the New York City–based Fire Family Transport Foundation, and to my surprise and delight they named it the "Lt. Dan Van." Many of the smaller town fire departments are volunteer and barely have any budget to fight fires or provide all that is necessary to keep their firefighters safe. So we try to help where needed, sometimes stepping into the most heartbreaking situations. We built a home for police officer Michael Flamion from Ballwin, Missouri. He was shot in the neck by an assailant during a routine traffic stop and is paralyzed from the neck down. His wife is now his full-time caregiver, and the home, built specifically for Michael's challenges, provides some much-needed support and relief.

My foundation's "Soaring Valor" program focuses on supporting our aging World War II veterans. Years ago, Tom Hanks asked me to lend my voice to a film called *Beyond All Boundaries* that Tom helped produce for the National World War II Museum in New Orleans. The forty-two-minute film lays out the entire broad picture of what happened in the war, and I portrayed the voice of Ernie Pyle, the famous war correspondent who wrote dispatches from the war zones in Europe and Asia. A special theater was built at the museum to showcase this film.

My involvement with the film sparked a relationship with the museum, and I called my uncle Jack who, at twenty-four, had been the navigator on a B-17 bomber during World War II. I thought about what I was doing when I was twenty-four years old. Uncle Jack was fighting a war at that age, and I was in a basement doing theater. Very different early years. I offered to fly him down to New Orleans to visit the museum for the first time. While he was there, museum staff recorded him on video, discussing the history of his war years. Uncle Jack passed away on October 27, 2014, and afterward I contacted the museum and asked them to send me the DVD my uncle had recorded. When I sat down and watched it, I choked up, grateful that I had this recorded history of Uncle Jack telling his story.

I thought every family of a World War II veteran should have a DVD like this—and every veteran should have the opportunity to see the museum and be recorded. I knew that time was short, because we're so rapidly losing our World War II veterans. So, in 2015, the foundation created our Soaring Valor program and arranged funding for one of the museum's historians to travel around the country to record the stories of our veterans who could not visit the museum in New Orleans.

We absolutely need to record and learn the lessons these veterans have to share. Never in the history of this country—and the world—has there been a more devastating and destructive war than World War II. With an estimated eighty to one hundred million people killed, it remains the most horrific conflict in human history. The line between freedom and tyranny was never so thin—and so clear—and all of us today are the beneficiaries of those who sacrificed in defense of freedom during those years. Had Nazi Germany, imperial Japan, and fascist Italy succeeded in their attempts at global conquest, each person alive today would be living very differently.

My uncle Jack flew with the Eighth Air Force 379th Bomb Group out of Kimbolton, England. His squadron, the 526th bombardment squadron, attacked enemy targets over Nazi Germany and occupied Europe that included bombing runs during the Battle of Northern France and the Battle of the Bulge. He told me that on many of his missions, as far as he could see—in front of him, behind him, and to the side—were airplanes. Hundreds of airplanes, sometimes more, all heading in the same direction. Many would not make it back. One time, just by chance, another navigator, Don Casey, switched missions with my uncle. On that mission, Don's B-17 was shot down and the crew had to bail out. Don was captured by the Germans and spent eighteen months in a prison camp before eventually being liberated by Patton's Third Army. He and Uncle Jack remained friends until their deaths, and Don always reminded Jack how lucky he was to swap flights that day. Of the 330 missions flown by his bomb group in B-17 Flying Fortresses, 141 were shot out of the sky. On one of Jack's runs, his B-17 was so shot up it only had one engine left, and they barely made it back over the English Channel, crash landing just as they reached the shore. Luckily all survived. It was truly a dangerous duty. Absolute hell above the earth.

I asked him if he felt scared going up in those bombers and having those big guns fired at him from the ground below, watching his buddies in other planes being shot down. Mission after mission, he went up and performed the same dangerous job. He said that when they approached the bomb site and the antiaircraft fire and flak were the most intense, as he looked through his scopes he was so focused on navigating for the bombardier that he didn't have much time to be scared. Nobody wanted to be in that horror, but he and his fellow troops knew what they needed to do to survive. They had only two outcomes possible during those years. It was either live under tyranny or live in freedom. It was either kill or be killed. And they did what they had to do.

While Uncle Jack was forthcoming in discussing his war experience, I always felt that there was a lot more he experienced that he didn't want to talk about, that he was simply unable to tell me about the many horrible things he'd witnessed during his time in World War II.

In addition to funding the historian, with the support of American Airlines we began flying groups of World War II veterans from all over the country to the museum. Sometimes we provide individual tickets for the veterans and their families, and other times the vets fly on special charters. In 2017, we began teaming each veteran with a high school student, so the older and younger generations could travel together. The older vets imparted lessons learned from the war years to the students. I have been on several of these trips myself, traveling with hundreds of veterans and many students since the program began, and it is such an honor to be able to do this. In time, after all our country's World War II veterans are gone, we hope to continue the program by providing field trips for high school students to the museum. The significance of what happened during this conflict can never be underestimated. Future generations must understand and appreciate the price paid during World War II and the tremendous cost of freedom. The story told at the National World War II Museum is invaluable for our students' education today, and I am so proud to be a supporter of this magnificent place.

As we grew as a foundation, we expanded our programs and outreach throughout the country. I contacted friends to ask if they'd become ambassadors for the foundation. If there's ever an event I can't attend, the ambassadors take my place and represent the foundation's mission.

They attend fund-raisers and ribbon cuttings. They write and speak. Each member of our Ambassadors Council is individually selected for exceptional character and patriotism.

Our first ambassador was comedian and actor Tom Dreesen, who'd served in the Marine Corps. Entertainers Joe Mantegna and D. B. Sweeney and celebrity chef Robert Irvine soon joined the council.

Medal of Honor recipients Sammy L. Davis, Drew Dix, and Jay Vargas joined, as did Mary Eisenhower from People to People International.

Prominent retired military personnel became ambassadors, including Lieutenant General Rick Lynch and his wife, Sarah Lynch; US Navy SEAL William Wagasy; Vietnam veteran Major Gary Weaver; and Captain John Woodall, a retired firefighter.

And wounded warriors round out the council today: Colonel Gregory Gadson, Sergeant Bryan Anderson, Staff Sergeant Travis Mills, Corporal Juan Dominguez, Corporal Garrett Jones, Master Sergeant Cedric King, Master Sergeant John Masson, Lieutenant Jason Redman, Sergeant First Class Mike Schlitz, and Captain Leslie Smith and her service dog, Isaac.

These friends all make an invaluable contribution to the outreach of the Gary Sinise Foundation.

Over the years, I've spent a lot of time visiting wounded troops in hospitals. Some of these men and women are in there a long time. One of the marines I met at Naval Medical Center San Diego was Staff Sergeant Jason Ross. In March 2011, during his second deployment to Afghanistan, Jason lost both of his legs and part of his pelvic bone when an IED exploded. Doctors gave him less than a 2 percent chance of survival, but Jason never stopped fighting. Complications set in, and surgeons kept needing to take more and more from his legs until eventually all his hips were gone. To date, he's undergone more than 240 surgeries. Basically, the entire lower half of his body is no longer there.

We built a smart home for Jason and his family in San Diego. When we handed over the keys to him in a ceremony, his six-year-old daughter, Stacy, asked to speak. "My daddy is Jason Ross," she said. "When I was little, my daddy got hurt in Afghanistan. He was in the hospital for a long time. My daddy is strong and brave." There wasn't a dry eye in the entire crowd.

I tried to imagine what it would be like to undergo more than 240 surgeries. In 2007, through friends at the USO, I was introduced to DC-based businessman and military supporter, Bob Pence. Later that year, and again in 2009, he and I produced Lt. Dan Band concerts at the old Walter Reed in Washington, DC, to give warriors like Jason a morale boost and a little relief from the daily grind of rehabilitation. We were able to bring many patients from their rooms for some fun and music. On one of my trips to the Naval Medical Center, I raised a question with Vice Admiral Forrest Faison, at the time the commander of ten hospitals and thirty clinics from the West Coast to the Indian Ocean. I asked the vice admiral what he would think if we brought my band out to San Diego to throw a huge party for the hospital. We could get some food and provide all the patients and their families with a day of appreciation. He loved the idea.

On October 20, 2012, my foundation produced a military appreciation day, an event that began our Invincible Spirit Festival program. Initially, we planned to get food trucks to bring the meal, but before the event I received a tweet from celebrity chef Robert Irvine. I'd seen Robert's show on the Food Network, *Restaurant: Impossible.* He knew of our work supporting the troops and said if there was anything he could do to help to please let him know. I wrote him back immediately, mentioned the festival, and asked him to come cook for everybody. He wrote, "I'm in. Give me the date." Robert brought a team of volunteers and arranged for the food to be donated. We set up a stage and barbecues. For the children of the wounded, we rented inflatable bounce houses and rock-climbing walls and brought in clowns and face painting. We created a real festival atmosphere and held a Lt. Dan Band concert. Everyone who could join us—the patients, their families, and the hospital staff—had a great time.

Since beginning this program in 2012, more than seventy-seven thousand people have come to our festivals at the Naval Medical Center in San Diego, Brooke Army Medical Center in San Antonio, and at Walter Reed and Fort Belvoir in the DC area. We've seen firsthand the importance of these festivals for the folks enduring long stays at the hospital. It's so easy to forget people going through long-term rehabilitation. Maybe they were wounded four years ago, and they're still in the hospital today. Or maybe they were wounded years ago and healed, but they need to return for follow-up work. The wounded troops and their family members tell me time and time again how getting out of the hospital for a day and being appreciated and loved is a tremendous encouragement to them.

My foundation's final program is called Relief and Resiliency Outreach. This is an umbrella program where we simply try to help veterans and their families in any way possible, including those recovering from trauma, injury, or loss.

Within the umbrella is a mentoring program. I've had a long relationship with the Disabled American Veterans (DAV) and know several wounded veterans who've lived with their injuries for decades, so I thought of providing an opportunity to introduce some of our younger wounded veterans from Iraq and Afghanistan to veterans from previous wars. I met with Jim Sursely, a Vietnam veteran triple amputee and a former national commander of the DAV, to gauge his interest and get his thoughts. He responded positively and said he would love to be involved and that he would discuss it with DAV leadership. I then proposed the idea to Ken Falke, founder of the Boulder Crest retreat centers, with locations in Bluemont, Virginia, and near Tucson, Arizona, and asked him to host the events. Ken was on board, the DAV was on board, and the mentoring program began. Several veterans have participated in the retreats, and it's been a positive experience for all.

The foundation established an emergency relief fund to help military veterans and first responders in need when times were tough. Many of these stories are so heartbreaking, and it is always tough, but it's also a joy for me to sit down and write letters to these deserving families as we send the small donations we are able to make through the generosity of the American people who support the Gary Sinise Foundation.

Emotional wounds need healing also. We recognize this and host uplifting events and group activities for vets and their families going through similar struggles. By building a community of strong friendships and forming joyful, lasting memories, these people can find new hope for the future together. We've been able to help more than eight thousand people this way.

The simple story here is that from its creation in 2011, the foundation has grown into a friendly giant. We've gone from one donor—just me in the beginning—to a base of more than forty-five thousand donors and an annual budget of nearly $30 million. In our early years, a terrific board of directors formed, and along with Judy Otter, these board members played a significant role in our expansion. Our growth has been terrific, and it is my sincere hope and belief that if I fell off the earth tomorrow, something important would be left behind that would continue to help people.

We're getting great things done. But there's lots more work to do, and we are always looking for more ways we can help our nation's defenders. I like to spread this message, a motto we've come to live by at the foundation. That motto holds that while we can never do enough to show our gratitude to our nation's defenders, veterans, first responders, and the families who serve alongside them, we can always *do a little more.*

CHAPTER 17

Why I'm Still on a Mission

Each person on this planet is here for a *purpose*. As the years have rolled on, I've come to believe that purpose is to care for other people and to help this world become a better place through service to others. This belief is part of my life's mission.

As I've gotten older, I have seen more clearly the fragility of life. How love and beauty and service and action and declining health and infirmity can all mix together. I've seen life's brevity too, hearing how the clock constantly ticks. I find myself getting up earlier and earlier and staying up later as time goes on, fearing that I won't be able to get in everything I'd like to do. And when you grasp how close we all are to the realities beyond the veil, you never want to waste another day.

In April 2014, my brother-in-law Jack Treese was diagnosed with stage 4 lung cancer. Jack had served as a medic in the army, and after Vietnam he became a physician's assistant. His wife, Amy, started teaching elementary school after her service in the army. Jack and I had grown very close over the years, and he and Amy had moved in with us a few years before the diagnosis. A month after he found out he had cancer, we moved to a new property with a guesthouse, and he and Amy moved into that. Jack had become my right-hand man before he got cancer, and I took him to Afghanistan with me, to Iraq twice, and all over the States. When I filmed *Ransom* in New York, he worked as my assistant. He became more like a brother than a brother-in-law. After the cancer diagnosis, Jack began chemo and radiation treatments. Gradually, he grew weaker and weaker.

Meanwhile, Sophie had fallen in love with a young man she'd known from their days in high school together, Bobby George, and they set their wedding for September 2014. All of us, including Jack, felt so happy for the young couple. After the ceremony at the church, we held the reception at our house. Jack was unable to attend because he was so weak from the cancer by then. From his room in our guesthouse, he could hear the festivities, and he gave us all his blessing. I know he wanted only the best for his niece. The entire day unfolded paradoxically, as we experienced both beauty and difficulty, joy and pain. Three days after the wedding, Jack passed away.

On the west side of our backyard, I built a memorial to Jack with a flagpole and a plaque to honor his service to our country. It reads: "In memory of Jack Lawrence Treese, CW2 US Army, Vietnam. Devoted husband, loving father and papa, beloved brother-in-law and uncle."

Our property rests on a small hill, and not long after the memorial was finished, I stood before the plaque and flagpole. Evening approached, the rare California rains had fallen earlier that day, and the winds from the Pacific had blown the sky free of clouds. As the sun set and the sky turned to purple and gold, I looked out beyond Jack's memorial to the horizon, and in between saw miles of tan hills and green canyons, fresh and renewed against the evening sky. Jack had known his purpose. He lived a life of service. In my own heart, mixed with the sorrow of his being gone, I felt immense waves of gratitude for having known him.

∞

Funny how the strongest emotions can be buried deep within the soul. They rise to the surface in times of pressure or intensity, in those infrequent moments of opportunity when we can draw closer to each other in service and dedication. When we understand anew the shortness of life.

Jack's passing reminded me of when my grandpa Dan died. He'd always been such a big, strong railroader, always working, always fixing something around the house. After retiring, he liked to golf, but one day while out walking the course, he succumbed to a stroke. A day later, when my father led me into my grandfather's hospital room, I saw Grandpa Dan bedridden, a thin sheet covering his chest, his once-strong body dressed only in a gown. He saw us and immediately burst into tears. I knew those tears meant something he couldn't express with words. I'd never seen my grandfather cry. He couldn't speak very well due to the stroke, and it was tough to see him looking so frail, trying to choke out some words to us. When my father and I left the hospital, we didn't speak much either. But as we rode back home together in silence, I knew we were both mulling the big questions of life.

In December 2015, I finished shooting the first season of my new television series, *Criminal Minds: Beyond Borders*. It was a wonderful experience working with a tremendous cast and crew. I was feeling great going into the new year when a few months later my father succumbed to a stroke. He and my mom had been living in Idaho near my sister, Lori, but doctors thought perhaps Dad would be better off in California with its lower elevation and warmer climate. So my parents had come to live with us. I jumped headlong into this new stage of life that allowed me to interact with them more closely than we had in years.

With Dad's various medical issues, I spent a lot of time taking him to different doctors. One day, while at an appointment, I received a call from our housekeeper. A pipe had burst at home, and water was pouring from our ceiling. My mom and daughter stayed with Dad at the doctor's office while I raced home to check things out. Repairmen had been working on our heating ducts, and by mistake one of the guys had hit a sprinkler pipe in the crawl space.

At the time, several other family members in addition to my parents lived with us. My nephew, Gavin Treese, had done two deployments to Afghanistan in the US Army and was now serving as a recruiter in Simi Valley. When his father, Jack, was diagnosed with cancer, Gavin was able to get reassigned to be near Jack in his final days. At the time the pipe broke, he, his wife, Kari, and their two kids, Aidan and Delilah, were staying with us. My daughter and her husband were also with us, and my sister-in-law Amy was still in the guesthouse where she had lived with Jack. Water can quickly wreak surprising amounts of damage. We needed to rip out all the damaged sections of our home, and the renovation became so extensive, we had to move everybody into a hotel, and then a rental house, until the work on the house could be finished.

Not long after the pipe burst, while we were still in the hotel, my phone rang. The clock read 3:30 a.m. My mom's voice came on the line. Dad felt miserable, she said. He was really in a lot of pain. I raced up to their hotel room where Dad lay moaning, foam edging the corners of his mouth. Within five minutes, the paramedics arrived and rushed him to the hospital. A scan showed massive bleeding on Dad's brain. He was eighty-five years old. The surgeon told me they needed to operate immediately. If they didn't, Dad would surely die that same night. I scribbled my signature on all the permission forms, and within two hours of my first running up to his room, Dad was undergoing emergency brain surgery.

For the next three and a half weeks, Dad remained in intensive care, hovering between life and death. I canceled everything else on my schedule, including a troop-support trip to Guantanamo Bay, Cuba, and stayed with him every day. He'd been intubated, and when they finally took the tube out, his throat ached. He tried to talk, but he was very emotional, as tearful as my grandpa Dan had been in the hospital.

After Dad had been in intensive care for some time, Moira asked our priest to come to the hospital. He prayed for my dad, then Moira and I walked out to a courtyard by the cafeteria to talk in private with him. He asked how we were holding up. My emotions, like Dad's and Grandpa's, overcame me and I started to cry. I'd been holding everything in so tightly—the pressure of trying to be a caregiver, the uncertainty of wondering if my father would pull through.

"I don't want my dad to go," I said through my tears. "I'm not ready yet."

We talked for some time, and it felt good to let everything out. I'm grateful our priest came that day.

In time, Dad recovered somewhat. Although he lost much of his balance and now is unable to do a few things, his memory remains sound. He can talk, and we're blessed and grateful to still have him with us.

One of the amazing things about the experience was the perfect timing of the burst pipe. If our pipe hadn't broken, we would have still been living at home when Dad needed emergency brain surgery. Our house is farther from the hospital than the hotel, and every minute counted in the rush to get him to the hospital. If not for the burst pipe, Dad might not have lived.

When I thought about that, I remembered something I have heard in church. We each have a purpose in life, and if we're serving God, following him, living out God's calling and purposes for our life, then we can have faith that God is leading us, and even difficult times can turn out all right. God can cause all things to work together for good.

Only a year after Dad's emergency brain surgery, Moira needed another back surgery, her sixth. Her back problems had begun more than a decade earlier. She had surgery on her spine, but the first surgeon had made a mistake, seriously damaging nerves in her right leg that would never properly heal. Three months later, she saw a different surgeon who was able to fix some of her issues with a spinal fusion, but in the following years she needed three more surgeries. Her fifth, in 2016, was another fusion of a few more discs that had fallen apart.

But this latest surgery was the most serious of all. At the end of this seven-hour surgery, Moira had fourteen inches of metal rods and screws in her spine, everything fused together, totally locked in place. In May 2017, she spent four and a half weeks in the hospital recovering, and I canceled everything to stay with her, sleeping on the room's tiny sofa at night. For the first two and a half weeks, Moira lay in terrible pain, and it took a while for the team to nail down the right mix of pain relievers. I've met a lot of families whose loved ones needed an extended hospital stay, and I couldn't help but think of all the families of our nation's defenders who have faced the same thing—multiple surgeries, lots of pain, trying to get their loved ones through it safely, staying by their side day after day, night after night.

Moira has recovered well, although she will never again be able to fully twist her torso from side to side. One thing lightened our load during those weeks in the hospital: our first grandchild. Sophie was due with the baby just before Moira's surgery, and since first babies often arrive late, Moira was afraid she would miss the birth. Amazingly, our granddaughter was born exactly on her due date at the end of May. Four days later, Moira went in for her surgery.

Before the baby was born, Moira and I went to a movie. As we climbed into our car after the show, the phone rang. "We were going to tell you this in person," Sophie said. "But we can't wait. We've decided on a name for our little girl. We're going to name her after you, Mom. Moira."

Moira burst into tears. My eyes filled too. We were so touched, so moved—so grateful.

———

I've had my own brush with life's frailty in recent years.

In March 2012, I landed at Reagan National Airport and jumped in a town car, headed to Walter Reed to visit wounded troops. A busy day was planned. After my visit to the hospital, I was scheduled to do an event with the chairman of the Joint Chiefs of Staff and folks from the USO. The following day I was to head out to Martinsville, Virginia, for a concert to raise funds to build a smart home for Marine Corps veteran and triple amputee, J. B. Kerns.

The driver of the town car cruised at the speed limit on the George Washington Memorial Parkway, a twenty-five-mile highway that runs along the Potomac River. I don't remember our car slowing. I was engrossed in plans for the next day's concert.

I didn't see anything. Feel anything. Hear anything.

The next thing I knew, I woke up in the emergency room. Ella, who attended nearby Catholic University of America, hovered above me with a concerned face. I felt her hand on my shoulder. I heard her voice. My neck ached terribly. I burst into tears and said, "I have to get to the hospital . . ." meaning, I need to get to Walter Reed to visit the wounded veterans.

"Dad! You gotta stay here," Ella said. "You were in an accident." Her voice echoed, like I was in a long tunnel.

Heavily sedated, I blurred in and out. I remember lying in the CT scanner. I remember a loud noise. I remember lots of faces I didn't know. Pieces of the past few hours shuffled through my mind. I vaguely remembered paramedics placing me on a spinal board and carrying me to an ambulance. I found out later that the driver had slowed to let a pedestrian cross the road where there was no crosswalk. A van had rammed us from behind at full speed. An off-duty firefighter happened to be driving by just as our car was hit. He'd stopped and called 911 for us and put a blanket over me so I wouldn't go into shock. My seat belt had snapped. Paramedics found me in the back seat, toppled to my left side, with the driver's seat lying on top of me. The driver of the van was fine. The driver of my ride, the town car, was injured and at the same hospital as I was. I was in and out, but they said I mumbled to the first responders to call my brother-in-law Jack. As it happened, Moira had just had her fourth back surgery. So we were both down for the count.

At the hospital, doctors apprised me of my injuries. My neck was fractured, so I was fitted with a thick neck brace. I also had a bad concussion, and my head ached. I remembered I was in a band when Kimo called to check on me. I told him to play the next day's concert without me, but he chuckled softly and said in a low voice, "No, Gary. Nobody wants to do this concert without you. You just heal up, buddy. Get better real soon."

For three days I stayed in the hospital. Ella slept on the couch in my room. The wounded veterans at Walter Reed who I'd been scheduled to visit found out about my accident and sent *me* a get-well card instead. The chairman of the Joint Chiefs of Staff, General Martin Dempsey, sent me a note saying he was sorry I missed the event with him and to get well soon.

My good friend Ben Robin, who'd been doing my makeup and hair for a long time, flew out from L.A. to DC to help. We'd just finished shooting *CSI: NY* for the season, but I had a full schedule of volunteer events. Everything needed to be canceled or rescheduled. My friend Dave McIntyre offered to pick me up in his plane and fly me home to L.A. This proved extremely helpful, because going through a commercial airport in my condition would have been difficult, plus we wanted to be careful how word got out to the press. Ben flew home with me.

We had just ordered a hospital bed for Moira so she wouldn't need to climb upstairs with her back surgery. We ordered another one for me and moved it in downstairs next to Moira's. Side by side, for the next month, we stayed in hospital beds in our living room—her with her back brace, me with my neck brace, fighting good-naturedly over the TV remote. I started rehabilitation within two weeks, and Moira soon went to her back appointments, and within a couple of weeks we were both back on schedule.

I'm grateful I woke up. I'm grateful I healed. Not everyone wakes up or heals.

For a month, I was off my feet and off the grid. When I finally came back toward the end of April, I played three concerts, one a military-appreciation event at Fort Drum, New York, plus two fund-raisers to build houses for wounded vets. Two months after the accident, I was back onstage at the National Memorial Day Concert. I invited the off-duty firefighter who'd stopped for me, plus the driver of my car, to be my guests. The driver had recovered well and was doing all right.

The entire experience made me see powerfully how quickly life can change. My schedule had been crazy. I had been going everywhere, doing everything. Moira chuckled at one point and said, "Well, you've been benched. Maybe this was the only way to get you to slow down." During those long days in our living room, I considered how one minute you're here and everything's going well. The next minute, even without expectation or awareness, life can completely change. You could be injured. You could be gone.

It made me think of our soldiers who have been wounded or have died in explosions. Some never knew what hit them. Just *kaboom,* and they were gone. Others went from one reality to another reality without remembering the middle. One minute they drove along in a Humvee. The next minute they lay in a hospital bed, with life forever changed.

I couldn't wait to get back to our mission.

In 2009, the evening after I'd helped pass out the Operation International Children (OIC) backpacks and school supplies at the Afghan school, I was staying at Bagram Air Base. I'd just finished the USO concert, and backstage General Mike Scaparrotti invited me to attend a send-off ceremony the following morning for what's called an "Angel Flight," the airplane trip that carries a fallen warrior home. Staff Sergeant Matthew Pucino, thirty-four, one of our special forces soldiers, had been killed shortly before our arrival at the base. He'd been on a patrol near Pashay Kala when his vehicle struck an IED, ending this warrior's mission. At 5:00 a.m. the next day, Matthew's body would be flown home to the United States.

I wanted to learn more about this hero. I found out that Matthew was as all-American as they came. He'd played baseball and football as a boy growing up in Plymouth and Bourne, Massachusetts. In high school, he quarterbacked his school's football team. After graduation, he went to university and earned a degree in criminal justice, intent on pursuing a career in law enforcement, but like so many others, his life's direction was changed forever by 9/11. He enlisted in 2002 and worked to become one of the best of the best, eventually becoming a Green Beret. He deployed twice to Iraq where he helped capture more than two hundred insurgents. Once, during a mission on Christmas Eve, his team came under heavy attack. Badly wounded, a sergeant needed blood to survive. Matthew quickly donated not just one, but *two* pints of blood to help his fellow soldier, then straightaway returned to the battle. After he came home to America, he reenlisted and deployed to Afghanistan to continue the fight against global terror. Those who knew him best simply called him "Uncle Matt."

I woke early, showered, and dressed. The general came to get me, and we arrived at the flight line shortly before 5:00 a.m. In the dark of the early morning we pulled up behind a giant C-17 with the back ramp down. Outside the airplane several military personnel stood quietly at attention in respect. It was a very still and somber scene. I could see into the belly of the plane. Bright lights lit the inside where a few soldiers stood watch over the flag-draped coffin of their fallen brother. The general and I got out of the car, and my throat had a lump that wouldn't go down. I stood motionless for a moment, staring at the casket, then followed the general onto the plane. Just the two of us. I looked at the sad faces of the soldiers quietly standing guard over their friend. Then I looked at the coffin.

General Scaparrotti knelt. He rested his hand on top of the coffin, and I knelt beside him and did the same. I closed my eyes, bowed my head, and said a silent prayer for this soldier and for his family who would be at Dover Air Force Base to receive their fallen loved one when he returned home.

After a moment, the general and I stood up and took a few steps back so there'd be space in front of the casket. One by one, the soldiers came on board the plane, each paying respects to this fallen brother. I choked back tears and thought of the hundreds if not thousands of families I have met over the years who have lost loved ones in military service, Gold Star families as they are known, and how hard it must have been for them when the Angel Flight arrived home. I pictured the casket being brought down the ramp as the dignified transfer took place. I felt so sad and sorry for these families. Far too many of them.

That moment is why I do what I do.

My mission is one of respect, of honor, of gratitude.

It's a mission of serving other people.

Of helping us never forget.

It's a mission I want to invite all American people to join. In fact, I invite all people from all countries who live their lives in freedom. We must ensure the sacrifices of freedom's defenders and their families are never forgotten. We must value freedom over tyranny, embrace the opportunities that freedom affords us, and support and remember those who provide it.

Today there's an organization called TAPS—Tragedy Assistance Program for Survivors—led by veteran Bonnie Carroll, the surviving spouse of Brigadier General Tom Carroll, who was killed in 1992 in a plane crash in Alaska along with seven other service members. Since 1994, TAPS has offered compassionate care to all those grieving the loss of a military loved one, and has helped more than eighty thousand military family members suffering and struggling with this terrible loss. TAPS supports mothers and fathers, brothers and sisters, sons and daughters, spouses and children. Military personnel can be lost through combat, in training accidents, from illness or suicide. The TAPS staff and volunteers don't differentiate how a military member dies. In March of 2018 I was privileged to receive their Guardian Angel Award for my support of their critically important work. I accepted the award by saying, in part, "I just hope that I can be a good steward of the freedom that has been provided to me, and all my fellow Americans, because of the sacrifices of so many guardian angels. It is my wish to do that for the rest of my life."

As I said those words, I remembered being on the tarmac in Afghanistan in 2009. I saw again Matthew Pucino's flag-draped coffin. I thought of the many warriors who have given their last full measure just like Matthew, and I thought, *God bless them and their families always.*

When I look at photographs of my trips, I often wonder about the men and women in those photographs. Did they make it back alive? Were they wounded? Over the years, more often than I can count, I have had a family member come up to me with a photo I took with their loved one in the war zone. Sometimes a final photo, as that person was killed shortly afterward. I made it a practice, when taking these photos, one after another and spending maybe only twenty or thirty seconds with each person, to try to make those seconds count. We are in a war zone, and anything can happen to these folks at any moment. After my 2017 trip to Baghdad, I received a very sad email from a friend informing me that a young woman, a soldier in a photo with me, had taken her own life shortly after that photo was taken. She was smiling and happy in the photo. You just don't know what is really going on sometimes.

After spending so much time with the grieving families of our fallen heroes, over and over I've been reminded that life can end at any time; that's why we all need to make the most of each day. We need to make each day purposeful, and for the past several years I've discovered that much of that purpose for me is in serving and honoring the needs of our defenders. That's why I'm still on a mission, a mission that's the driving reason I've told my story. All my experiences—the places I came from, my years of formation, the people I met along the way, the mistakes I made and learned from, the challenges of my career and the ways I overcame— all my life has culminated in my ongoing service work.

There is an unfortunate disconnect between most Americans and our military. Unless we have a family member or close friend who is serving, most of us go about our daily lives with little understanding of who is actually defending us. The majority of Americans will never have a chance to see what our military does on a daily basis. Our service members are exceptional in so many ways. And not just at fighting our wars. When disasters such as hurricanes, fires, floods, and earthquakes strike, our carriers, helicopters, and hospital ships (floating medical treatment facilities) offer aid and support in countless ways to nations far and wide. Our military and first responders go into harm's way in service to others over and over again. I want to know what they do, how they do it, and why they do it, and they have allowed me some special privileges over the years as I have visited them around the world. Our amazing pilots have taken me to seventy-two thousand feet in a U-2 spy plane over northern California, and pushed my body to 7 Gs in an F-16 in Aviano, Italy. I have landed in a C-2 Greyhound on the aircraft carrier USS *Ronald Reagan* in the Persian Gulf, and in the cockpit of an F-18 Super Hornet onto the carrier USS *Theodore Roosevelt* off the coast of San Diego. I've experienced training with US Army Special Forces in Germany and have witnessed firsthand how Navy SEALs complete BUD/S class and Hell Week on Coronado Island. I have seen American sons and daughters wearing the cloth of this nation as they serve in war zones. Year after year I have walked the halls of our military hospitals and witnessed our wounded as they face their challenges with great strength and courage, supported by the selfless caregivers who stand by day after day, month after month, year after year, helping them through. And I have seen the extraordinary care with which the members of the military and first responder communities honor their fallen brothers and sisters. Each time I have been allowed the privilege of participating in these types of experiences, it has helped me to become a more educated advocate, as I try to help bridge that disconnect. If only all of our fellow citizens could get to know them as I have, the difficult issues and challenges our veterans face would be greatly reduced as more of us would be inspired to take up the charge to support them. As a public figure, I am grateful that I have been able to use my platform to pass on what I have learned about who our military is, how skilled they are, and how fortunate we all are to have men and women like these serving our country.

Ronald Reagan once said, "Freedom is never more than one generation away from extinction. We didn't pass it to our children in the bloodstream. It must be fought for, protected, and handed on for them to do the same."

Those words have stuck with me. As I have traveled the world, sometimes visiting countries that have not known the blessings of liberty, I have realized more and more the high cost of preserving that freedom, and the sacrifices of those who have provided it for us over the years. Freedom is not something all human beings simply get to have and enjoy. A price must be paid, and I am grateful to those who are willing to pay that price, sometimes the ultimate price. Because of these special Americans, I have been able to live out my dreams, succeed at my chosen career, and turn that success into something positive for others.

I am thankful for the many inspirational individuals and friends I have met over the years who have helped me and supported me. I am grateful for my loving family and for the fact that we have overcome the many challenges faced along the way and are stronger for it. And I am most fortunate to have met the love of my life, my beautiful Moira, my best friend through all our ups and downs, who has showed me how God's grace truly works.

At the conclusion of the film *Saving Private Ryan*, James Ryan—having fought through and survived the terrible world war of the 1940s and now an old man—stands among the thousands of graves of our buried dead in Normandy. After looking down at the grave of the man who gave his life to save him and with his own life now near its natural end, Ryan looks into the eyes of his wife and says to her, "Tell me I've led a good life . . . Tell me I'm a good man." She answers him with a quiet and passionate, "You are."

For those who have sacrificed for me, for those who have inspired me, for those who have supported me in the many endeavors over the years that I've shared in these pages, and for those who have loved me and who I love, I hope to continue to make the most of that love, that support, that inspiration, and that sacrifice for as long as I live. I want to lead a good life, not just for myself, but also for my fellow man. A life of service, to try to make the world a better place. America has given me this opportunity, and for that, I will always be grateful.

Called to Action

The United Service Organizations (USO)
The Aleethia Foundation/Friday Night Dinners
The Fire Department of New York (FDNY)
The Fire Family Transport Foundation
Friends of Firefighters (NY)
Disabled American Veterans
The Coalition to Salute Americas Heroes
The Wounded Warrior Project
The Dancing Angels Foundation
Operation Gratitude
Injured Marine *Semper Fi* Fund
Navy SEAL Foundation
Operation Home Front
"A Million Thanks" Letter Writing Campaign
Chicago Police Memorial Foundation
Operation Support Our Troops Illinois/America
Congressional Medal of Honor Society and Foundation
Special Operations Warrior Foundation
The American Veterans Disabled for Life Memorial
National Memorial Day Concert and Parade
Unmet Needs, a program of the Veterans of Foreign Wars (VFW)
The National 9/11 Pentagon Memorial
The Brooklyn Wall of Remembrance

The Lansing Veterans Memorial

America Supports You

The documentary "Brothers at War"

The GI Film Festival

Hope for the Warriors

Snowball Express

Tragedy Assistance Program for Survivors (TAPS)

Fort Worth Air Power Foundation and American Airlines Skyball

The Independence Fund

The Intrepid Foundation

Tunnel to Towers Foundation

United States Veterans Arts Program

Fisher House Foundation

Golden Coral and Camp Coral

My Good Deed (a 9/11 Day of Service and Volunteerism)

Various Public Service Announcements for Military and Veterans' Causes

Visits of the Wounded at Military Hospitals

GARY SINISE AND THE LT. DAN BAND

Ben Lewis (keyboards)

Ernie Denov (lead guitar)

Danny Gottlieb (drums)

Elizabeth Gottlieb (percussion)

Jeff Vezain (vocals/rhythm guitar)

Dan Myers (violin/vocals)

Mari Anne Jayme (vocals)

Julie Myers (vocals)

Molly Callinan (vocals)

Kirk Garrison (trumpet)

Mitch Paliga (saxophone)

Tom "Bones" Malone (trombone)

Gary Sinise (bass guitar)

THE CREW

James Stuckman (tour/production manager)

Scott Steiner (sound mixer)

Tristan Beache (monitor engineer)

Art Beresheim (production coordinator)

Acknowledgments

The writing of *Grateful American* was a stimulating and challenging process—and it would have been far more challenging had I not had the support, love, and friendship of so many wonderful people over the years, people who have enriched my life and encouraged me to keep going when times were tough.

And there have been many. A whole other book's worth, in fact. But here I'd like to acknowledge a select group who played a specific role in supporting me in a number of my current endeavors—some of the key moments highlighted in the book—as well as those without whom I would not have taken on the task of writing this memoir.

First, my family. I dedicate this first book to my beloved wife, Moira, the love of my life who has supported and helped me, and who read the first draft, giving me feedback and responses that were vital in the development of the book. I love you, honey. Thank you. I also dedicate the book to my children: Sophia, McCanna (Mac), and Ella. I am so proud of them and grateful for them. You are the best kids a dad could ask for. And to my parents, Bob and Millie Sinise, whose love and support has always been there: thanks, Mom and Dad. And to my sister, Lori, and my brother, Craig: thank you for being you. Love you both.

It was Cait Hoyt at Creative Artists Agency who put a bug in my ear about doing the book in the first place and who originally discussed the idea with my manager, Marc Gurvitz, and my agent, Matt Delpiano. Cait is a terrific book agent who gave me excellent notes on the first draft, and Marc and Matt are dear friends who have been with me and supported me for over twenty years. All three were great champions of this project. Thank you, folks.

Cait introduced me to Marcus Brotherton, and it was a great pleasure to work with Marcus. A wonderful writer, Marcus has a tremendous ear and is a great listener who was able to sort through my thoughts and help me get them organized. With my schedule so busy all the time, working with Marcus made it possible for me to get this done a lot sooner than I would have without his keen insight and excellent skill, and I thank him very much for the great work.

Matt Baugher and Brian Hampton at Thomas Nelson were eager to support the book, and our editor, Webster Younce, was great to work with. Webb was a steady voice and patient ear, and he gave me great advice in crafting the final drafts. Thank you, gents, as well as everyone at Thomas Nelson who supported this project.

My great executive assistant, Cristin Bartter, and my wonderful son, Mac, were also very helpful in research and helping me find key historical information. Thank you, Cristin and Mac, for your hard work.

Staci Wolfe has been my friend and publicist for over twenty years, doing a superb job at both. She has a keen eye and was very helpful with notes on the second draft. Thanks to both Staci and her colleague Greg Longstreet for doing a great job and for being wonderful friends and supporters.

At the Gary Sinise Foundation, thank you to Judy Otter, our staff, our Ambassadors Council, our Advisory Board, and members of our board of directors Jim Shubert and Pat Velasco, as well as former board members Jim Palmersheim and Bob Pence, for their support of my efforts over the years to serve and honor the needs of our veterans. Having a great team in place keeping the ship sailing along gave me the peace of mind and confidence that I could take the time required to write the book.

Finally, thank you to the inspirational first responders, military veterans, and family members who are the focus of much of this book. Your service to our country is very much appreciated by this grateful American.

God bless you.

About the Author

GARY SINISE, actor, director, musician, and humanitarian, has been an advocate for America's veterans for nearly forty years. He's best known for his roles in the award-winning movies *Forrest Gump*, *Apollo 13*, *Ransom*, *Of Mice and Men*, *Truman*, *George Wallace*, and *The Green Mile*, and in the hit TV shows *CSI: NY* and *Criminal Minds: Beyond Borders*.

Gary has won an Emmy Award, a Golden Globe Award, and a star on the Hollywood Walk of Fame, and was nominated for an Oscar.

He's the founder of the Gary Sinise Foundation, which serves and honors America's defenders, veterans, first responders, their families, and those in need. He's the leader and bass player for the Lt. Dan Band, which has entertained more than half a million troops around the world. He is the cofounder of the prestigious Steppenwolf Theatre of Chicago.

Gary has been presented with many awards, including the Spirit of Hope Award by the Department of Defense. He was named an honorary Chief Petty Officer by the United States Navy, was pinned as an honorary marine, and received the Sylvanus Thayer Award at West Point, given to a civilian "whose character, service, and achievements reflect the ideals prized by the US Military Academy." He's the recipient of the Presidential Citizens Medal, the second-highest civilian honor awarded to citizens for "exemplary deeds performed in service of the nation."

Gary lives with his wife, actress Moira Harris, outside of Los Angeles.

garysinisefoundation.org

ABOUT THE AUTHOR

MARCUS BROTHERTON is the *New York Times* bestselling author or coauthor of more than twenty-five books, including *Tough as They Come* with SSG Travis Mills, and *We Who Are Alive and Remain: Untold Stories from the Band of Brothers*. He has won the Christopher Award for literature that "affirms the highest value of the human spirit."

marcusbrotherton.com

Receiving the Disabled American Veterans Commander's Award, August 1994, at the Conrad Hilton Hotel in Chicago. Pictured with disabled veteran and 1994 DAV National Commander Richard Marbes.

(DAV/J. CHANEY)

My great-grandparents Vito Sinise and Anna Maria Fusco. Photo taken in Italy, late 1800s.

(AUTHOR'S PERSONAL COLLECTION)

My dad, Robert Sinise, in the early 1950s, serving as a photo mate in the US Navy.

(AUTHOR'S PERSONAL COLLECTION)

Family shot, 1964, in front of our first house in Highland Park, Illinois. L-R: Grandpa Dan, me with baseball glove, Mom and my sister Lori, Dad, my brother Craig, and Grandma Betty.

(AUTHOR'S PERSONAL COLLECTION)

Me, age 5, 1960. The uniform was a gift from an uncle serving in the US Army.

(AUTHOR'S PERSONAL COLLECTION)

My sixth grade band playing at a party in our backyard in Highland Park, 1966. I'm second from the right in white socks and penny loafers.

(AUTHOR'S PERSONAL COLLECTION)

Jeff Perry (left) and me acting in *Rosencrantz and Guildenstern Are Dead*, the third Steppenwolf production, June 1974.

My mom snapped this picture of me in 1976 outside the Catholic school basement theater. I'm 21 years old. This is the first Steppenwolf sign, ever.

Steppenwolf ensemble pictured on the elevated train tracks, north side of Chicago, fall 1980. Left of sign, from back to front: Glenne Headly, Tom Irwin, John Mahoney, Joan Allen, Terry Kinney, Alan Wilder, Rondi Reed. Right of sign, from back to front: John Malkovich, Francis Guinan, Moira Harris, Jeff Perry, me, Laurie Metcalf.

(LISA HOWE-EBRIGHT)

Playing a character named "Dopey"
in *Balm in Gilead*, 1980.

(LISA HOWE-EBRIGHT)

Moira and me on our wedding
night, July 21, 1981, at a party at our
apartment after a performance of
Balm in Gilead.

(© DOROTHEA JACOBSON-WENZEL)

Moira and me making our entrance at the 2012 Congressional Medal of Honor Society's Celebration of Freedom event at the Reagan Library. I cohosted this event for five years.

(TRIWEST HEALTHCARE ALLIANCE)

With John Malkovich in the New York production of *True West*, October 1982, off-Broadway, Cherry Lane Theater. This is the final scene of the play. All hell's about to break loose.

(MARTHA SWOPE, NEW YORK PUBLIC LIBRARY DIGITAL COLLECTION)

Here I am in December 1983 at our bootcamp for the cast of *Tracers* at the closed down summer camp in Sawyer, Michigan.

(AUTHOR'S PERSONAL COLLECTION)

With John Malkovich and Elaine Steinbeck, fall 1991, on the set of *Of Mice and Men*.

Directing and acting in *Of Mice and Men* in Santa Ynez, California, fall 1991.

A production still of me as Lieutenant Dan on the set of *Forrest Gump*, shot in Beaufort, SC, fall 1993.

Before a flight on the KC 135, known as the "Vomit Comet," during training for *Apollo 13* at Johnson Space Center in Houston in 1994. L-R: me, Ron Howard, producer Todd Hallowell, Kevin Bacon, Tom Hanks, Bill Paxton. Notice the two white plastic bags in each of our front pockets in case we got sick on the flight. Guess who returned with only one bag?

On the set of *Apollo 13* playing naval aviator and astronaut Ken Mattingly.

Moira, me, and the kids, 1994, at our home in Pasadena. That Hawaiian shirt was one of my favorites back then. It was my personal shirt, but I ended up wearing it in a scene in *Forrest Gump*.

(AUTHOR'S PERSONAL COLLECTION)

With my family at a candlelight vigil in our neighborhood, three days after the attacks of September 11, 2001.

(JAN CRANE / *MALIBU TIMES*)

A production still from *Truman*, 1995, shot in and around Kansas City, Missouri. The makeup took 4.5 hours each day to apply.

(HBO MEDIA RELATIONS DIGITAL LIBRARY)

Visiting Ground Zero in New York in 2008. This photo was taken from the documentary film, *Lt. Dan Band: For the Common Good.*
(LAMPLIGHT ENTERTAINMNENT, INC. / JONATHAN FLORA, PRODUCER/DIRECTOR)

Speaking to thousands of troops, November 2003, at a USO show at Camp Anaconda, Balad, Iraq.
(SARAH FARNSWORTH)

Me with Wayne Newton, Neal McCoy, Chris Isaak, and Iraqi schoolkids at the Abu Hassan School in Balad, Iraq, November 2003. The idea of sending school supplies to the troops to distribute to kids began to take shape in my head that day.
(LES MARTINES)

In 2006 with President Bush in a meeting in the Roosevelt Room at the White House along with representatives of various military support nonprofit organizations. I was there representing Operation Iraqi Children (OIC).

(WILLIAM D. MOSS)

In Baghdad in 2008, sitting in one of Saddam Hussein's palaces, which he called the Victory over America palace. It was bombed in early 2003 during the shock and awe campaign at the beginning of the Iraq war.

(AUTHOR'S PERSONAL COLLECTION)

Distributing Operation International Children (OIC) school supplies at a school near the border of Afghanistan and Pakistan, November 2009.
(WILLIAM W. SEO)

Me and the Lt. Dan Band playing for the Marines at Camp Leatherneck on our 2009 tour to Afghanistan. A very dusty day. We're on a makeshift stage on a flatbed truck.
(TOMAS R. DELVALLE)

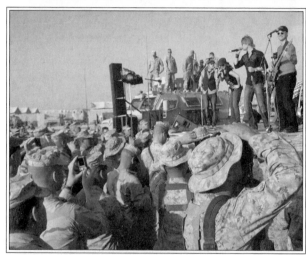

On the set of *CSI: NY*, season 7, with Hill Harper (l) and Eddie Cahill, 2011.
(AUTHOR'S PERSONAL COLLECTION)

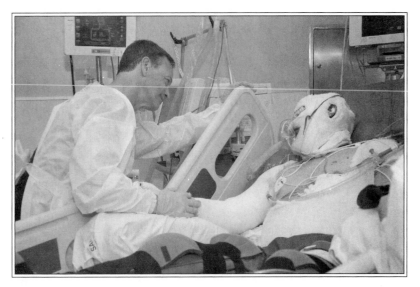

Visiting USMC Lt. Col. Bryan Forney in the intensive care burn unit at Brooke Army Medical Center in San Antonio, March 7, 2013. He had just been brought to the hospital after a helicopter crash.

(JENNIE FORNEY)

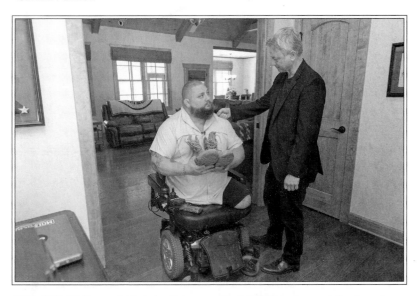

With USMC Corporal Christian Brown on April 9, 2017, in the specially adapted home donated by the Gary Sinise Foundation as part of the R.I.S.E. program. December 13, 2011, Christian stepped on an improvised explosive device (IED) in Afghanistan, losing both his legs and sustaining multiple traumas to both hands and arms.

(© JULIA ROBINSON)

At the 2016 Snowball Express event for children of our fallen heroes. They've been through so much. Wonderful to see them smiling and laughing, so I let them jump all over me. Anything for these kids!

December 21, 2017, in Ninawa, Iraq, visiting with soldiers of the Texas National Guard. I had the pleasure on that trip of traveling to both Iraq and Afghanistan with my friend General Mark Milley, Chief of Staff of the Army, on my left.

With World War II veteran Carmen Schiavoni at one of our Gary Sinise Foundation's Soaring Valor events in 2017. He flew 30 combat missions over Europe with the 8th Air Force as a waist gunner on a B-17. It's always an honor to be with these heroes.

Here I am serving baked beans to our troops at Naval Base Ventura County in 2018 as part of the Gary Sinise Foundation Serving Heroes program. Always a pleasure to let them know they're appreciated.

Onstage October 7, 2014, with the navy at a concert at Walter Reed National Military Medical Center in Bethesda, MD. One of the Gary Sinise Foundation's Invincible Spirit festivals.

(TIM LUNDIN/ TDLPHOTO.COM © TIMOTHY LUNDIN PHOTOGRAPHY 2018)

Just outside the base hospital at Camp Anaconda, Balad Air Base, Iraq, 2007. I'd just visited troops in the hospital, then came out and wrote this message on a busted concrete wall.

(US AIR FORCE PHOTO)

Thanks from a grateful American.

(US AIR FORCE PHOTO)

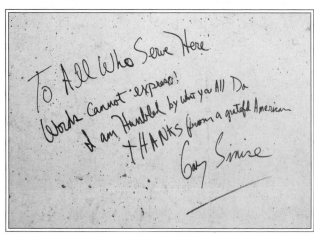